Test Book

ELEMENTS OF LITERATURE

THIRD COURSE

Test Book

ELEMENTS OF LITERATURE

THIRD COURSE

HOLT, RINEHART AND WINSTON, INC.

AUSTIN NEW YORK SAN DIEGO CHICAGO TORONTO MONTREAL

ACKNOWLEDGMENTS

For permission to reprint copyrighted material, grateful acknowledgment is made to the following sources:

Albert I. Da Silva, as agent for Neil Simon: From *Brighton Beach Memoirs* by Neil Simon. Copyright © 1984 by Neil Simon.

Doubleday, a division of Bantam, Doubleday, Dell Publishing Group, Inc.: From *The Illiad* by Homer, translated by Robert Fitzgerald. Copyright © 1974 by Robert Fitzgerald.

Harcourt Brace Jovanovich, Inc.: From *1984* by George Orwell. Copyright 1949 by George Orwell; copyright renewed 1977 by Sonia Brownell Orwell. "The Downward Path to Wisdom" from *The Learning Tower and Other Stories* by Katherine Anne Porter. Copyright © 1939, 1967 by Katherine Anne Porter.

Harvard University Press, Inc., and the Trustees of Amherst College: "She Sweeps With Many-Colored Brooms" from *The Poems of Emily Dickinson*, edited by Thomas H. Johnson. Copyright 1951, © 1955, 1979, 1983 by The President and Fellows of Harvard College. Published by the Belknap Press of Harvard University Press, Cambridge, MA.

Ellen C. Masters: "Mabel Osborne" from *Spoon River Anthology, New Edition with New Poems* by Edgar Lee Masters. Copyright 1944 by Edgar Lee Masters; copyright renewed 1972 by Ellen Masters.

Printed in the United States of America

ISBN 0-03-023273-2

90123456 085 98765432

USING THE TEST BOOK

This Test Book accompanies ELEMENTS OF LITERATURE, Third Course.

For each unit in the literature anthology, there is an **introductory test.** For units which are subdivided in the anthology according to various literary elements, there are sub-unit introduction tests. Following these introductory tests are individual **selection tests** for each major selection and a number of tests on short, grouped selections such as poetry. At the end of each unit are a **word analogy test, a unit review test,** and a **critical thinking and writing test.**

The individual selection tests are comprised of the following parts:

A. **Understanding What Happened** or **Recognizing Elements** (of Plot, Character, Theme, etc.). In this section, multiple-choice or true-false questions are structured to test your students' *reading comprehension* and/or *understanding of a particular literary element.*

B. **Interpreting Meanings** or **Recognizing Elements** (of Plot, Character, Theme, etc.). In this section of the selection test are a series of multiple-choice questions designed to *develop interpretive skills,* to *understand an author's style* and *grasp each writer's point of view,* and to further develop understanding of the specific literary element or technique under discussion.

Sometimes B. sections are divided into two parts. In such cases, Part 2 offers a writing assignment emphasizing critical and interpretive skills.

C. **Developing Vocabulary.** This section is devoted to vocabulary words found in the selections just studied.

The three end-of-unit tests further develop vocabulary, reading comprehension, and critical and interpretive skills.

1. **Word Analogies / Extending Vocabulary Skills.** Twenty words drawn from the literature of each unit provide the basis for this *extra vocabulary-extending exercise.*

For assistance in teaching analogies, in helping students to read, solve, and create analogies, and to understand the various types of relationships that are commonly used in analogies, a special feature, entitled **"Introduction to Word Analogy Tests"** is provided on pages 245-246 of this Test Book. This unique feature will be helpful in teaching your students the art of inferring word correspondencies.

2. **Unit Review/Applying Skills I.** This comprehensive unit test asks your students
   - *to read* a brief selection similar to those just studied
   - *to respond* to multiple-choice questions which test comprehension
   - *to write* about the selection
   - *to analyze* language and test understanding of the vocabulary in the selection.

3. **Critical Thinking and Writing / Applying Skills II.**

Referring to the specific literature selections in the unit just studied, this test asks your students to *write one or two paragraphs summarizing, comparing, analyzing, evaluating*—in short, sharpening the critical thinking and writing skills which have been introduced in the unit just studied.

Other features of this Test Book:

- Except for the essential, occasional essay questions, *objective questioning,* requiring only a letter answer, has been employed.
- All tests are written in a conversational tone and have been designed to be *"user friendly"* for both you and your students.
- All tests are prepared for *easy scoring:* the component parts always add up to a perfect score of 100.
- Objective test questions—short and incisive—have been carefully designed to *instill careful reading habits* (see the **A. Understanding What Happened** section of each

test), *to promote thoughtful interpretive and analytical skills* (see **B. Interpreting Meanings**), and to *extend vocabulary skills* (see **C. Developing Vocabulary**).

- Although your students' answers to non-objective essay questions will of course vary, suggested or probable *answers are provided* as a handy basic checklist for you.
- Tests which require reference to the anthology (as a rule, most selection tests including essay questions) are marked for easy referral with the *symbol of an open book* in the upper right-hand corner. Before deciding whether to assign any test as, "open book," you may want to evaluate the individual needs and abilities of your students, or consider the amount of classroom time spent on any particular selection or unit.

Answers to all test questions, including essay questions, are given in the Answer Key on pages 247-268 of this book.

TABLE OF CONTENTS

UNIT 1: THE ELEMENTS OF A SHORT STORY

Introduction / Understanding Plot 1
Poison Roald Dahl 3
The Adventure of the Speckled Band Arthur Conan Doyle 5
The Birds Daphne du Maurier 7

Introduction / Understanding Character 9
A Christmas Memory Truman Capote 11
María Tepache Amado Muro 13
Thank You, M'am Langston Hughes 15
Blues Ain't No Mockin Bird Toni Cade Bambara 17

Introduction / Understanding Setting 19
Top Man James Ramsey Ullman 21
Antaeus Borden Deal 23
A Man Called Horse Dorothy M. Johnson 25

Introduction / Understanding Point of View 27
Correspondence Carson McCullers 29
The Hat Jessamyn West 31
The Old Demon Pearl S. Buck 33

Introduction / Understanding Theme 35
The Scarlet Ibis James Hurst 37
The Bridge Nicolai Chukovski 39
Red Dress Alice Munro 41

Introduction / Understanding Irony 43
The Little Girl and the Wolf / The Princess and the Tin Box James Thurber 45
The Sniper Liam O'Flaherty 47
The Cask of Amontillado Edgar Allan Poe 49
The Necklace Guy de Maupassant 51

Word Analogies / Extending Vocabulary Skills 53
Unit Review / Applying Skills I 55
Critical Thinking and Writing / Applying Skills II 59

UNIT 2: THE ELEMENTS OF POETRY

Unit Introduction / Understanding the Elements of Poetry 61

Introduction / Understanding Imagery 63
Imagery: Seeing Things Freshly 65

Introduction / Understanding Similes and Metaphors 67
Similes and Metaphors: Seeing Connections 69

Introduction / Understanding Personification 71
Personification: Making the World Human 73

Introduction / Understanding Rhythm 75
The Sounds of Poetry: Rhythm 77

Introduction / Understanding Rhyme and Other Sound Effects 79
The Sounds of Poetry: Rhyme and Other Sound Effects 81

Introduction / Understanding Tone 83
Tone: Revealing an Attitude 85

Introduction / Understanding Ballads and Lyrics 87
Two Kinds of Poetry: Ballads and Lyrics 89

Word Analogies / Extending Vocabulary Skills 91
Unit Review / Applying Skills I 93
Critical Thinking and Writing/Applying Skills II 97

UNIT 3: THE ELEMENTS OF NON-FICTION

Unit Introduction / Understanding the Elements of Nonfiction 99

Introduction / Understanding Personal Essays 101
The Giant Water Bug Annie Dillard 103

The Night the Bed Fell James Thurber 105
The Washwoman Isaac Bashevis Singer 107
Charley in Yellowstone John Steinbeck 109

Introduction / Understanding Reports on People and Events 111
FROM Coming Into the Country John McPhee 113
Everything in Its Path Kai Erickson 115
Annapurna Maurice Herzog 117

Introduction / Understanding Biography and Autobiography 119
"Annie" Joseph P. Lash 121
Barrio Boy Ernesto Galarza 123
The Phantom of Yazoo Willie Morris 125
I Know Why the Caged Bird Sings Maya Angelou 127
Life on the Mississippi Mark Twain 129

Word Analogies / Extending Vocabulary Skills 131
Unit Review / Applying Skills I 133
Critical Thinking and Writing / Applying Skills II 137

UNIT 4: THE ELEMENTS OF DRAMA

Unit Introduction / Understanding the Elements of Drama 139
The Miracle Worker, Act One William Gibson 141
The Miracle Worker, Act Two William Gibson 143
The Miracle Worker, Act Three William Gibson 145
Visitor from Forest Hills Neil Simon 147
The Mother Paddy Chayefsky 149

Word Analogies / Extending Vocabulary Skills 151
Unit Review / Applying Skills I 153
Critical Thinking and Writing / Applying Skills II 157

UNIT 5: WILLIAM SHAKESPEARE

Unit Introduction / Understanding Shakespeare 159
The Tragedy of Romeo and Juliet, Act I William Shakespeare 161
The Tragedy of Romeo and Juliet, Act II William Shakespeare 163
The Tragedy of Romeo and Juliet, Act III William Shakespeare 165
The Tragedy of Romeo and Juliet, Act IV William Shakespeare 167
The Tragedy of Romeo and Juliet, Act V William Shakespeare 169

Word Analogies / Extending Vocabulary Skills 171
Unit Review / Applying Skills I 173
Critical Thinking and Writing / Applying Skills II 177

UNIT 6: THE ELEMENTS OF THE EPIC

Unit Introduction/Understanding the Elements of an Epic 179
The Odyssey, Books 1-4 Homer 181
The Odyssey, Book 5 Homer 183
The Odyssey, Books 6-8 Homer 185
The Odyssey, Book 9 Homer 187
The Odyssey, Books 10-11 Homer 189
The Odyssey, Book 12 Homer 191
The Odyssey, Books 16-17 Homer 193
The Odyssey, Book 19 Homer 195
The Odyssey, Book 21 Homer 197
The Odyssey, Book 22 Homer 199
The Odyssey, Book 23 Homer 201
The Odyssey, Book 24 Homer 203

Word Analogies / Extending Vocabulary Skills 205
Unit Review / Applying Skills I 207
Critical Thinking and Writing / Applying Skills II 211

UNIT 7: THE ELEMENTS OF THE NOVEL

Unit Introduction / Understanding the Elements of the Novel 213
Animal Farm, Chapter I George Orwell 215
Animal Farm, Chapter II George Orwell 217
Animal Farm, Chapter III George Orwell 219
Animal Farm, Chapter IV George Orwell 221
Animal Farm, Chapter V George Orwell 223

Animal Farm, Chapter VI
George Orwell 225
Animal Farm, Chapter VII
George Orwell 227
Animal Farm, Chapter VIII
George Orwell 229
Animal Farm, Chapter IX
George Orwell 231
Animal Farm, Chapter X
George Orwell 233
Word Analogies / Extending Vocabulary Skills 235
Unit Review / Applying Skills I 237
Critical Thinking and Writing / Applying Skills II 241

ANSWER KEY

Using the Answer Key 243
Introduction to Word Analogy Tests 245
ANSWER KEY 247

NAME ______________________ CLASS __________ DATE __________ SCORE __________

UNIT 1: THE ELEMENTS OF A SHORT STORY

INTRODUCTION / Understanding Plot

Directions: For each question, place the letter of the best answer in the space provided. *(10 points each)*

1. The quotation by E.M. Forster in the introductory quotation suggests that an important element in the art of storytelling is
a. suspense
b. a pleasant voice
c. an interested audience
d. a comfortable room

1. ______

2. The series of related events in a story—"the hook of curiosity"—is its
a. characters
b. plot
c. setting
d. climax

2. ______

3. The basic situation, or exposition, of a story
a. introduces the characters and their conflict
b. predicts what ultimately will happen
c. summarizes all important occurrences
d. is always presented in the first paragraph

3. ______

4. Conflict in a story may occur between
a. two characters
b. a character and his or her environment
c. a character and his or her conscience
d. all of the above

4. ______

5. An internal conflict takes place
a. indoors
b. between two characters
c. among the members of a family
d. in a character's mind

5. ______

6. The greater the conflict in a story is,
a. the more we care about the outcome
b. the more the characters in the story fight
c. the longer the story is
d. the more difficult the story is to read

6. ______

7. The "bare bones" of a plot include all of the following *except* the
a. exposition
b. complication and climax
c. resolution, or denouement
d. characterization

7. ______

8. In the complication of a plot, the
   a. conflict is resolved
   b. character encounters problems
   c. character is introduced
   d. reader realizes the outcome of the story

8. ______

9. The climax of a story
   a. always comes in the final sentence
   b. occurs when the reader realizes the outcome of the conflict
   c. directly follows the exposition
   d. refers to its message

9. ______

10. The resolution, or denouement, occurs at the
   a. beginning of the story
   b. middle of the story
   c. end of the story
   d. moment of crisis

10. ______

NAME ________________ CLASS ________ DATE ________ SCORE ________

UNIT 1: THE ELEMENTS OF A SHORT STORY

THE ADVENTURE OF THE SPECKLED BAND   Arthur Conan Doyle

A. RECOGNIZING ELEMENTS OF PLOT

Directions: For each question, place the letter of the best answer in the space provided. *(5 points each)*

1. Which of the following statements does Helen Stoner make to "hook" your curiosity?
a. "I am living with my stepfather."
b. "It is fear, Mr. Holmes. It is terror."
c. "You know me, then?"
d. "I started from home before six."
1. ______

2. In "The Adventure of the Speckled Band," the basic situation of the plot is that
a. Dr. Grimesby Roylott has died
b. Sherlock Holmes has risen early for a change
c. Helen's stepfather has gone to Calcutta
d. Holmes and Dr. Watson try to solve the murder of Helen's sister
2. ______

3. The main conflict in this story is the struggle that takes place between
a. Dr. Roylott and his stepdaughters
b. Dr. Watson and Helen
c. Holmes and Helen
d. Helen and the gypsies
3. ______

4. The climax occurs in the scene in which Holmes and Watson see
a. Dr. Roylott and his stepdaughters
b. the tassel of the bell rope lying on the pillow
c. the cheetah drink a saucer of milk
d. the swamp adder rise from Dr. Roylott's hair
4. ______

5. The story's resolution is presented when
a. Holmes explains how he solved the mystery
b. Holmes throws the snake into the safe
c. Holmes and Watson enter Dr. Roylott's room
d. Holmes and Watson hear the whistle
5. ______

B. INTERPRETING MEANINGS

Part 1. *Directions:* For each question, place the letter of the best answer in the space provided. *(4 points each)*

1. At the beginning of the story, a trembling Helen Stoner speaks softly as she moves to a seat by the fire and says, "It is not cold which makes me shiver." What is she feeling?
a. anticipation **b.** enthusiasm **c.** fear **d.** sleepiness
1. ______

2. The plot is complicated by
a. the political climate of 1883
b. the detective who followed Helen to London
c. the boy driving Dr. Roylott's carriage
d. Dr. Roylott's violent temper
2. ______

3. Dr. Roylott's visit to Baker Street causes Holmes to feel
   a. challenged **b.** threatened **c.** uninterested **d.** frightened — 3.______

4. Holmes's attitude toward Dr. Roylott's death can be described as
   a. guilty **b.** not very guilty **c.** amused **d.** angry — 4.______

5. This passage occurs near the end of the story:

> He had ceased to strike, and was gazing up at the ventilator, when suddenly there broke from the silence of the night the most horrible cry to which I have ever listened. It swelled up louder and louder, a hoarse yell of pain and fear and anger all mingled in the one dreadful shriek. They say that away down in the village, and even in the distant parsonage, that cry raised the sleepers from their beds. It struck cold to our hearts, and I stood gazing at Holmes, and he at me, until the last echoes of it had died away into the silence from which it rose.

What can you infer from this scene?
a. Holmes and Watson will never participate in so horrible a mystery again.
b. An innocent bystander has been hurt.
c. Helen will receive her inheritance.
d. Dr. Roylott has finally paid for his evil actions. — 5.______

Part 2. Arthur Conan Doyle includes many false clues and extra details that have nothing to do with the solution of the mystery. His purpose is to interest you and deepen the mystery. Readers who regard these details as clues to the murder might reach the wrong solution. What are some of these details? How could a detective less astute than Sherlock Holmes have misunderstood the clues?

Directions: On a separate sheet of paper, write a paragraph explaining how an ordinary detective might have solved the mystery incorrectly. Cite parts of the story that might influence this detective. *(15 points)*

C. DEVELOPING VOCABULARY

Directions: In the spaces provided, mark each true statement **T** and each false statement **F**. *(4 points each)*

1. A *metropolis* is a large city. — 1.______
2. A *deduction* is a logical solution. — 2.______
3. A *premature* event takes place at its proper time. — 3.______
4. A *dense* fog is thin and scattered. — 4.______
5. A *tiara* is a crown. — 5.______
6. *Manifold* evils of the human heart are many and varied. — 6.______
7. A *pauper* has a great deal of money. — 7.______
8. A *morose* person feels gloomy. — 8.______
9. The *hubbub* of a gale makes a quiet, peaceful sound. — 9.______
10. When a person's face is *blanched* with terror, it becomes red and flushed. — 10.______

NAME ______________________ CLASS ________ DATE ________ SCORE ________

UNIT 1: THE ELEMENTS OF A SHORT STORY

THE BIRDS **Daphne du Maurier**

A. UNDERSTANDING WHAT HAPPENED

Directions: In the spaces provided, mark each true statement **T** and each false statement **F**. *(2 points each)*

1. Nat Hocken earns his living as a farmer. **1.** ______

2. Nat first realizes that the birds are acting strangely when they attack his children in their bedroom at night. **2.** ______

3. Jim, the cowman, has no time for Nat because Nat is said to read books. **3.** ______

4. At first, Nat mistakenly thinks that the gulls sitting on the sea are the white caps of the waves. **4.** ______

5. Nat has the impression that, despite warnings on the radio, people in London would be going to parties. **5.** ______

6. The children at the bus stop laugh at Nat because he is carrying a dead bird. **6.** ______

7. After being attacked by the birds as he crossed the field, Nat has trouble entering his house because the door is jammed. **7.** ______

8. The BBC stops broadcasting at night because there is a power shortage. **8.** ______

9. During the night, Nat and his family hear the distant crash of aircraft. **9.** ______

10. Nat worries that pouring paraffin on the fire might cause the chimney to catch fire. **10.** ______

B. RECOGNIZING ELEMENTS OF PLOT

Directions: For each question, place the letter of the best answer in the space provided. *(6 points each)*

1. Which event does Daphne du Maurier use to hook your curiosity at the beginning of the story?
a. The noisy birds follow the plow.
b. Gulls nearly knock off the farmer's cap.
c. A message comes to the birds.
d. The gulls race and run on the beach. **1.** ______

2. Between which of the following does the external conflict take place in this story?
a. Nat and the birds
b. Nat and the farmer
c. Nat and his wife
d. the jackdaws and the gulls **2.** ______

3. Nat's internal conflict develops when
   a. the birds attack him
   b. the birds attack the children
   c. his wife seems not to believe him
   d. the draft blows out his candle

3.______

4. The plot is complicated by
   a. Nat's midday snacking
   b. Nat's wartime disability
   c. Nat walking the children to the bus stop
   d. the radio station going off the air

4.______

5. At the conclusion of the story,
   a. Nat continues to devise ways to keep out the birds
   b. the birds break down the doors and windows
   c. the British Navy sails down the channel
   d. Nat gives up hope

5.______

C. DEVELOPING VOCABULARY

Directions: In the space provided, place the letter of the word that best matches each definition. (*5 points each*)

1. a person's nature or temperament
   a. disability b. disposition c. repose d. nationality

1.______

2. a loud outcry
   a. clamor b. urge c. curlew d. rustling

2.______

3. a disturbed feeling of fear or doubt
   a. bluster b. apprehend c. irritation d. misgiving

3.______

4. the top or highest point
   a. crest b. creeper c. ledge d. breaker

4.______

5. a long, narrow hollow
   a. hedgerow b. wireless c. trough d. pit

5.______

6. to come in contact with, to collide
   a. to pinpoint b. to exempt c. to jostle d. to protrude

6.______

7. a place where food supplies are stored
   a. larder b. lanyard c. lard d. boarder

7.______

8. gloomy
   a. mellow b. downcast c. solitary d. pasty

8.______

9. slyly secret
   a. ominous b. ashen c. spent d. furtive

9.______

10. without pity
   a. risky b. ruthless c. hysterical d. cautious

10.______

NAME ______________________ CLASS __________ DATE __________ SCORE __________

UNIT 1: THE ELEMENTS OF A SHORT STORY

INTRODUCTION / Understanding Character

Directions: For each question, place the letter of the best answer in the space provided. *(10 points each)*

1. The primary purpose in writing a story is to
a. express personal opinions
b. earn money
c. create new literary works
d. reveal various aspects of human nature
1. ______

2. For a character to be realistic, he or she must
a. be closely based on an actual person
b. combine characteristics of many people
c. demonstrate a variety of emotions and actions
d. resemble the author
2. ______

3. Authors show their characters undergoing changes in order to
a. confuse the reader
b. reveal something about the characters' inner selves
c. entertain the reader
d. hold the reader's attention
3. ______

4. A character's manner of speech
a. is relatively unimportant
b. depicts modern life
c. reflects the author's self-image
d. helps reveal his or her nature
4. ______

5. Scrooge's frigid appearance is an example of the fact that
a. a character's nature often is reflected in his appearance
b. appearance always corresponds to inner worth
c. exaggeration is necessary in good literature
d. the Christmas season is approaching
5. ______

6. Knowing a character's inner thoughts enables the reader to determine
a. the truth
b. the writer's fantasies
c. the character's mind
d. the action of the story
6. ______

7. Characters are often revealed through
a. techniques of plot construction
b. other characters' feelings about them
c. geographical descriptions
d. the writer's good intentions
7. ______

8. Characters reveal themselves most vividly through their
a. names
b. actions
c. ages
d. places of birth

8. ______

9. Indirect characterization
a. is the author's explanation of a character's motives
b. is a summary of a character's role in a plot
c. involves the reader's interpretation of character
d. is another term for denouement

9. ______

10. Direct characterization
a. is used infrequently by modern writers
b. provides direct statements about a character's motives
c. reveals a character's nature
d. all of the above

10. ______

NAME ____________ CLASS ________ DATE ________ SCORE ________

UNIT 1: THE ELEMENTS OF A SHORT STORY

A CHRISTMAS MEMORY Truman Capote

A. RECOGNIZING ELEMENTS OF CHARACTER

Directions: For each question, place the letter of the best answer in the space provided. *(6 points each)*

1. Buddy's friend can best be described as
a. mature
b. cold-hearted
c. intellectual
d. innocent
1. ______

2. The interaction between Buddy and his friend demonstrates that
a. they are extremely close
b. she is a good baby sitter
c. they are rivals
d. neither likes to share
2. ______

3. The sour relatives are characterized by their
a. emotional supportiveness
b. financial extravagance
c. frequent demands upon Buddy and his friend
d. vicious acts of violence
3. ______

4. Which statement *indirectly* reveals how Buddy and his friend feel on Christmas Eve?
a. "I kick the covers and turn my pillow as though it were a scorching summer's night."
b. "Her excitement is equaled by my own."
c. "Somewhere a rooster crows."
d. "My mind's jumping like a jack rabbit."
4. ______

5. Capote's narration indicates that his experience at military school
a. was rewarding
b. was unrewarding
c. taught him necessary skills
d. was a family tradition
5. ______

B. INTERPRETING MEANINGS

Part 1. *Directions:* For each question, place the letter of the best answer in the space provided. *(5 points each)*

1. For Buddy and his friend, the most important part of Christmas is
a. shopping in town
b. saving a bone for Queenie
c. making and giving gifts
d. sharing time with relatives
1. ______

2. Buddy points out several of his friend's accomplishments, for they made him feel
   a. frightened   b. sad   c. proud   d. amused   2. ______

3. Which character(s) believe that whiskey is "sinful"?
   a. Buddy's friend
   b. Mrs. Haha
   c. the cafe's patrons
   d. Buddy's relatives   3. ______

4. This paragraph appears after Buddy and his friend have drunk a little whiskey and are busy singing and dancing:

   > Enter: two relatives. Very angry. Potent with eyes that scold, tongues that scald. Listen to what they have to say, the words tumbling together into a wrathful tune: "A child of seven! whiskey on his breath! are you out of your mind? feeding a child of seven! must be loony! road to ruination! remember Cousin Kate? Uncle Charlie? Uncle Charlie's brother-in-law? shame! scandal! humiliation! kneel, pray, beg the Lord!"

   From this passage, you learn that the relatives
   a. are impatient with Buddy's friend
   b. are religious leaders in their community
   c. never drink alcohol
   d. intend to put Buddy's friend in an institution   4. ______

5. Buddy's friend eventually
   a. marries   b. dies   c. becomes famous   d. moves away   5. ______

Part 2. Truman Capote tells you that Buddy's friend is "still a child." What do you think that means?

Directions: On a separate sheet of paper, write a paragraph explaining your point of view. Cite parts of the story that influence your opinion. *(15 points)*

C. DEVELOPING VOCABULARY

Directions: Match each word in the left-hand column with the best meaning in the right-hand column. Write the letter of the best definition in the space provided. *(3 points each)*

______ 1. dilapidated
______ 2. paraphernalia
______ 3. accumulated
______ 4. conspiracy
______ 5. somber
______ 6. carnage
______ 7. festooned
______ 8. simultaneous
______ 9. potent
______ 10. burnished

a. bloody and extensive slaughter
b. powerful
c. a collection of things
d. shabby and neglected
e. made shiny by rubbing
f. piled up or gathered together
g. dark, gloomy
h. decorated in loops or curves
i. a secret plan
j. occurring at the same time
k. having a thin skin
l. a craving for sweet food

NAME ______________________ CLASS __________ DATE __________ SCORE __________

UNIT 1: THE ELEMENTS OF A SHORT STORY

MARÍA TEPACHE **Amado Muro**

A. UNDERSTANDING WHAT HAPPENED

Directions: In the spaces provided, mark each true statement **T** and each false statement **F**. *(3 points each)*

1. The narrator of "María Tepache" is a drifter. **1.** ______

2. When the traveler arrives in San Antonio, he is hungry and tired. **2.** ______

3. When María Tepache thinks back on her youth, she does not remember her father. **3.** ______

4. Apparently, the narrator speaks no Spanish. **4.** ______

5. The stranger has visited many homes like María's before. **5.** ______

6. María lives in a simple house with only her husband and a dog. **6.** ______

7. María first meets her husband in Mexico. **7.** ______

8. In return for food, the traveler fetches water and chops wood for María. **8.** ______

9. The traveler plans to stay two or three days. **9.** ______

10. María frequently eats chocolate and other rich foods. **10.** ______

B. RECOGNIZING ELEMENTS OF CHARACTER

Directions: For each question, place the letter of the best answer in the space provided. *(8 points each)*

1. Amado Muro characterizes the old woman in "María Tepache" through all of the following *except*
a. her actions
b. her thoughts
c. her appearance
d. her speech
1. ______

2. María Tepache says "I'm not one of those women meant to live in homes that would be like cathedrals if they had bells." This shows that she
a. is accepting of her life
b. hates her family
c. feels deprived
d. has sad memories of her youth
2. ______

3. You sense that María is a good woman because
a. her home is clean
b. she is old
c. her eyes are untroubled
d. lettuce heads are displayed in her window
3. ______

4. After María discusses her husband, she looks "older than I'd thought at first seeing her." Remembering her husband makes María feel
   a. sad
   b. happy
   c. younger
   d. untroubled
   4. ______

5. By giving the traveler food for his journey, María shows that she is
   a. extremely poor
   b. secretly wealthy
   c. generous
   d. foolish
   5. ______

C. DEVELOPING VOCABULARY

Directions: In the space provided, place the letter of the word that best matches each definition. (*3 points each*)

1. distorted; twisted, bent
   a. warped b. warmed c. smoky d. burdened 1. ______

2. to coat with a golden color
   a. gild b. gold c. scald d. gall 2. ______

3. thoughtful
   a. respectful b. weighty c. intelligent d. reflective 3. ______

4. short and thick
   a. stamped b. stumpy c. outspread d. tangled 4. ______

5. a dark, gloomy covering
   a. corrugate b. primitive c. pall d. humble 5. ______

6. loaded or weighed down, oppressed
   a. chilled b. corrugated c. burdened d. crooked 6. ______

7. piece of candy
   a. bonbon b. bin c. lard d. chunk 7. ______

8. low in position, modest, not proud or vain
   a. short b. burdened c. crucified d. humble 8. ______

9. a coarse fabric
   a. burlap b. curtains c. velvet d. cottonwood 9. ______

10. will to succeed
    a. smart b. reflective c. ambition d. desirous 10. ______

NAME ______________________ CLASS __________ DATE __________ SCORE __________

UNIT 1: THE ELEMENTS OF A SHORT STORY

THANK YOU, M'AM **Langston Hughes**

A. RECOGNIZING ELEMENTS OF CHARACTER

Directions: For each question, place the letter of the best answer in the space provided. *(5 points each)*

1. Roger is best characterized as a
a. vicious criminal terrorizing the elderly
b. troubled boy in need of guidance
c. thrill-seeker out to prove himself
d. desperate thief supporting his family **1.** ______

2. You first realize that Mrs. Jones cares for the boy when she
a. offers to wash his face
b. gives him a clean towel
c. asks his name
d. makes dinner for him **2.** ______

3. The climax of "Thank You, M'am" occurs when
a. Roger tries to steal the purse
b. Mrs. Jones gives the boy ten dollars
c. the woman kicks Roger
d. Roger washes his face **3.** ______

4. At the end of "Thank You, M'am," Roger probably feels
a. angry
b. proud and manly
c. frightened
d. respectful **4.** ______

5. Throughout the story, Mrs. Jones thinks Roger
a. is nothing but a hoodlum
b. needs someone to act as his mother
c. will harm her
d. will run away **5.** ______

B. INTERPRETING MEANINGS

Part 1. *Directions:* In the spaces provided, mark each true statement **T** and each false statement **F**. *(3 points each)*

1. Mrs. Jones carries a large hammer in her purse for protection. **1.** ______

2. Roger's fear causes him to bungle the robbery attempt. **2.** ______

3. Despite her size, Mrs. Jones is a weak woman. **3.** ______

4. Roger doesn't really mean to grab Mrs. Jones's purse. **4.** ______

5. Mrs. Jones viciously kicks the young thief before calming down. 5. ______

6. Mrs. Jones says the boy "ought to be" her son because he resembles one of her own children. 6. ______

7. Mrs. Jones tells Roger he will remember her because she is going to teach him a lesson about life. 7. ______

8. Roger is surprised to hear Mrs. Jones say that he could have asked her for money. 8. ______

9. Mrs. Jones teaches Roger by scolding and lecturing him. 9. ______

10. Near the end of the story, Langston Hughes writes:

> She heated some lima beans and ham she had in the icebox, made the cocoa, and set the table. The woman did not ask the boy anything about where he lived, or his folks, or anything else that would embarrass him. Instead, as they ate, she told him about her job in a hotel beauty shop that stayed open late, what the work was like, and how all kinds of women came in and out, blondes, redheads, and Spanish. Then she cut him a half of her ten-cent cake.

Mrs. Jones does what she can to make Roger feel more at ease. 10. ______

Part 2. Langston Hughes tells you that Roger never sees Mrs. Jones again. Do you think he is glad or unhappy about this fact?

Directions: On a separate sheet of paper, write a paragraph explaining your point of view and citing parts of the story that influence your opinion. *(15 points)*

C. DEVELOPING VOCABULARY

Directions: Match each word in the left-hand column with the best meaning in the right-hand column. Place the letter of the best definition in the space provided. *(3 points each)*

______ 1. frail
______ 2. to contact
______ 3. furnished
______ 4. suede
______ 5. to dash
______ 6. presentable
______ 7. icebox
______ 8. barren
______ 9. stoop
______ 10. combined

a. refrigerator
b. to rush
c. empty and unattractive, or uninteresting
d. entrance stairway or small porch
e. supplied
f. joined together
g. weak, fragile
h. leather with a soft, velvety surface
i. to get in touch with
j. fit to be seen
k. a small dish
l. to correct

NAME ______________________ CLASS __________ DATE __________ SCORE __________

UNIT 1: THE ELEMENTS OF A SHORT STORY

BLUES AIN'T NO MOCKIN BIRD **Toni Cade Bambara**

A. UNDERSTANDING WHAT HAPPENED

Directions: In the spaces provided, mark each true statement **T** and each false statement **F.** *(5 points each)*

1. At the beginning of the story, Cathy and the narrator are breaking ice with their feet. **1.** ______

2. Judging from the narrator's description of Cathy, she is more mature than the other children. **2.** ______

3. The camera men treat Granny with proper respect. **3.** ______

4. Granny says, "Go tell that man we ain't a bunch of trees" because she does not want to be photographed. **4.** ______

5. The camera men tell Granny that she should apply for food stamps. **5.** ______

6. When Granny tells the film crew, "I don't know about the thing, the it, and the stuff. Just people here is what I tend to consider," she is admitting that she doesn't understand their job. **6.** ______

7. Granny tells the children the story about the man on the bridge to teach them the meaning of sin. **7.** ______

8. Granny makes the family move a lot because she becomes enraged by the inconsiderate behavior of other people. **8.** ______

9. Granddaddy Cain appears, carrying over his shoulder a dead chicken hawk. **9.** ______

10. Granny is humming at the end of the story because she always hums when she bakes. **10.** ______

B. RECOGNIZING ELEMENTS OF CHARACTER

Directions: For each question, place the letter of the best answer in the space provided. *(6 points each)*

1. Granny is
a. proud and independent
b. a bad hostess
c. cold and mean
d. a constant complainer
1. ______

2. Granddaddy's character is revealed primarily by
a. his speech
b. the attitudes of the other characters
c. his actions
d. the author's direct characterization
2. ______

3. Toni Cade Bambara's narrator describes Granddaddy as tall and silent to indicate his
a. strength and dignity **b.** simplicity **c.** height **d.** handsomeness **3.** ______

4. The main conflict in "Blues Ain't No Mockin Bird" takes place between Granny and
   a. Granddaddy b. the children c. the film crew d. the hawks 4.______

5. This passage appears before the climax of the story:

> The camera man duckin and bendin and runnin and fallin, jigglin the camera and scared. And Smilin jumpin up and down swipin at the huge bird, tryin to bring the hawk down with just his raggedy ole cap. Granddaddy Cain straight up and silent, watchin the circles of the hawk, then aimin the hammer off his wrist. The giant bird fallin, silent and slow. Then here comes Camera and Smilin all big and bad now that the awful screechin thing is on its back and broken, here they come.

   This excerpt compares and contrasts Granddaddy's
   a. aim with the hammer with the men's aim with the camera
   b. fear with the men's courage
   c. hammer with Smilin's cap
   d. behavior with that of the film crew 5.______

C. DEVELOPING VOCABULARY

Directions: Complete each sentence by placing the letter of the best answer in the space provided. *(2 points each)*

1. Alan looks _____ wearing that old mask.
   a. wired b. weird c. wield d. wheeled 1.______

2. The stacks of glasses rise like a mountain of _____.
   a. circle b. censure c. census d. crystal 2.______

3. The waiter serves the soup to the guests with a _____.
   a. ladle b. hawser c. ledger d. hammer 3.______

4. The students are visiting the _____ to see the cows.
   a. dairy b. daily c. derry d. dare 4.______

5. At the factory we see big _____ filled with chemicals.
   a. pliers b. vetches c. vats d. oilskins 5.______

6. The crowd at the rodeo cheers when the rider _____ the calf.
   a. drools b. squawks c. jiggles d. lassoes 6.______

7. We have to admit that Professor Cheng's new idea is _____.
   a. ardent b. original c. arduous d. ordinal 7.______

8. The farmers must harvest the nuts from the _____ trees.
   a. pudding b. orange c. pecan d. pelican 8.______

9. The candidates begin to _____ a year before the election.
   a. campaign b. canteen c. construct d. cartel 9.______

10. When the girls drive in a _____ manner, I begin to worry about their safety.
   a. ruthless b. reckless c. roofless d. rectified 10.______

NAME ______ CLASS ______ DATE ______ SCORE ______

UNIT 1: THE ELEMENTS OF A SHORT STORY

INTRODUCTION / Understanding Setting

Directions: For each question, place the letter of the best answer in the space provided. *(10 points each)*

1. In the introductory quotation, Eudora Welty points out that
a. all characters are basically the same
b. authors borrow each other's plots
c. all characters and plots are different
d. setting is crucial to a story
1. ______

2. One of the easy pleasures of reading is
a. escape to new sights and scenes
b. learning new vocabulary
c. testing one's reading speed
d. improving one's reading level
2. ______

3. A story's setting tells us
a. about the characters' motivations
b. where and when the story takes place
c. about the author's background
d. about the language of the story
3. ______

4. Information about where characters live and act is supplied by
a. characterization
b. plot
c. setting
d. conflict
4. ______

5. When characters battle against nature, the setting of the story also provides the story's
a. conflict
b. introduction
c. conclusion
d. climax
5. ______

6. The atmosphere or mood of a story
a. depends solely on the reader's interpretation
b. is greatly influenced by its setting
c. is unrelated to the setting
d. should be obvious in the first sentence
6. ______

7. A believable setting depends upon
a. characters based on real people
b. detailed statistical research
c. the writer's selection of appropriate details and images
d. color photographs or illustrations
7. ______

8. Ordinary settings
a. produce colorless fiction
b. dull the imagination
c. come alive with vivid imagery
d. are generally avoided by writers

8. ______

9. The imagination of the reader
a. plays a central role in a successful story
b. confuses the writer's purpose
c. is unnecessary if a story is well written
d. is less important than the writer's

9. ______

10. In comparison to watching television, reading
a. demands less effort
b. requires more imagination
c. offers fewer rewards
d. takes less time

10. ______

NAME________________ CLASS________ DATE________ SCORE________

UNIT 1: THE ELEMENTS OF A SHORT STORY

TOP MAN James Ramsey Ullman

A. RECOGNIZING ELEMENTS OF SETTING

Directions: For each question, place the letter of the best answer in the space provided. *(6 points each)*

1. The mountain setting in which "Top Man" takes place gives us an opportunity to gain important information about the
a. character of the climbers
b. narrator's character
c. politics of India
d. geology of England
1.______

2. K3 is described as having a "sweeping skirt of glaciers; the monstrous vertical precipices of the face and the jagged ice line of the east ridge; finally the symmetrical summit pyramid that transfixed the sky." These words warn you that the climb will be
a. fun **b.** simple **c.** triumphant **d.** dangerous
2.______

3. The main conflict of "Top Man" is between
a. Paul Osborn and Martin Nace
b. Nace and his dead friend, John Furness
c. the narrator and Osborn
d. the men and the mountain
3.______

4. The climax of "Top Man" occurs when
a. Osborn disobeys Nace
b. Nacc and thc narrator follow Osborn
c. Nace falls off the mountain
d. Nace's ax is found at the summit
4.______

5. Which of the following statements provides a clue to Nace's character?
a. "The youngster started at Nace..."
b. "Nace...[was] the only one among us who was not staring at K3 for the first time."
c. "His lean British face...was expressionless."
d. "Nace did not seem to hit the snow: he simply disappeared through it..."
5.______

B. INTERPRETING MEANINGS

Part 1. *Directions:* For each question, place the letter of the best answer in the space provided. *(5 points each)*

1. Why does James Ramsey Ullman set Nace off from the other mountaineers?
a. He is older.
b. He has the most experience.
c. He is the only Englishman.
d. He has witnessed death on this mountain.
1.______

2. The narrator describes K3 as first appearing "unreal—a dream image" and then as "no longer an image at all. It was a mass, solid, imminent, appalling." What do these details suggest about the account to follow?
a. The narrative will sound like a fairy tale.
b. The climbers will be unable to remember their ascent.
c. The climb will deal with issues of life and death.
d. The story will be humorous.
2.______

3. The conflict between Nace and Osborn is established at the beginning of the story. Ullman's purpose is to
   a. strengthen the climax and denouement of the story
   b. show how much he dislikes both men
   c. change the mood throughout the story
   d. indicate the narrator's character

3. ______

4. At the story's end, a combined English-Swiss expedition finds Nace's ax at the summit of K3. What does this detail reveal about Osborn?
   a. He felt proud of reaching the summit himself.
   b. He remained defiant until the end.
   c. He was angry at Nace.
   d. He had been humbled by Nace's sacrifice.

4. ______

5. Toward the close of the story, the following passage appears:

> I stayed where I was, and the hours passed. The sun reached its zenith above the peak and sloped away behind it. And at last I heard above me the sound of Osborn returning. As I looked up, his figure appeared at the top of the chimney and began the descent. His clothing was in tatters, and I could tell from his movements that only the thin flame of his will stood between him and collapse. In another few minutes he was standing beside me.

In this passage, Ullman suggests Osborn's
   a. failure   b. success   c. sadness   d. joy

5. ______

Part 2. The narrator of "Top Man" states, "If fate were to grant that the ax of any one of us should be planted upon the summit of K3, I hoped it would be his." He is referring to Martin Nace. As you read the story, did you agree?

Directions: On a separate sheet of paper, write a paragraph explaining your point of view and citing parts of the story that influence your opinion. *(15 points)*

C. DEVELOPING VOCABULARY

Directions: In the spaces provided, mark each true statement **T** and each false statement **F**. *(3 points each)*

1. A *gorge* is a wide valley. 1. ______
2. A *taciturn* man likes to talk. 2. ______
3. *Ominous* clouds usually threaten rain. 3. ______
4. A *desolated* area looks deserted or uninhabited. 4. ______
5. A *spasm* is a slow steady pain. 5. ______
6. A *laborious* climb is difficult. 6. ______
7. The *summit* of a mountain is one of its steepest sides. 7. ______
8. An *imminent* event is likely to happen without delay. 8. ______
9. Two *simultaneous* crashes occur one after the other. 9. ______
10. A *taut* rope is tightly stretched. 10. ______

NAME ____________ CLASS ______ DATE ______ SCORE ______

UNIT 1: THE ELEMENTS OF A SHORT STORY

ANTAEUS **Borden Deal**

A. UNDERSTANDING WHAT HAPPENED

Directions: In the spaces provided, mark each true statement **T** and each false statement **F**. *(3 points each)*

1. T. J. lives by himself in an old car. **1.** ______

2. The narrator introduces T. J. to the gang. **2.** ______

3. The boys decide to plant a garden on the roof of an apartment building. **3.** ______

4. The boys spend most of their time in the park. **4.** ______

5. T. J.'s friends give him credit for coming up with the idea of a roof garden. **5.** ______

6. The garden is the gang's most organized project. **6.** ______

7. The boys carry most of the dirt from the park. **7.** ______

8. T. J. manages to keep his new friends interested in the garden project. **8.** ______

9. When Blackie steps on the grass, the garden is ruined. **9.** ______

10. T. J. is used to dealing with adults who want to destroy his work. **10.** ______

B. RECOGNIZING ELEMENTS OF SETTING

Directions: For each question, place the letter of the best answer in the space provided. *(8 points each)*

1. In this story, the industrial setting of T. J.'s new home is contrasted with the
- **a.** crowded apartment in which he lived
- **b.** Alabama countryside he left
- **c.** tarred roof on the factory next door
- **d.** vacant lots from which he gathered soil **1.** ______

2. The climax in "Antaeus" occurs when T. J.
- **a.** moves into the building
- **b.** interests the others in his idea
- **c.** throws the soil off the roof
- **d.** runs away **2.** ______

3. Which of the following statements reveals T.J.'s character?
- **a.** "Only rich people had roof gardens."
- **b.** "His voice was resolute with the knowledge of his rightness."
- **c.** "I slapped T.J. on the shoulder."
- **d.** "T.J. kept looking at the tar under his feet." **3.** ______

4. T. J.'s friends begin to understand his feelings
   a. when they meet him
   b. after the rain
   c. when they steal the grass seed
   d. before the men appear on the roof 4. ______

5. This passage appears at the end of "Antaeus:"

   Then the Nashville police caught him just outside the Nashville freight yards. He was walking along the railroad track, still heading South, still heading home.
   As for us, who had no remembered home to call us, none of us ever again climbed the escapeway to the roof.

   This part of the story is called the
   a. denouement
   b. basic situation
   c. hook of curiosity
   d. conflict 5. ______

C. DEVELOPING VOCABULARY

Directions: Place in the space provided the letter of the word that best matches each definition. *(3 points each)*

1. a low wall or railing to protect the edge of a room or bridge
   a. parquet b. parapet c. paraffin d. parable 1. ______

2. having a fixed, firm purpose; determined
   a. resolute b. dissolute c. desolate d. saline 2. ______

3. hard to understand, not clear
   a. obscene b. obstinate c. obsessed d. obscure 3. ______

4. unexcitable
   a. solid b. stolid c. stilted d. stooped 4. ______

5. land owned solely by one ruler or owner
   a. remains b. reins c. feign d. domain 5. ______

6. to think about intently
   a. to concentrate b. to contemplate c. to conciliate d. to conclude 6. ______

7. seemingly lifeless, lacking the power to move or act
   a. inert b. intent c. invert d. inept 7. ______

8. to make or become larger or wider
   a. to retract b. to rebuke c. to dilate d. to refract 8. ______

9. to treat without reverence
   a. to deprive b. to descend c. to desert d. to desecrate 9. ______

10. knowledge understood or designed for a small, select group of people
    a. predetermined b. esoteric c. anonymous d. vacant 10. ______

NAME ______ CLASS ______ DATE ______ SCORE ______

UNIT 1: THE ELEMENTS OF A SHORT STORY

A MAN CALLED HORSE **Dorothy M. Johnson**

A. RECOGNIZING ELEMENTS OF SETTING

Directions: For each question, place the letter of the best answer in the space provided. *(5 points each)*

1. All of the following words describe the young man's Boston home *except*
a. discontented **b.** gracious **c.** comfortable **d.** privileged **1.** ______

2. When Horse arrives at the Crow camp as a captive, the setting in which he finds himself is
a. joyful
b. peaceful
c. horrible
d. mysterious **2.** ______

3. The descriptions of how Greasy Hand and her family live and behave contribute to our understanding of the story's
a. theme
b. suspense
c. climax
d. setting **3.** ______

4. The main conflict in "A Man Called Horse" takes place between
a. Horse and Old Greasy Hand
b. the Crow Indians and nature
c. Horse and the Crow culture
d. Horse and the white man's culture **4.** ______

5. At the end of the story, the narrator says that Horse "was the equal of any man on earth" because he
a. took revenge on the Crow Indians
b. progressed from behaving like a dog to behaving like a full member of Crow society
c. killed a Crow enemy and captured his horses
d. accepted Old Greasy Hand as his mother **5.** ______

B. INTERPRETING MEANINGS

Part 1. *Directions:* In the spaces provided, mark each true statement T and each false statement F. *(3 points each)*

1. In the West, the young man hires four men as companions, but continues to feel lonely. **1.** ______

2. The Crows have mercy on the white man when he is naked and unarmed. This is because they never kill anyone who cannot fight back. **2.** ______

3. The young man escaped from an Indian tribe once before. **3.** ______

4. The old woman gives him stinking, rancid grease so he will smell like the re[obscured] the tribe. ______

5. Indian men behave cautiously to avoid getting killed. ______

6. People laugh when Horse gives the old woman flowers because they see h[obscured] learning to behave like a Crow. ______

7. The old woman allows Horse to remain in the tepee because she is beginning to consider him a human being. 7. ______

8. Horse calls Pretty Calf "Freedom" because he loves and treasures her, and freedom is what he values most. 8. ______

9. After his marriage, Horse feels comfortable living with the tribe. 9. ______

10. At the end of the story, Horse cuts his arms to assure the Crows that he will not run away. 10. ______

Part 2. In "A Man Called Horse," the author writes, "He could afford to be magnanimous, for he knew he was a man." What do you think this means?

Directions: On a separate sheet of paper, write a paragraph explaining your point of view and citing parts of the story that influence your opinion. *(15 points)*

C. DEVELOPING VOCABULARY

Directions: Match each word in the left-hand column with the best meaning in the right-hand column. Place the letter of the best definition in the space provided. *(3 points each)*

______1. forestall
______2. regalia
______3. brandishing
______4. prosperous
______5. rancid
______6. docile
______7. detractor
______8. to deviate
______9. piteous
______10. querulous

a. having the taste or smell of spoiled fat or oil
b. a thin slice of bacon
c. obedient, submissive
d. complaining, whining
e. arousing or deserving pity
f. to prevent by taking action first
g. fancy clothes, often the symbols and emblems of royalty
h. successful, thriving
i. to move away from an accepted norm of behavior
j. waving triumphantly or threateningly
k. a person who speaks ill of someone
l. empty

NAME ________________ CLASS ________ DATE ________ SCORE ________

UNIT 1: THE ELEMENTS OF A SHORT STORY

INTRODUCTION / Understanding Point of View

Directions: For each question, place the letter of the best answer in the space provided. *(20 points each)*

1. The term "point of view" refers to the way the writer has chosen to
- **a.** create conflict
- **b.** present dialogue
- **c.** express his opinions
- **d.** see and tell the story

1. ______

2. The omniscient narrator
- **a.** is a character in the story
- **b.** knows everything about the characters
- **c.** uses the first-person pronoun, "I"
- **d.** resolves conflicts

2. ______

3. In the third-person limited point of view, the narrator
- **a.** describes the innermost feelings of every character
- **b.** analyzes the past, present, and future
- **c.** focuses on the thoughts and emotions of one character
- **d.** relates the entire story in flashback

3. ______

4. When one character tells the story, the point of view is called
- **a.** third-person omniscient
- **b.** second person
- **c.** first person
- **d.** third-person limited

4. ______

5. The narrator and the writer
- **a.** are always the same
- **b.** are never the same
- **c.** are not necessarily the same
- **d.** present different points of view in each story

5. ______

NAME________________________________ CLASS__________ DATE__________ SCORE__________

UNIT 1: THE ELEMENTS OF A SHORT STORY

CORRESPONDENCE **Carson McCullers**

A. UNDERSTANDING WHAT HAPPENED

Directions: In the spaces provided, mark each true statement **T** and each false statement **F**. *(5 points each)*

1. Henky Evans hopes to begin a pen pal correspondence with a South American student. **1.** ______

2. Henky knows what Manoel looks like from his photograph. **2.** ______

3. Henky feels she is different from other freshmen in her high school because she thinks about serious subjects. **3.** ______

4. When Henky writes that her Airedale is a "one-man dog," she means that he is her best friend. **4.** ______

5. Henky expects to receive from Manoel a letter that is written in perfect English. **5.** ______

6. When she grows up, Henky wants to be an Arctic explorer or a writer. **6.** ______

7. In November, Henky stays home from school because she is afraid of flunking Latin. **7.** ______

8. Henky's biggest mistake is assuming that Manoel will be her friend. **8.** ______

9. The last letter reveals Henky's hurt and angry feelings. **9.** ______

10. In the end, Manoel finally responds to Henky. **10.** ______

B. RECOGNIZING POINT OF VIEW

Directions: For each question, place the letter of the best answer in the space provided. *(6 points each)*

1. In "Correspondence," the story is told from the point of view called
a. third-person omniscient
b. third-person limited
c. second person
d. first person
1. ______

2. The point of view used in "Correspondence" is that of
a. Manoel García
b. Henky's English teacher
c. Henrietta Evans
d. Thomas
2. ______

3. Carson McCullers's choice of viewpoint enables her to suggest
   a. Brazilians' attitudes about Americans
   b. Manoel's attitude toward Thomas
   c. Manoel's feelings about Henky
   d. Henky's views of herself — 3. ______

4. One indication of the changes in Henky's attitude toward Manoel is
   a. the increasingly informal endings to her letters
   b. her addressing Manoel as "Mr."
   c. her omission of P.S.'s
   d. the fact that her letters grow longer — 4. ______

5. In her first letter to Manoel, Henky writes:

   > I thought a long time about you, Manoel, before writing this letter. And I have this strong feeling we would get along together. Do you like dogs? I have an airedale named Thomas and he is a one-man dog. I feel like I have known you for a very long time and that we could discuss all sorts of things together. My Spanish is not so good naturally as this is my first term on it. But I intend to study diligently so that between us we can make out what we are saying when we meet each other.

   This passage contains a clue about why Manoel may be reluctant to answer Henky's letters. The explanation could be that
   a. he does not like to write letters
   b. Henky assumes too much about a person she has never met
   c. Manoel can't stand dogs
   d. Manoel dislikes studious girls — 5. ______

C. DEVELOPING VOCABULARY

Directions: In the spaces provided, mark each true statement **T** and each false statement **F**. *(2 points each)*

1. *Correspondence* refers to letters that people exchange. — 1. ______
2. When students *ponder* an idea, they fail to think carefully about it. — 2. ______
3. A step taken *in vain* is usually successful. — 3. ______
4. A *diligent* student is hardworking. — 4. ______
5. A task performed *exceedingly* well is overdone. — 5. ______
6. *Reincarnation* is the rebirth of the soul in a new body. — 6. ______
7. A *hunch* is an educated guess based on specific knowledge. — 7. ______
8. A person who goes *astray* is on the wrong path. — 8. ______
9. A *raffle* is an interesting game of skill. — 9. ______
10. *Fulfilling* an agreement involves carrying it out as promised. — 10. ______

NAME ________________ CLASS ________ DATE ________ SCORE ________

UNIT 1: THE ELEMENTS OF A SHORT STORY

THE HAT **Jessamyn West**

A. RECOGNIZING POINT OF VIEW

Directions: For each question, place the letter of the best answer in the space provided. *(6 points each)*

1. The point of view used in "The Hat" is best described as that of
a. the Delahanty family
b. Cress and Edwin
c. third-person limited
d. third-person omniscient
1. ______

2. Cress can best be characterized as
a. mature
b. self-centered
c. brave
d. beautiful
2. ______

3. All of the following complicate the basic situation of "The Hat" *except*
a. Mrs. Delahanty's opposition to the hat
b. Cress's difficulty in balancing her large hat on her head
c. Edwin's failure to show up right away
d. Cress's letting her hat fall into the fish tank
3. ______

4. The climax of the story occurs when
a. Cress lets her hat fall into the aquarium
b. the aquarium owner loses his temper
c. Edwin defends Cress
d. Cress's new hat is ruined
4. ______

5. Cress's refusal to throw away the hat represents the story's
a. tone
b. climax
c. main complication
d. resolution
5. ______

B. INTERPRETING MEANINGS

Part 1. *Directions:* For each question, place the letter of the best answer in the space provided. *(5 points each)*

1. Mrs. Delahanty argues against Cress buying the hat because
a. it reminds her of her own youth
b. she thinks it will make Cress look cheap
c. she doesn't want Cress to grow up so fast
d. she considers the hat ugly
1. ______

2. Cress is determined to have the hat because she thinks it will
a. impress her girlfriends
b. win her parents' respect
c. satisfy her love of flowers
d. force Edwin to behave like a strong man
2. ______

3. It is clear that Cress doesn't feel the heat with the car window rolled up because
   a. the hat keeps her cool
   b. she is nervous
   c. she is lost in her fantasies
   d. the sea breeze is blowing 3.______

4. We gather that Mrs. Delahanty understands what her daughter is experiencing when she
   a. compares Cress's hat to table decorations
   b. protests when her husband agrees to look at the hat in the store
   c. steers the car for her husband while he removes his coat
   d. tells Cress, "...I don't know that I'd want a daughter of mine trigged out like everyone else." 4.______

5. At first, Cress reacts to the destruction of her hat with
   a. humiliation
   b. rage
   c. good humor
   d. tears 5.______

Part 2. In "The Hat," Cress's mother says to her husband, "She wanted to be such a lady—for him." Do you think this is what Cress wanted? Mrs. Delahanty is surprised that Cress wants to keep the hat to remember the day by. Why do mother and daughter react to the day's events so differently?

Directions: On a separate sheet of paper, write a paragraph stating your point of view. Cite specific parts of the story that influence your decision. *(15 points)*

C. DEVELOPING VOCABULARY

Directions: Match each word in the left-hand column with the best meaning in the right-hand column. Place the letter of the best definition in the space provided. *(5 points each)*

______ 1. becoming

______ 2. instinctive

______ 3. languorous

______ 4. gait

______ 5. malicious

______ 6. crux

a. a way of walking, stepping, or running

b. having a natural talent, skill, or ability

c. showing or having ill will, spiteful

d. suitable, attractive

e. tired, listless, or dreamy

f. the most important or significant point

g. energetic

h. tenant

NAME ____________________ CLASS __________ DATE __________ SCORE __________

UNIT 1: THE ELEMENTS OF A SHORT STORY

THE OLD DEMON **Pearl S. Buck**

A. UNDERSTANDING WHAT HAPPENED

Directions: In the spaces provided, mark each true statement **T** and each false statement **F**. *(5 points each)*

1. Mrs. Wang thinks she knows what a Japanese person looks like because she remembers having seen a foreigner once. **1.** ______

2. Mrs. Wang is frightened of the river because it is full of snakes. **2.** ______

3. The villagers respect Mrs. Wang because the village is named after her. **3.** ______

4. Mrs. Wang thinks that her husband was lazy. **4.** ______

5. The villagers of Three Mile Wangs never bothered to repair the dikes. **5.** ______

6. Mrs. Wang believes that the river is full of good and evil together. **6.** ______

7. According to Mrs. Wang, the Japanese will avoid her village because the river is so dangerous. **7.** ______

8. While the village is being bombed, Mrs. Wang lets her family leave without her so that she can protect her house. **8.** ______

9. Mrs. Wang cannot understand the pilot's speech because he is from the South. **9.** ______

10. When Mrs. Wang opens the sluice gate, she is worried about the pain of dying. **10.** ______

B. RECOGNIZING POINT OF VIEW

Directions: For each question, place the letter of the best answer in the space provided. *(4 points each)*

1. "The Old Demon" is told from the following point of view:
a. first-person
b. omniscient
c. third-person
d. all of the above **1.** ______

2. Because of the point of view used in this story, you see not only what happens to Mrs. Wang but know
a. what she is thinking
b. what the narrator is thinking
c. what the Japanese are thinking
d. that the river will rise **2.** ______

3. Mrs. Wang is characterized indirectly through her actions as
   a. foolish and superstitious
   b. cheerful and optimistic
   c. strong and respectful
   d. dictatorial

3. ______

4. By the end of the story, Mrs. Wang's attitude toward the river changes from watchful to
   a. welcoming
   b. angry
   c. threatening
   d. suspicious

4. ______

5. The following passage appears at the end of the story:

> Then she felt it seize her and lift her up to the sky. It was beneath her and around her. It rolled her joyfully hither and thither, and then, holding her close and enfolded, it went rushing against the enemy.

   This passage illustrates the fact that
   a. Mrs. Wang is a good swimmer
   b. the conflict between Mrs. Wang and the river is less important to her in the end than the conflict between her people and the Japanese
   c. the water seized her and lifted her to the top of the dike
   d. none of the above

5. ______

C. DEVELOPING VOCABULARY

Directions: Match each word in the left-hand column with the best meaning in the right-hand column. Place the letter of the best definition in the space provided. *(3 points each)*

______ 1. hearsay	a. dark and gloomy
______ 2. to disconcert	b. severe, sharp
______ 3. to deprecate	c. an evil spirit or demon
______ 4. to wheedle	d. with a firm purpose
______ 5. quavering	e. rumor
______ 6. dike	f. trembling
______ 7. demon	g. to belittle
______ 8. somber	h. to persuade by flattery or coaxing
______ 9. acute	i. a dam to hold back river or sea water from low land
______ 10. resolute	j. to upset or embarrass
	k. to see clearly
	l. intentionally harmful

NAME ____________________ CLASS ________ DATE ________ SCORE ________

UNIT 1: THE ELEMENTS OF A SHORT STORY

INTRODUCTION / Understanding Theme

Directions: For each question, place the letter of the best answer in the space provided. *(20 points each)*

1. The central idea of a story is called its
a. theme
b. subject
c. conclusion
d. introduction
1. ______

2. The subject of a story is simply its
a. theme
b. topic
c. climax
d. resolution
2. ______

3. Usually, a theme
a. preaches a moral lesson
b. presents an educational fact
c. reveals a truth about human behavior
d. provides entertainment only
3. ______

4. Fiction writers present their main ideas through
a. the actions of their characters
b. direct statements
c. persuasion
d. informal writing
4. ______

5. "Formula," or "slick," fiction is weak because of its
a. controversial subject matter
b. lack of depth
c. unhappy endings
d. writing style
5. ______

NAME ______________________ CLASS ________ DATE ________ SCORE ________

UNIT 1: THE ELEMENTS OF A SHORT STORY

THE SCARLET IBIS **James Hurst**

A. RECOGNIZING ELEMENTS OF THEME

Directions: For each question, place the letter of the best answer in the space provided. *(6 points each)*

1. The theme of "The Scarlet Ibis" can best be described as which of the following?
a. Parents never know what their children can achieve.
b. All brothers hate each other.
c. Personal pride can destroy those we love.
d. Love overcomes all obstacles. **1.** ______

2. Doodle resembles the scarlet ibis because
a. both die when forced to live in a way they were not meant to
b. both live in the deep South
c. the narrator understands neither one
d. both are beautiful **2.** ______

3. The scene in which Doodle lies bloodstained under a red bush echoes
a. the orange sun at the tops of the pines
b. the red-feathered bird lying under the bleeding tree
c. the color of the petunias in the front yard
d. the color of the wildflowers at the swamp **3.** ______

4. The subject of "The Scarlet Ibis" is
a. pride
b. death
c. honesty
d. religion **4.** ______

5. The narrator's greatest conflict is primarily with
a. his parents
b. the Southern way of life
c. Doodle's inability to be like other boys his age
d. Doodle's lying **5.** ______

B. INTERPRETING MEANINGS

Part 1. *Directions:* In the spaces provided, mark each true statement **T** and each false statement **F**. *(2 points each)*

1. The narrator uses a grindstone to symbolize the passage of time. **1.** ______

2. The narrator wants to kill his newborn brother when he learns that he has been born handicapped. **2.** ______

3. Doodle's efforts to learn to walk are a failure. **3.** ______

4. Doodle's name caused people to expect little from him and made even his smallest achievements seem very important. **4.** ______

5. The narrator and Doodle have their best times together in the swamp. 5. ______

6. The narrator admits that sometimes he was mean to his brother. 6. ______

7. Doodle finally learns to walk so that his brother will stop bothering him. 7. ______

8. Doodle's "lies" involve birds and people with wings who fly wherever they want to go. 8. ______

9. The narrator does not tell his parents about the development program he has planned for Doodle. 9. ______

10. As he runs through the thunderstorm, the narrator ignores the cries of his brother. 10. ______

Part 2. At one point in "The Scarlet Ibis," the narrator says, "I did not know then that pride is a wonderful, terrible thing, a seed that bears two vines, life and death."

Directions: On a separate sheet of paper, write a paragraph explaining what the narrator of the story means by this comment. Cite incidents from the story to support your findings. *(20 points)*

C. DEVELOPING VOCABULARY

Directions: Complete each sentence by placing the letter of the best answer in the space provided. *(3 points each)*

1. The ____ smell is offensive.
   a. hank b. rank c. stank d. lank 1. ______

2. The field of wheat ____ towards us like a wave.
   a. pillows b. bellows c. mellows d. billows 2. ______

3. The ____ of the whirling wind nearly knocks us over when it reaches us.
   a. vortex b. index c. ibex d. helix 3. ______

4. He is so sure of his ____ that he thinks he can do no wrong.
   a. gullibility b. infallibility c. reliability d. culpability 4. ______

5. The politician ____ his statements over and over again.
   a. remits b. rehabilitates c. relapsed d. reiterates 5. ______

6. Her movements were completely ____ after her long bus ride.
   a. uncoordinated b. uncooperative c. uncommon d. uncordial 6. ______

7. The ____ of boats completely surrounds the island.
   a. armor b. armada c. armament d. armature 7. ______

8. We watch the mechanic ____ the two pieces of metal together.
   a. soldier b. sodden c. solidify d. solder 8. ______

9. Throughout the valley, the mist and fog ____ until the air is completely clear.
   a. evacuate b. evaded c. evanesce d. evaluate 9. ______

10. The tropical bird was a brilliant shade of ____ .
    a. vermin b. vermilion c. vertical d. vermicelli 10. ______

IAME ______________________ CLASS __________ DATE __________ SCORE __________

JNIT 1: THE ELEMENTS OF A SHORT STORY

HE BRIDGE   Nicolai Chukovski

UNDERSTANDING WHAT HAPPENED

Directions: In the spaces provided, mark each true statement **T** and each false statement **F**. *(5 points each)*

1. Kostya is excited and happy about leaving home. **1.** ______

2. Kosty's mother has been dead for over a year. **2.** ______

3. Kostya must leave his hometown because he did poorly at school. **3.** ______

4. Kostya is afraid of leaving his grandmother. **4.** ______

5. The bicycle ride takes place on a narrow mountain path. **5.** ______

6. Kostya begins to pedal faster when he notices a colored dot in the distance. **6.** ______

7. During the chase, Kostya is able to overtake the girl because she lets him catch up with her. **7.** ______

8. Kostya is unfrightened as he pursues the girl on his bicycle. **8.** ______

9. The girl plunges off the bridge because Kostya shouts at her. **9.** ______

10. Kostya enjoys recovering the girl's bicycle from the bridge because the girl is watching him admiringly. **10.** ______

B. RECOGNIZING ELEMENTS OF THEME

Directions: For each question, place the letter of the best answer in the space provided. *(4 points each)*

1. Which of the following quotations best illustrates the main theme of the story?
a. "Gramma was the only one with whom he felt at ease, unafraid. But now he'd have to leave her...."
b. "The zeal of achievement had made him feel light and fearless."
c. "He felt like being extremely generous; as a matter of fact, he was sorry he couldn't give her his bike."
d. "He had suddenly made a discovery--he found out something about himself he had never known: he could accomplish tasks." **1.** ______

2. A secondary theme of this story describes how
a. young people can be reckless
b. fear can make people do strange things
c. maturity brings an awareness of love
d. the happiest years are adolescence **2.** ______

3. The main physical conflict in "The Bridge" takes place between Kostya and the river. His principal internal conflict is a struggle against
   a. the young girl
   b. his grandmother
   c. his immaturity
   d. his love for his hometown
   3.______

4. After his adventure, Kostya has changed. Which of the following words or phrases would you use to describe Kostya at the end of the story?
   a. conceited
   b. doubtful
   c. expectant and hopeful
   d. fearful
   4.______

5. The basic situation in "The Bridge" is that of a youth who
   a. must face leaving home and moving to his uncle's home in Siberia to learn a profession
   b. chases a young girl on a bicycle through the countryside
   c. dives into a dangerous river to save a young girl's life
   d. begins to regard his future in a new and more promising light
   5.______

C. DEVELOPING VOCABULARY

Directions: Place in the space provided the letter of the word that best matches each definition. *(3 points each)*

1. to lift with an effort
   a. joist b. rouse c. hoist d. baste
   1.______

2. like frosted glass
   a. transparent b. translucent c. transient d. transcendent
   2.______

3. to increase by adding elements
   a. compound b. impound c. compress d. impress
   3.______

4. a small stream that flows into a larger one
   a. tribulation b. trickle c. trilogy d. tributary
   4.______

5. what is left over, the remainder
   a. remedy b. remission c. remittance d. remnant
   5.______

6. the force of motion
   a. impetus b. impetuous c. inertia d. impetigo
   6.______

7. the top or highest point
   a. cleft b. crater c. crest d. crisis
   7.______

8. temporary wooden or metal framework
   a. baffling b. embankment c. abutment d. scaffolding
   8.______

9. to prevent from acting or moving freely
   a. refer b. hamper c. confer d. pamper
   9.______

10. imposing, impressive
    a. grandiose b. granular c. grandee d. grandiloquent
    10.______

NAME ______________________ CLASS __________ DATE __________ SCORE __________

UNIT 1: THE ELEMENTS OF A SHORT STORY

RED DRESS **Alice Munro** 

A. RECOGNIZING ELEMENTS OF THEME

Directions: For each question, place the letter of the best answer in the space provided. *(6 points each)*

1. The rite of passage described in "Red Dress" involves
a. graduating from high school
b. attending the Christmas dance
c. smoking a cigarette
d. wearing a homemade dress **1.** ______

2. Which one of the following ideas best expresses the central theme of "Red Dress"?
a. Experiences of adolescence help you to mature.
b. Some parents misunderstand their children.
c. Physical conflict is a fact of life.
d. High school dances can be painful. **2.** ______

3. The point of view used in "Red Dress" is
a. first-person
b. third-person limited from the narrator's point of view
c. third-person limited from the mother's point of view
d. third-person omniscient **3.** ______

4. The red dress is a symbol of
a. the narrator's feelings about boys
b. the narrator's relationship with her mother
c. adolescent embarrassment
d. the dance **4.** ______

5. Which quotation does the narrator use to characterize her mother?
a. "She worked at an old treadle machine pushed up against the window to get the light and also to let her look out."
b. "...the style my mother had chosen was not easy either."
c. "My mother pulled me about and pricked me with pins."
d. "...there were no patterns made to match the ideas that blossomed in her head." **5.** ______

B. INTERPRETING MEANINGS

Part 1. *Directions:* For each question, place the letter of the best answer in the space provided. *(5 points each)*

1. The narrator dislikes the dresses her mother makes because her mother
a. always uses velvet
b. refuses to make finished buttonholes
c. does not sew as well as the narrator would like
d. argues with her about styling **1.** ______

2. The "disguise" Lonnie wears around adults is an expression best described as
   a. angry   b. polite   c. sarcastic   d. sullen   2. ______

3. The narrator does not want to attend the Christmas dance because
   a. she made a pact with Lonnie
   b. Lonnie would get icy hands and palpitations
   c. Lonnie has not said that she wants to go to the dance
   d. she is embarrassed about her dress and uncomfortable at school   3. ______

4. Mary Fortune hides in the girl's washroom because
   a. she feels faint
   b. she wants a cigarette
   c. no boy has asked her to dance
   d. she hates the band   4. ______

5. Near the end of the story, this paragraph appears:

   > It was a good thing, I thought, that I had done that, for at my gate, when I said, "Well, goodnight," and after he said "Oh, yeah. Goodnight," he leaned toward me and kissed me, briefly, with the air of one who knew his job when he saw it, on the corner of my mouth. Then he turned back to town, never knowing he had been my rescuer, that he had brought me from Mary Fortune's territory into the ordinary world.

   To the narrator, the "ordinary world" is the world
   a. in which boys ask girls to dance
   b. in which the narrator is constantly embarrassed
   c. of the narrator's mother
   d. of independence and self-respect   5. ______

Part 2. At the end of "Red Dress" the narrator says, "I understood what a mysterious and oppressive obligation I had, to be happy, and how I had almost failed it, and would be likely to fail it, every time, and she would not know." What does she mean by this?

Directions: On a separate sheet of paper, write a paragraph explaining your point of view and citing parts of the story that influence your opinion. *(15 points)*

C. DEVELOPING VOCABULARY

Directions: In the spaces provided, mark each true statement **T** and each false statement **F.** *(3 points each)*

1. After harvesting, fields are often filled with *stubble.*   1. ______
2. A *ferocious* animal is difficult to manage.   2. ______
3. If you *accentuate* a word, you emphasize it.   3. ______
4. If a boxer *inflicts* a blow on his opponent, he makes him feel better.   4. ______
5. A *rapt* listener pays little attention to the speaker.   5. ______
6. A *premonition* is a feeling that something is going to happen, often something unpleasant.   6. ______
7. Cool and collected thoughts are symptoms of *delirium.*   7. ______
8. An *inanimate* object is endowed with life.   8. ______
9. *Languid* people lack vigor or vitality.   9. ______
10. If a group of children has *barbaric* manners, they are wild, crude, or uncivilized.   10. ______

NAME ______________________________ CLASS ____________ DATE ____________ SCORE ____________

UNIT 1: THE ELEMENTS OF A SHORT STORY

INTRODUCTION / Understanding Irony

Directions: For each question, place the letter of the best answer in the space provided. *(20 points each)*

1. Irony is
a. the logical chain of events in a story
b. the difference between what we expect and what actually happens in a story
c. the most important element in a story
d. the writer's expression of personal opinions
1. ________

2. The essence of irony is
a. fear
b. surprise
c. pride
d. hope
2. ________

3. When a character says one thing but means something else, there is
a. verbal irony
b. situational irony
c. dramatic irony
d. critical thinking
3. ________

4. In cases of situational irony,
a. the expected happens
b. comical moments always develop
c. chance often plays a profound role
d. tragedy is inevitable
4. ________

5. Dramatic irony occurs when
a. the characters shock the audience
b. the writer tricks the audience
c. the audience knows something that the characters do not know
d. tragedy is inevitable
5. ________

NAME ______________________ CLASS __________ DATE __________ SCORE __________

UNIT 1: THE ELEMENTS OF A SHORT STORY

THE LITTLE GIRL AND THE WOLF / THE PRINCESS AND THE TIN BOX — James Thurber

A. UNDERSTANDING WHAT HAPPENED

Directions: In the spaces provided, mark each true statement **T** and each false statement **F**. *(3 points each)*

1. The little girl in "The Little Girl and the Wolf" must walk through a forest to reach her grandmother's house. **1.** ______

2. The little girl does not recognize the wolf in the bed because he looks exactly like her grandmother. **2.** ______

3. The story of "The Little Girl and the Wolf" has the same ending as "Little Red Riding Hood." **3.** ______

4. James Thurber's moral to "The Little Girl and the Wolf" indicates his sympathy for the wolf. **4.** ______

5. As a child, the heroine of "The Princess and the Tin Box" plays only with toys made from precious materials. **5.** ______

6. The blackbird in the story has a flute made of boxwood. **6.** ______

7. Four of the Princess's suitors bring her gifts made of jewels and precious metals. **7.** ______

8. The fifth prince is ugly and stupid as well as poor. **8.** ______

9. The Princess is fascinated by the fifth prince's gift. **9.** ______

10. This paragraph appears near the end of the story:

> "The way I figure it," she said, "is this. It is a very large and expensive box, and when I am married, I will meet many admirers who will give me precious gems with which to fill it to the top. Therefore, it is the most valuable of all the gifts my suitors have brought me, and I like it the best."

This excerpt suggests that the Princess makes her choice on the basis of how she has been reared by her father, the King. **10.** ______

B. RECOGNIZING IRONY

Directions: For each question, place the letter of the best answer in the space provided. *(8 points each)*

1. An example of situational irony from "The Little Girl and the Wolf" is:
- **a.** "...she saw that there was somebody in bed with a nightcap and nightgown on."
- **b.** "...the little girl took an automatic out of her basket and shot the wolf dead."
- **c.** "...a wolf does not look any more like your grandmother than the Metro-Goldwyn lion looks like Calvin Coolidge."
- **d.** "...the wolf asked her where her grandmother lived and the little girl told him..." **1.** ______

2. The irony used in "The Princess and the Tin Box" is an example of
   a. verbal irony
   b. situational irony
   c. dramatic irony
   d. foolish irony

2. ______

3. "The Princess and the Tin Box" is ironic because you expect
   a. the story to end like a traditional fairy tale
   b. the Princess to choose one of the wealthy princes
   c. the princes to be asked to perform difficult deeds
   d. the story to be longer

3. ______

4. The climax of "The Princess and the Tin Box" occurs when
   a. the Princess attends her brother's wedding
   b. the King announces the Princess's wedding
   c. the princes arrive
   d. the Princess makes her choice

4. ______

5. In "The Princess and the Tin Box," the moral can best be described as:
   a. Humble presents are better than rich presents.
   b. One who is accustomed to diamonds will never be satisfied with stones.
   c. He who laughs last laughs best.
   d. Fathers know best, even if they are kings.

5. ______

C. DEVELOPING VOCABULARY

Directions: Match each word in the left-hand column with the best meaning in the right-hand column. Place the letter of the best definition in the space provided. *(3 points each)*

______ 1. lyre
______ 2. nightingale
______ 3. topaz
______ 4. ebony
______ 5. realm
______ 6. mica
______ 7. to disdain
______ 8. tawdry
______ 9. to glut
______ 10. revelry

a. to supply more than there is demand for
b. showy and cheap
c. a small harp
d. noisy merrymaking
e. a sweet-singing bird
f. a white material made from bone or tusk
g. a hard, black wood
h. kingdom, sphere, or domain
i. to laugh about
j. to scorn
k. a thin, transparent, layered mineral
l. a hard, gem-like mineral, yellow to brownish in color

NAME ______________________ CLASS __________ DATE __________ SCORE __________

UNIT 1: THE ELEMENTS OF A SHORT STORY

THE SNIPER **Liam O'Flaherty**

A. RECOGNIZING IRONY

Directions: For each question, place the letter of the best answer in the space provided. *(6 points each)*

1. The surprise twist used by Liam O'Flaherty occurs when the sniper
a. fires at the old woman
b. is hit after shooting the woman
c. tricks the other sniper
d. recognizes the man he has killed — **1.** ______

2. "The Sniper" is an example of
a. dramatic irony
b. situational irony
c. inferred irony
d. verbal irony — **2.** ______

3. The theme of "The Sniper" could be stated as:
a. War is difficult.
b. War turns brother against brother.
c. In combat you must follow your heart.
d. Only the smart survive. — **3.** ______

4. In this story, the purpose of irony is to create feelings of
a. admiration
b. indifference
c. horror
d. satisfaction — **4.** ______

5. One of the many ironies of the "The Sniper" is that the young assassin
a. possesses no political beliefs
b. was trained by his brother
c. is a religious man
d. utters a cry of joy upon shooting his brother — **5.** ______

B. INTERPRETING MEANINGS

Part 1. *Directions:* For each question, place the letter of the best answer in the space provided. (*5 points each*)

1. The Republican sniper has not eaten since morning because
a. this is his first combat experience
b. his commander is angry
c. he has had no food
d. he was too excited to think of food — **1.** ______

2. The sniper shoots the old woman because
a. she is an informer
b. she threatens him physically
c. she is an easy target
d. his orders are to shoot at anything that moves — **2.** ______

3. The sniper's actions under fire indicate that he is
   a. an inexperienced soldier
   b. fearless and devoid of emotion
   c. an experienced fighter
   d. riddled with fear and guilt
   3.______

4. The Republican sniper wants to identify the enemy sniper because
   a. he wonders if he knows him
   b. he thinks he recognizes him
   c. his commander needs the information
   d. he likes to take risks
   4.______

5. After the Republican sniper shoots his enemy, this paragraph appears:

   > The sniper looked at his enemy falling and he shuddered. The lust of battle died in him. He became bitten by remorse. The sweat stood out in beads on his forehead. Weakened by his wound and the long summer day of fasting and watching on the roof, he revolted from the sight of the shattered mass of his dead enemy. His teeth chattered, he began to gibber to himself, cursing the war, cursing himself, cursing everybody.

   The author's purpose in this passage is to show
   a. the effects of fasting
   b. the sniper's weakened physical condition
   c. that the sniper is really a coward
   d. that the sniper still had human feelings
   5.______

Part 2. Liam O'Flaherty writes about people who are living in the middle of a civil war. How would you describe his feelings about war?

Directions: On a separate sheet of paper, write a paragraph explaining your point of view and citing parts of the story that influence your opinion. *(15 points)*

C. DEVELOPING VOCABULARY

Directions: Place in the space provided the letter of the word that best matches each definition. *(3 points each)*

1. to wrap, cover, or hide
   a. entrench b. envelop c. envelope d. environs
   1.______
2. soft and woolly
   a. fleet b. flaxen c. fleecy d. flinty
   2.______
3. to harass, besiege
   a. beleaguer b. befog c. belabor d. benight
   3.______
4. sudden, and often intense
   a. sporadic b. spasmodic c. specious d. spurious
   4.______
5. a person who practices unusual self-denial or discipline
   a. ascorbic b. aseptic c. anesthetic d. ascetic
   5.______
6. torn or ragged
   a. transposed b. truncated c. tattered d. transpired
   6.______
7. broken or cracked
   a. fractionate b. fractured c. fractious d. fragile
   7.______
8. a sudden severe attack
   a. paroxysm b. paradigm c. parallax d. parlance
   8.______
9. deep, painful regret for having done wrong
   a. deplore b. morose c. bemoan d. remorse
   9.______
10. to go without food
   a. feast b. fault c. fasten d. fast
   10.______

NAME ______________________ CLASS ________ DATE ________ SCORE ________

UNIT 1: THE ELEMENTS OF A SHORT STORY

THE CASK OF AMONTILLADO **Edgar Allan Poe**

A. UNDERSTANDING WHAT HAPPENED

Directions: In the spaces provided, mark each true statement **T** and each false statement **F**. *(6 points each)*

1. The narrator of "The Cask of Amontillado" wants revenge on Fortunato because he has been insulted by him. **1.** ______

2. The narrator tells Fortunato about a cask of amontillado in order to entice him into the vaults. **2.** ______

3. Fortunato is drunk when Montresor leads him to the vaults **3.** ______

4. The niche in which Fortunato is walled up is a former wine vault. **4.** ______

5. The following passage appears near the beginning of the story:

> It must be understood that neither by word nor deed had I given Fortunato cause to doubt my good will. I continued, as was my wont, to smile in his face, and he did not perceive that my smile *now* was at the thought of his immolation.

This excerpt illustrates the central element of dramatic irony in the plot. **5.** ______

B. RECOGNIZING IRONY

Directions: For each question, place the letter of the best answer in the space provided. *(6 points each)*

1. In "The Cask of Amontillado," an example of dramatic irony occurs when
- **a.** Fortunato dresses like a jester
- **b.** you know that Montresor plans revenge, but Fortunato does not
- **c.** the narrator urges Fortunato to test the amontillado even though he is already intoxicated
- **d.** the crime is committed during carnival season **1.** ______

2. All of the following are examples of verbal irony used by the narrator *except:*
- **a.** "My dear Fortunato, you are luckily met."
- **b.** "How remarkably well you are looking today!"
- **c.** "I will not impose upon your good nature."
- **d.** "The Montresors...were a great and numerous family." **2.** ______

3. The carnival atmosphere in which Poe sets the crime contributes to the tale's
- **a.** conflict
- **b.** irony
- **c.** plot
- **d.** point of view **3.** ______

4. The first-person point of view enhances the dramatic irony by
   a. revealing the narrator's evil nature and his plot firsthand
   b. making the background of the story clear
   c. explaining Fortunato's motives
   d. demonstrating Montresor's verbal irony

4. ______

5. The climax of "The Cask of Amontillado" occurs when
   a. Montresor meets Fortunato
   b. Fortunato agrees to enter the catacombs
   c. Montresor walls up the entrance of the niche
   d. Fortunato says, "For the love of God, Montresor!"

5. ______

C. DEVELOPING VOCABULARY

Directions: In the spaces provided, mark each true statement **T** and each false statement **F**. *(4 points each)*

1. To *preclude* is to make impossible, to prevent. 1. ______

2. To *redress* a wrong is to make it right. 2. ______

3. A person who is guilty of *imposture* pretends to be something he or she is not. 3. ______

4. Someone who *accosts* you hits you with a large stick. 4. ______

5. To *abscond* is to dance about wildly. 5. ______

6. Audiences watching actors *gesticulate* see them use their hands to express ideas or feelings. 6. ______

7. A *crypt* is a simple grave dug in the ground. 7. ______

8. To *circumscribe* an object, a line is drawn straight through it. 8. ______

9. Runners who *endeavor* to finish a race give up before they start. 9. ______

10. An *obstinate* person is stubborn. 10. ______

NAME ______________________ CLASS __________ DATE __________ SCORE __________

UNIT 1: THE ELEMENTS OF A SHORT STORY

THE NECKLACE **Guy de Maupassant**

A. RECOGNIZING IRONY

Directions: For each question, place the letter of the best answer in the space provided. *(6 points each)*

1. In "The Necklace," the greatest situational irony occurs when Mme. Loisel
a. is born into the wrong class
b. convinces her husband to let her buy a new dress
c. attends the kind of party she had always dreamed of
d. discovers that she has wasted ten years of her life to replace a cheap necklace **1.** ______

2. One of the principal themes of this story is that
a. we suffer for our vanities
b. it is unwise to borrow jewelry
c. parties can lead to trouble
d. friends should be honest with each other **2.** ______

3. Guy de Maupassant tells his story in
a. the first-person from Mme. Loisel's point of view
b. the third-person limited from Mme. Loisel's point of view
c. the third-person limited from M. Loisel's point of view
d. the third-person omniscient **3.** ______

4. We realize that Mme. Loisel's experience has failed to change her character when the author writes:
a. "She played her part, however, with sudden heroism."
b. "She became heavy, rough, harsh, like one of the poor."
c. "And now that everything was paid off, she would tell her the whole story. Why not?"
d. "'Yes, I've [Mathilde] had a hard time....And plenty of misfortunes and all on account of you!'" **4.** ______

5. Mme. Forestier's final words, "Why, at most it was worth only five hundred francs!" can be best summed up as
a. verbal irony
b. logical irony
c. situational irony
d. theatrical irony **5.** ______

B. INTERPRETING MEANINGS

Part 1. *Directions:* In the spaces provided, mark each true statement **T** and each false statement **F**. *(3 points each)*

1. M. Loisel never puts his wife's interests before his own. **1.** ______

2. The author believes that beauty, grace, and charm can make up for lack of money and status. **2.** ______

3. At the beginning of the story, Mme. Loisel grieves constantly because she feels she lives a deprived life. **3.** ______

4. Mme. Loisel is always satisfied with what she gets. 4. ______

5. M. Loisel makes a personal sacrifice so that his wife can have a new dress. 5. ______

6. Seeing her friend distresses Mme. Loisel because she envies her. 6. ______

7. At first, Mme. Loisel rejects the invitation to the reception so that her husband will feel guilty and buy her a new dress. 7. ______

8. Mme. Loisel rushes from the party to avoid being seen in her inexpensive coat. 8. ______

9. After ten years of labor, Mme. Loisel remains very attractive. 9. ______

10. This sentence appears near the end of the story:

> But, sometimes, while her husband was at work, she would sit near the window and think of that long-ago evening when, at the dance, she had been so beautiful and admired.

This excerpt indicates that Mme. Loisel had been successful and contented throughout her life. 10. ______

Part 2. When Mme. Loisel takes the necklace to Mme. Forestier, the author writes that Jeanne Forestier speaks "frostily." Is this an accurate characterization of Mme. Forestier, or does it reflect something else?

Directions: On a separate sheet of paper, write a paragraph explaining your point of view and citing parts of the story that influence your opinion. *(10 points)*

C. DEVELOPING VOCABULARY

Directions: Complete each sentence by placing the letter of the best answer in the space provided. *(3 points each)*

1. The young woman brought her family's house as a _____ to her marriage.
a. cowry b. dowry c. salary d. bower 1. ______

2. The _____ of the apartment was depressing..
a. dissertation b. diversion c. dubiousness d. dinginess 2. ______

3. It is the goose's _____ drives that help it find its flock.
a. instinctive b. inhuman c. initial d. instructive 3. ______

4. The constant sound of the rain _____ drumming on the tin roof drove the man crazy.
a. increasingly b. incessantly c. incapably d. incidentally 4. ______

5. My brother is so _____ that nothing will relieve his misery.
a. disgraced b. discreet c. disconsolate d. discordant 5. ______

6. Her _____ is made worse when the girls begin to annoy her.
a. vexation b. vector c. vaccination d. vixen 6. ______

7. The _____ is finding it difficult to make a living.
a. paper b. popper c. polar d. pauper 7. ______

8. After being rescued, Russell and Jane now find themselves in another _____.
a. predicate b. predicament c. prediction d. predilection 8. ______

9. The children's _____ clothing is not warm enough for winter.
a. scarce b. scanty c. scented d. scattered 9. ______

10. We feel that the restaurant's _____ prices are too high for students.
a. exacting b. exceeding c. exceptional d. exorbitant 10. ______

NAME ______________________ CLASS ________ DATE ________ SCORE ________

UNIT 1: THE ELEMENTS OF A SHORT STORY

WORD ANALOGIES / Extending Vocabulary Skills

Directions: In the space provided, write the letter of the pair of words that best describes a *relationship* that is closest to that of the capitalized pair of words. (*5 points each*)

1. HAGGARD : GAUNT ::
   a. ragged : trim
   b. weak : strong
   c. happy : sad
   d. stout : burly
   1. ______

2. METROPOLIS : COUNTRYSIDE ::
   a. urbane : sophisticated
   b. urban : rural
   c. simple : complicated
   d. nation : continent
   2. ______

3. TRIBUTARY : RIVER ::
   a. tribute : captors
   b. payment : ransom
   c. root : tree
   d. dam : flood
   3. ______

4. BLUSTER : WORDS ::
   a. brandish : weapons
   b. brace : support
   c. blithe : spirits
   d. brash : actions
   4. ______

5. RESOLUTE : INDOMITABLE ::
   a. dissolve : evaporate
   b. resolution : domination
   c. dogged : stubborn
   d. sunshine : cloudiness
   5. ______

6. BELEAGUER : SURROUND ::
   a. hasten : hesitate
   b. falter : succeed
   c. hamper : interfere
   d. sustain : diminish
   6. ______

7. UNIFORM : SIMILAR ::
   a. clothing : rules
   b. unison : combination
   c. formally : informally
   d. unique : distinctive
   7. ______

8. POTENCY : LANGUOR ::
   a. power : vigor
   b. strength : weakness
   c. intrepid : brave
   d. laziness : sloth
   8. ______

9. PITTANCE : ABUNDANCE ::
   a. much : more
   b. scanty : plenty
   c. harvest : famine
   d. part : whole
   9. ______

10. SUMMIT : DEPRESSION ::
    a. mountain : hollow
    b. sad : happy
    c. extreme : common
    d. memory : impression
    10. ______

11. AMBLE : CAREEN ::
    a. journey : walk
    b. stroll : lurch
    c. traverse : wander
    d. stalk : strut
    11. ______

12. OPPRESSIVE : SEVERE ::
    a. harsh : compassionate
    b. tyrannical : docile
    c. sullen : cheerful
    d. ruthless : pitiless
    12. ______

13. INANIMATE : LANGUID ::
    a. lifeless : listless
    b. mild : tepid
    c. faint : feeble
    d. decayed : rotten
    13. ______

14. IMPRUDENT : DISSOLUTE ::
    a. precipitate : dissolve
    b. wise : foolish
    c. barbaric : savage
    d. rude : kind
    14. ______

15. STOLID : TACITURN ::
a. lethargic : apathetic
b. docile : excited
c. exuberant : verbose
d. immobile : animate **15.** ______

16. DISCONSOLATE : WOEFUL ::
a. desolate : lonely
b. desolation : destruction
c. privation : sufficiency
d. poverty : wealth **16.** ______

17. MOROSE : SULLEN ::
a. more : less
b. impudent : wise
c. gloomy : sulky
d. cheerful : glum **17.** ______

18. PREMONITION : FUTURE ::
a. intuition : hunch
b. superstition : present
c. caution : now
d. reminiscence : past **18.** ______

19. IMMINENT : IMPENDING ::
a. former : following
b. simultaneous : concurrent
c. prior : forthcoming
d. preceding : succeeding **19.** ______

20. VULNERABLE : PRECARIOUS ::
a. insecure : uncertain
b. intelligent : ignorant
c. intolerable : endurable
d. offensive : defensive **20.** ______

NAME ____________________ CLASS ________ DATE ________ SCORE ________

UNIT 1: THE ELEMENTS OF A SHORT STORY

UNIT REVIEW / Applying Skills I

A. READING A STORY

Directions: Read the passage below carefully, then answer the questions that follow.

In the square bedroom with the big window Mama and Papa were lolling back on their pillows handing each other things from the wide black tray on the small table with crossed legs. They were smiling and they smiled even more when the little boy, with the feeling of sleep still in his skin and hair, came in and walked up to the bed. Leaning against it, his bare toes wriggling in the white fur rug, he went on eating peanuts which he took from his pajama pocket. He was four years old.

"Here's my baby," said Mama. "Lift him up, will you?"

He went limp as a rag for Papa to take him under the arms and swing him up over a broad, tough chest. He sank between his parents like a bear cub in a warm litter, and lay there comfortably. He took another peanut between his teeth, cracked the shell, picked out the nut whole and ate it.

"Running around without his slippers again," said Mama. "His feet are like icicles."

"He crunches like a horse," said Papa. "Eating peanuts before breakfast will ruin his stomach. Where did he get them?"

"You brought them yesterday," said Mama, with exact memory, "in a grisly little cellophane sack. I have asked you dozens of times not to bring him things to eat. Put him out, will you? He's spilling shells all over me."

Almost at once the little boy found himself on the floor again. He moved around to Mama's side of the bed and leaned confidingly near her and began another peanut. As he chewed he gazed solemnly in her eyes.

"Bright-looking specimen, isn't he?" asked Papa, stretching his long legs and reaching for his bathrobe. "I suppose you'll say it's my fault he's dumb as an ox."

"He's my baby, my only baby," said Mama richly, hugging him, "and he's a dear lamb." His neck and shoulders were quite boneless in her firm embrace. He stopped chewing long enough to receive a kiss on his crumby chin. "He's sweet as clover," said Mama. The baby went on chewing.

"Look at him staring like an owl," said Papa.

Mama said, "He's an angel and I'll never get used to having him."

"We'd be better off if we never *had* had him," said Papa. He was walking about the room and his back was turned when he said that. There was silence for a moment. The little boy stopped eating, and stared deeply at his Mama. She was looking at the back of Papa's head, and her eyes were almost black. "You're going to say that just once too often," she told him in a low voice. "I hate you when you say that."

Papa said, "You spoil him to death. You never correct him for anything. And you don't take care of him. You let him run around eating peanuts before breakfast."

"You gave him the peanuts, remember that," said Mama. She sat up and hugged her only baby once more. He nuzzled softly in the pit of her arm. "Run along, my darling," she told him in her gentlest voice, smiling at him straight in the eyes. "Run along," she said, her arms falling away from him. "Get your breakfast."

FROM "The Downward Path to Wisdom" by Katherine Anne Porter

B. ANALYZING A STORY

Directions: For each question, place the letter of the best answer in the space provided. *(5 points each)*

1. This excerpt is most likely from
a. the exposition of the story
b. the climax of the story
c. the resolution of the story
d. none of the above

1. ______

2. The primary conflict established is
a. the parents' external conflict with each other
b. an external conflict between the parents and the society in which they live
c. the mother's internal conflict over whether she has properly cared for the boy
d. an external conflict between the boy and his father

2. ______

3. The characterization of Mama and Papa is provided mainly through
a. the little boy's thoughts about them
b. their speech
c. their thoughts
d. their appearance

3. ______

4. Imagery is used in paragraph 3 to appeal to the reader's sense of
a. smell
b. taste
c. sight and touch
d. hearing

4. ______

5. The mood of the excerpt might be described as
a. tender
b. humorous
c. tense
d. upbeat

5. ______

6. The point of view from which this excerpt is told is
 a. first person
 b. third person omniscient
 c. third person limited
 d. none of the above **6.** ______

7. The title "The Downward Path to Wisdom" foreshadows
 a. the painful inner growth of a central character
 b. the family's plummeting finances
 c. the family's move downtown
 d. the family's mountain climbing experience **7.** ______

8. The author's reference to the child as Mama's "only baby" at the end of the excerpt in an example of
 a. mood
 b. conflict
 c. imagery
 d. irony **8.** ______

9. Irony is established by the contrasts between
 a. the little boy's comfort and the parents' conversation
 b. the cozy setting and the parents' behavior
 c. Mama's words and her actions
 d. all of the above **9.** ______

10. The author's attitude toward Mama and Papa is
 a. sympathetic
 b. disapproving
 c. condescending
 d. affectionate **10.** ______

C. WRITING ABOUT A STORY

Which character is portrayed most sympathetically in this excerpt? How can you tell? Find evidence in the excerpt to support your opinion.

Directions: Using the evidence you have found in the excerpt, write *one* paragraph, perhaps beginning with a statement such as: "The author sympathizes with ______________. This is clear because ______________." *(25 points)*

____

____

____

____

____

____

____

D. ANALYZING LANGUAGE AND DEVELOPING VOCABULARY

Directions: In the spaces provided, mark each true statement **T** and each false statement **F**. *(5 points each)*

1. Judging from the context, *lolling* (paragraph 1) probably refers to a sharp, quick action. **1.** ______

2. The use of the word *grisly* (paragraph 6) helps the reader to understand Mama's mood. **2.** ______

3. Paragraphs 4 and 5 contain figurative language. **3.** ______

4. Judging from the context, the meaning of *litter* in paragraph 3 is "wastepaper." **4.** ______

5. In paragraph 3, *broad* and *tough* are examples of homonyms. **5.** ______

NAME ______________________ CLASS __________ DATE __________ SCORE __________

UNIT 1: THE ELEMENTS OF A SHORT STORY

CRITICAL THINKING AND WRITING / Applying Skills II

A. SUMMARIZING A PLOT

Directions: In *one* paragraph, summarize the plot of "Thank You, M'am." Be sure to organize your paragraph in time sequence (that is, the order in which events occurred) and to explain causes and their effects clearly. *(40 points)*

____

____

____

____

____

____

____

____

____

B. EXPLAINING THE FUNCTION OF SETTING

Directions: Write *two* paragraphs to describe the setting of "The Hat." In the first paragraph, explain how setting functions in the story. In the second paragraph, explain how the setting seems to change with the changes in the main character's feelings. *(30 points)*

____

____

____

____

____

____

____

____

____

C. RESPONDING TO A STORY

Directions: Write *one* paragraph that describes your response to any *two* of the following stories: "Poison," "Antaeus," "The Sniper." Begin your paragraph by stating which story you like better. Follow this with details that compare the two stories and support your opinion. You might wish to comment on elements such as the story's plot, setting, characterization, or use of language. *(30 points)*

NAME ______________________ CLASS __________ DATE __________ SCORE __________

UNIT 2: THE ELEMENTS OF POETRY

UNIT INTRODUCTION / Understanding the Elements of Poetry

Directions: For each question, place the letter of the best answer in the space provided. *(10 points each)*

1. Poets impart their ideas and feelings by
a. using words and meanings imaginatively
b. following the rules of language
c. always writing about uplifting themes
d. using rhythms seriously
1. ______

2. Poets play with the sounds of language through their use of
a. personification
b. rhymes and rhythms
c. serious messages
d. metaphors and similes
2. ______

3. In punning, poets use a word that
a. they have made up
b. twists your tongue
c. has two meanings
d. sounds funny
3. ______

4. Poetry differs from other kinds of writing because it
a. has no message
b. is unclear
c. is written plainly
d. doesn't have to be literal
4. ______

5. Poetry is important to a civilization because it
a. reflects the values and character of a people
b. includes statistics and charts
c. presents vital economic data
d. offers a literal record of a country's history
5. ______

6. The antennae of poets
a. record interesting comments
b. capture the dreams and beliefs of a nation
c. promote the work of elected legislators
d. gather details to add to their work
6. ______

7. Percy Bysshe Shelley called poets "unacknowledged legislators" because
a. few people read poetry
b. the poets were unpaid lawmakers
c. poets express the laws of our spiritual life
d. making laws is really a poetic experience
7. ______

8. The various forms of poetry
a. are just like plays
b. are similar to stories
c. rarely have sentences
d. are written in lines

8. ______

9. Good poets use
a. well-chosen words
b. few comparisons
c. confusing punctuation
d. too many words

9. ______

10. A poem is meant to be understood
a. with your eyes and ears only
b. with your mind and heart
c. through silent reading
d. after one reading

10. ______

NAME ______________________ CLASS __________ DATE __________ SCORE __________

UNIT 2: THE ELEMENTS OF POETRY

INTRODUCTION / Understanding Imagery

Directions: For each question, place the letter of the best answer in the space provided. *(10 points each)*

1. Imagery is one of the elements that contribute to a poem's
a. forcefulness
b. exactness
c. perfection
d. structure
1. ______

2. Images in poetry can best be described as
a. exact copies of objects
b. approximate copies of objects
c. actual objects
d. symbols for objects
2. ______

3. Poetic images help us to
a. think logically
b. understand history
c. read carefully
d. see things freshly
3. ______

4. Images appeal to
a. any one of our five senses
b. our sense of color
c. our sense of motion
d. our sense of texture
4. ______

5. To create an image, a poet requires
a. an entire stanza
b. a whole poem
c. only a single word or phrase
d. a complete sentence
5. ______

6. In addition to providing insights, images also can help us to
a. evaluate plans
b. make decisions
c. calculate distances
d. appreciate all of our senses
6. ______

7. Imagery is the product of the poet's
a. intelligence
b. family history
c. own way of seeing the world
d. religious beliefs
7. ______

8. The type of imagery a poet uses is determined by
   a. the length of his work
   b. the time and place in which he lives
   c. his education
   d. his financial situation

8.______

9. Poets who live in rural areas are likely to write about
   a. street scenes
   b. industrial landscapes
   c. nautical subjects
   d. country matters

9.______

10. The way an image is phrased can have an effect on our
   a. feelings and emotions
   b. financial decisions
   c. ability to learn
   d. choice of careers

10.______

NAME ________________ CLASS ________ DATE ________ SCORE ________

UNIT 2: THE ELEMENTS OF POETRY

IMAGERY: Seeing Things Freshly

A. RECOGNIZING IMAGERY

Directions: For each question, place the letter of the best answer in the space provided. *(6 points each)*

1. In "If the Owl Calls Again," the imagery suggests
- **a.** the loneliness of an Arctic night
- **b.** the terror of the owl's prey
- **c.** the night flight of an owl
- **d.** jungle warfare

1. ______

2. In "The Bat," imagery is used chiefly to contrast
- **a.** a comfortable sight with an alarming one
- **b.** the appearance of mice and bats
- **c.** the faces of bats and humans
- **d.** daytime and nighttime occurrences

2. ______

3. The total impact of the imagery in "Poem To Be Read at 3 A.M." suggests that
- **a.** night drivers are virtually blind
- **b.** motorists in trouble at night are helpless
- **c.** people are sadly separated and alone
- **d.** driving provides poets with good ideas

3. ______

4. The images in "In a Mirror" add up to a picture of
- **a.** the plight of many handicapped people
- **b.** a missed opportunity to reach out to another person
- **c.** the danger of walking alone on an icy street
- **d.** a completely self-centered person

4. ______

5. Through the imagery in "Southbound on the Freeway," you see
- **a.** the probability that aliens are observing us
- **b.** a new view of an ordinary aspect of our lives
- **c.** the ignorance of motorists and highway engineers
- **d.** a helpless driver trapped in a traffic jam

5. ______

B. INTERPRETING POETRY

Directions: In the spaces provided, mark each true statement **T** and each false statement **F**. *(3 points each)*

Part 1. Finding Facts

1. In Haines's poem, the setting is a cold land. **1.** ______

2. Roethke describes how a bat's behavior changes at night. **2.** ______

3. Justice knew immediately for whom he would be writing his poem. **3.** ______

4. Stubbs's poem is told from the blind man's point of view. 4. ______

5. The tourist in Swenson's poem is observing the scene from above. 5. ______

Part 2. Understanding Moods and Meanings

6. Haines presents night as a time of fulfillment and union. 6. ______

7. Roethke feels threatened by the bat while it is flying around at a distance. 7. ______

8. Both Haines and Roethke feel close to the animals about which they write. 8. ______

9. For Justice and Stubbs, driving alone takes on the same symbolic value. 9. ______

10. Swenson's poem expresses her admiration of modern-day travel. 10. ______

Part 3. Writing About Poetry

Statement: The title of a poem may take on its full meaning only after you have read the poem.

Directions: On a separate sheet of paper, write a paragraph to support this statement, using examples from a poem in this section. *(10 points)*

C. LEARNING THE LANGUAGE OF POETRY

Directions: Match each phrase in the left-hand column with the best meaning in the right-hand column. Place the letter of the best definition in the space provided. *(3 points each)*

______ 1. "morning climbs the limbs"

______ 2. "hooded against the frost"

______ 3. "drifts toward Asia"

______ 4. "take wing"

______ 5. "fingers make a hat"

______ 6. "brushes up against"

______ 7. "but for"

______ 8. "listening for the ground"

______ 9. "in a broken sequence"

______ 10. "transparent parts"

a. touches

b. finding out what's around

c. except for

d. windows

e. headlights

f. the sun rises

g. flies off

h. moves westward

i. protected by feathers

j. has difficulty with

k. in a series of images

l. wings cover his face

NAME ______________________ CLASS__________ DATE__________ SCORE__________

UNIT 2: THE ELEMENTS OF POETRY

INTRODUCTION / Understanding Similes and Metaphors

Directions: For each question, place the letter of the best answer in the space provided. *(10 points each)*

1. *Figurative language* involves expressions that emphasize
- **a.** imaginative connections
- **b.** literal meanings
- **c.** unusual definitions
- **d.** clever rhymes

1. ______

2. A *figure of speech* is always based on a
- **a.** conversation
- **b.** conclusion
- **c.** comparison
- **d.** complication

2. ______

3. Figurative language can be thought of as similar to
- **a.** typing
- **b.** shorthand
- **c.** word processing
- **d.** cost accounting

3. ______

4. Using figures of speech makes it possible for communication to be
- **a.** more complex
- **b.** clearer
- **c.** literal
- **d.** instantaneous

4. ______

5. In everyday life, figures of speech are used
- **a.** rarely
- **b.** constantly
- **c.** by poets only
- **d.** on formal occasions only

5. ______

6. *Similes* make comparisons by using words such as
- **a.** *by* or *through*
- **b.** *rhyme* or *rhythm*
- **c.** *like, as, than,* or *resembles*
- **d.** *objects* or *feelings*

6. ______

7. A *metaphor* is a comparison in which one thing becomes another without using
- **a.** a regular rhyme scheme
- **b.** irony
- **c.** the words *yet* or *but*
- **d.** the words *like, as, than,* or *resembles*

7. ______

8. The difference between a simile and a metaphor is largely a matter of
- **a.** taste
- **b.** skill
- **c.** emphasis
- **d.** intuition

8.______

9. A *direct metaphor* compares two things by using a verb such as
- **a.** *likes*
- **b.** *is*
- **c.** *resembles*
- **d.** *owns*

9.______

10. An *implied metaphor* expresses a comparison by
- **a.** omission of the verb *is*
- **b.** addition of the verb *seems*
- **c.** the use of symbolism
- **d.** the insertion of colorful adjectives

10.______

NAME ______________________ CLASS __________ DATE __________ SCORE __________

UNIT 2: THE ELEMENTS OF POETRY

SIMILES AND METAPHORS: Seeing Connections

A. RECOGNIZING SIMILES AND METAPHORS

Directions: For each question, place the letter of the best answer in the space provided. *(6 points each)*

1. In "Harlem" the similes describe
- **a.** decaying garbage in Harlem
- **b.** a black family's problem
- **c.** an unfulfilled dream
- **d.** a vivid nightmare

1. ______

2. The metaphors in Dickinson's poem "A Narrow Fellow in the Grass" convey mainly
- **a.** what wildlife hides in the grass
- **b.** how a snake makes the speaker feel
- **c.** what a snake is like in the sun
- **d.** the sensation of bare feet in moving grass

2. ______

3. The metaphors in Walker's "Women" and Wordsworth's poem "She Dwelt Among Untrodden Ways" describe women who
- **a.** lacked something essential in their own lives
- **b.** received no recognition for their efforts
- **c.** are mothers determined to help their children
- **d.** are remembered mostly for their deaths

3. ______

4. The pilot in Hall's poem, " The Old Pilot's Death," is closest to Shakespeare's metaphor in " The Seven Ages of Man"
- **a.** of "the soldier full of strange oaths"
- **b.** of "second childishness and mere oblivion"
- **c.** for "the sixth age"
- **d.** for "the whining schoolboy"

4. ______

5. Sandburg in "Fog" and Eliot in "The Yellow Fog" use a similar metaphor to describe
- **a.** the movements of a cat on a gray day
- **b.** the way day becomes night in foggy weather
- **c.** how fog clings to everything in its path
- **d.** the soft fog descending on a city

5. ______

B. INTERPRETING POETRY

Directions: In the spaces provided, mark each true statement **T** and each false statement **F**. *(3 points each)*

Part 1. Finding Facts

1. Dickinson's poem is told from the point of view of the snake. **1.** ______

2. The women in Walker's poem are stronghearted. **2.** ______

3. The old pilot in Hall's poem flies off in a jet fighter. **3.** ______

4. Eliot's poem shows how fog changes a spring night. 4. ______

5. The speaker in Shakespeare's poem dwells on the dignity of each age of life. 5. ______

Part 2. Understanding Moods and Meanings

6. Hughes uses italics in the last line to suggest barely repressed anger. 6. ______

7. The snake in Dickinson's poem represents a kind of i[illegible] fear. 7. ______

8. Wordsworth's poem indicates that he was impressed by Lucy's sophistication. 8. ______

9. Sandburg's poem reveals a comfortable acceptance of fog. 9. ______

10. Both Shakespeare and Hall view death with bitterness. 10. ______

Part 3. Writing about Poetry

Statement: A powerful simile or metaphor can take the place of many words.

Directions: On a separate sheet of paper, write a paragraph explaining your point of view about this statement and citing parts of the story that influence your opinion. *(10 points)*

C. LEARNING THE LANGUAGE OF POETRY

Directions: Match each poetic phrase in the left-hand column with the best meaning in the right-hand column. Place the letter of the best definition in the space provided. *(3 points each)*

______ 1. "crust and sugar over"

______ 2. "divides as with a comb"

______ 3. "unbraiding"

______ 4. "stout of step"

______ 5. "beam of late sun"

______ 6. "ceased to be"

______ 7. "corners of the evening"

______ 8. "being seven ages"

______ 9. "bubble reputation"

______ 10. "shrunk shank"

a. straightening out

b. just before nightfall

c. soapy name

d. last ray of sunshine

e. quick and easily lost fame

f. thinning leg

g. form a firm topping

h. wide shoe

i. heavy

j. are seven stages

k. died

l. parts

NAME ____________________ CLASS __________ DATE __________ SCORE __________

UNIT 2: THE ELEMENTS OF POETRY

INTRODUCTION / Understanding Personification

Directions: For each question, place the letter of the best answer in the space provided. *(20 points each)*

1. Personification is a special kind of
a. symbol
b. image
c. metaphor
d. rhyme scheme

1. ______

2. Personification gives human qualities to
a. people who lack courage
b. something that is not human
c. individuals without imagination
d. people who behave unkindly

2. ______

3. An example of personification is when we
a. attribute feelings to a car
b. name our pets
c. criticize politicians
d. gossip about friends

3. ______

4. In everyday speech, personification is used by
a. computer programmers
b. TV reporters
c. writers
d. all of us

4. ______

5. Giving life, feelings, and meaning to lifeless objects requires the use of our
a. intellect
b. sense of humor
c. maturity
d. imagination

5. ______

NAME ______________________ CLASS __________ DATE __________ SCORE __________

UNIT 2: THE ELEMENTS OF POETRY

PERSONIFICATION: Making the World Human

A. RECOGNIZING PERSONIFICATION

Directions: For each question, place the letter of the best answer in the space provided. *(6 points each)*

1. In Haines's poem, "The Legend of the Paper Plates," paper plates are made to seem like
a. people having fun at a picnic
b. old-timers telling stories of their past
c. children telling parents about hard times
d. abused and unappreciated humans
1. ______

2. The wisdom of old people is best personified in
a. Spivack's "March 1st"
b. Ratti's "My Mother Remembers Spanish Influenza"
c. Hillyer's "A Pastoral"
d. Stafford's "Fifteen"
2. ______

3. Ratti's poem personifies chiefly
a. the mysterious comings and goings of a disease
b. the pain and fever of influenza
c. a fan brought to a child as a gift
d. wheels of trolley cars and roller skates
3. ______

4. In Inez's "Slumnight," night is personified as a
a. violent person temporarily at rest
b. combative person waking up
c. bringer of nightmares about war
d. peacemaker bringing rest and relaxation
4. ______

5. In Stafford's "Fifteen," a machine is personified as
a. threatening and dangerous
b. friendly and adventurous
c. injured and in need of help
d. seeking its true owner
5. ______

B. INTERPRETING POETRY

Directions: In the spaces provided, mark each true statement **T** and each false statement **F**. *(3 points each)*

Part 1. Finding Facts

1. Spivack's poem is set in a snowstorm. **1.** ______

2. In Hillyer's poem, the speaker is an ancient tree. **2.** ______

3. Ratti's poem tells about his own childhood illness. **3.** ______

4. The setting of Inez's poem is confined to a single room. **4.** ______

5. The setting of Haines's poem moves from place to place. **5.** ______

Part 2. Understanding Moods and Meanings

6. Both Stafford and Inez view the city as unfriendly. 6. ______
7. Unlike Haines, Hillyer feels that destruction by humans can be avoided. 7. ______
8. Ratti sympathizes with his mother's feelings. 8. ______
9. Spivack is saddened by winter's lingering on. 9. ______
10. "Fifteen" portrays a skeptical and unimaginative young man. 10. ______

Part 3. Writing About Poetry

Statement: It is easier for poets to personify things that are alive than things that are not alive.

Directions: On a separate sheet of paper, write a paragraph in which you support or refute this statement. Support your argument with specific examples from the poems in this section. *(10 points)*

C. LEARNING THE LANGUAGE OF POETRY

Directions: Match each poetic phrase in the left-hand column with the best meaning in the right-hand column. Place the letter of the best definition in the space provided. *(3 points each)*

______ 1.	**a.** bringing noise with it	"the patriarchs crashed"
______ 2.	**b.** fan slats	"a crown of such fantastic blooming"
______ 3.	**c.** the oldest trees fell	"our memories send shoots"
______ 4.	**d.** a realization of possible excitement	"garlanded itself disgracefully with powder"
______ 5.	"furred with a fine fringe"	**e.** headpiece of gems
______ 6.	"running inside my head, metal on metal"	**f.** daylight fading
______ 7.	"carved ivory fingers"	**g.** the upper limbs in full flower
______ 8.	"pulsing gleam"	**h.** was left with patches of snow
______ 9.	"a forward feeling"	**i.** bringing pain and fever
______ 10.	"time scuffling into night"	**j.** trimmed with
		k. the shine and vibration of a vehicle
		l. we tell what we recall

NAME ______________________ CLASS __________ DATE __________ SCORE __________

UNIT 2: THE ELEMENTS OF POETRY

INTRODUCTION / Understanding Rhythm

Directions: For each question, place the letter of the best answer in the space provided. *(10 points each)*

1. Rhythm is based on
a. originality
b. variation
c. creativity
d. repetition

1. ______

2. Poetry having a regular pattern of stressed and unstressed syllables in each line is written in
a. meter
b. free verse
c. dialogue
d. imagery

2. ______

3. A poem that uses an unstressed syllable followed by a stressed syllable (da DAH) is composed in
a. similes
b. metaphors
c. iambs
d. symbols

3. ______

4. The basic building block of meter is called a
a. iamb
b. anapest
c. poetic foot
d. trochee

4. ______

5. A foot utilizing a stressed syllable followed by an unstressed syllable (DAH da) is a
a. trochee
b. iamb
c. anapest
d. spondee

5. ______

6. A foot made up of three syllables in which two unstressed syllables are followed by a stressed syllable (da da DAH) is
a. offbeat
b. on target
c. a trochee
d. an anapest

6. ______

7. One stressed syllable followed by two unstressed syllables (DAH da da) is a(n)
a. anapest
b. anarchist
c. dactyl
d. dagger

7. ______

8. A foot containing two stressed syllables (DAH DAH) is known as a
   a. spondee
   b. anapest
   c. refrain
   d. repetition

8. ______

9. Taking apart a poem to analyze its meter is known as
   a. scattering
   b. scanning
   c. scaling
   d. scheming

9. ______

10. Poetry that uses no strict pattern of stressed and unstressed syllables is called
    a. opera
    b. oratory
    c. meterless
    d. free verse

10. ______

NAME ________________ CLASS ________ DATE ________ SCORE ________

UNIT 2: THE ELEMENTS OF POETRY

THE SOUNDS OF POETRY: Rhythm

A. RECOGNIZING RHYTHM

Directions: For each question, place the letter of the best answer in the space provided. *(6 points each)*

1. In the line "Though three men dwell on Flannan Isle," the stressed syllables are

a.	Though	men	on	-nan
b.	three	dwell	Flan-	Isle
c.	Though	three	Flan-	on
d.	men	dwell	-nan	Isle

1. ______

2. In "The Pear Tree," the stressed syllables of "In this squalid, dirty dooryard" are found in the words

a. squalid dirty dooryard
b. squalid dirty
c. this squalid
d. In dooryard

2. ______

3. In "Woman Work," Angelou creates rhythm chiefly by using

a. a consistent meter in every line
b. the use of apostrophe
c. pairs of rhyming lines
d. repetition of sentence patterns

3. ______

4. In "The Fury of Overshoes," each line of the poem reflects Sexton's

a. invention of a new meter
b. sense of poetic phrasing
c. reliance on one stressed syllable
d. imitation of children's speech

4. ______

5. When reading a run-on line, you should

a. think of the punctuation the poet intended
b. understand that the poem is free verse
c. not pause before going to the next line
d. change the meter of the next line

5. ______

B. INTERPRETING POETRY

Directions: In the spaces provided, mark each true statement **T** and each false statement **F**. *(3 points each)*

Part 1. Finding Facts

1. In "Flannan Isle" you are never told how many men make up the search party. **1.** ______
2. Millay says that the pear tree is aware of its own beauty. **2.** ______
3. Angelou's poem shifts from a catalog of chores to a series of requests. **3.** ______
4. Sexton's poem refers to uncaring parents as "big fish." **4.** ______
5. Sexton uses apostrophe twice in her poem. **5.** ______

Part 2. Understanding Moods and Meanings

6. As they begin their trip to Flannan Isle, the searchers are already frightened. 6. ______

7. The searchers in Gibson's poem eventually worry about their own safety. 7. ______

8. The pear tree seems "incredible" to Millay mainly because of its environment. 8. ______

9. In "Woman Work," the speaker finds nothing to console or comfort her. 9. ______

10. Sexton suggests that most of us will outgrow our childhood fears. 10. ______

Part 3. Writing About Poetry

In "Woman Work," Maya Angelou uses one rhythm to list the "hard facts" of life, and another to describe her own needs and dreams.

Directions: On a separate sheet of paper, write a paragraph describing how the two different rhythms suit the two different subject matters. As examples, quote and scan two lines from the poem. *(10 points)*

C. LEARNING THE LANGUAGE OF POETRY

Directions: Match each poetic phrase in the left-hand column with its meaning in the right-hand column. Place the letter of the correct meaning in the space provided. *(3 points each)*

______ 1. "wonder all too dread for words"	a. hardly daring to breathe
______ 2. "a chill clutch on our breath"	b. feel burdens lifted
______ 3. "and each with black foreboding eyed"	c. snowflakes
______ 4. "takes the sun"	d. flourishing in the sunlight
______ 5. "vain of its new holiness"	e. too heavy to swim
______ 6. "float across the sky"	f. inexpressible fear
______ 7. "white cold icy kisses"	g. captures the sun
______ 8. "tears running down like mud"	h. laboring at life's tasks
______ 9. "like a stone frog"	i. making dark puddles
______ 10. "taking giant steps"	j. with fear of what lay ahead
	k. flowing thickly
	l. proud of its splendor

NAME ______________________ CLASS__________ DATE__________ SCORE__________

UNIT 2: THE ELEMENTS OF POETRY

INTRODUCTION / Understanding Rhyme and Other Sound Effects

Directions: For each question, place the letter of the best answer in the space provided. *(20 points each)*

1. Repetition of the sound of a stressed syllable and any syllables that follow is called
a. rhythm
b. meter
c. rhyme
d. lyrics
1. ______

2. Poetry that does not rhyme exactly but that repeats only some sounds uses
a. approximate rhymes
b. head-on rhymes
c. awkward rhymes
d. internal rhymes
2. ______

3. Rhymes that occur inside a line of poetry are
a. slant rhymes
b. half rhymes
c. internal rhymes
d. imperfect rhymes
3. ______

4. "Fitting the sound of the words to the sense of the words" describes
a. metaphor
b. onomatopoeia
c. parallelism
d. personification
4. ______

5. A poet who repeats the same letters of the alphabet in the first letters of several words is using
a. blank verse
b. alliteration
c. internal rhyme
d. approximate rhyme
5. ______

NAME ______________________ CLASS ________ DATE ________ SCORE ________

UNIT 2: THE ELEMENTS OF POETRY

THE SOUNDS OF POETRY: Rhyme and Other Sound Effects

A. RECOGNIZING RHYME AND OTHER SOUND EFFECTS

Directions: For each question, place the letter of the best answer in the space provided. *(6 points each)*

1. Which of the following can be found in the line "herring boxes without topses, sandals were for Clementine"?
- **a.** internal rhyme
- **b.** onomatopoeia
- **c.** approximate rhyme
- **d.** simile

1. ______

2. In "Robinson Crusoe's Story," the words "tough and dry" and "beetle-pie" are examples of
a. alliteration **b.** approximate rhyme **c.** onomatopoeia **d.** rhyme

2. ______

3. Alliteration is most evident in the line
- **a.** "Some say the world will end in fire"
- **b.** "Forever rolling, with a hollow sound"
- **c.** "Seeing the snowman standing all alone"
- **d.** "Some say in ice"

3. ______

4. In "I Never Saw a Moor," the words "heaven" and "given" are examples of
a. rhythm **b.** off-rhyme **c.** internal rhyme **d.** imperfect rhyme

4. ______

5. In "The Shell," Stephens uses onomatopoeia in the line
- **a.** "Whipped by an icy breeze"
- **b.** "And waves that journeyed blind"
- **c.** "And straightway, like a bell"
- **d.** "To wonder at the moon"

5. ______

B. INTERPRETING POETRY

Directions: In the spaces provided, mark each true statement **T** and each false statement **F**. *(3 points each)*

Part 1. Finding Facts

1. Both Montrose and Carryl use a consistent rhyme scheme. **1.** ______

2. Dickinson describes places she has visited. **2.** ______

3. Wilbur's poem is set at twilight. **3.** ______

4. Robert Frost says that perishing by ice is less painful than death by fire. **4.** ______

5. Stephens presents visual images as well as images of what he hears. **5.** ______

Part 2. Understanding Moods and Meanings

6. In "The Shell," Stephens experiences the sea as a place of beauty and serenity. 6.______

7. The child in Wilbur's poem is more perceptive than the snowman. 7.______

8. To Frost, desire is a destructive emotion. 8.______

9. The dominant message in Dickinson's poem is that faith is as important as experience. 9.______

10. Montrose and Carryl take traditional values seriously. 10.______

Part 3. Writing About Poetry

Both Dickinson (in "I Never Saw a Moor") and Frost (in "Fire and Ice") deal with the end of life. Yet these two poets have different feelings about what that "end" will be.

Directions: On a separate sheet of paper, write a paragraph in which you contrast the moods of the two poems. Quote lines from the poems to support your presentation of the contrasting moods. *(10 points)*

C. LEARNING THE LANGUAGE OF POETRY

Directions: Match each poetic phrase in the left-hand column with its meaning in the right-hand column. Place the letter of the correct meaning in the space provided. *(3 points each)*

______ 1. "foaming brine"

______ 2. "droop and pine"

______ 3. "yet know I how"

______ 4. "his tearful sight"

______ 5. "a trickle of the purest rain"

______ 6. "bright pane"

______ 7. "tasted of"

______ 8. "sunless strand"

______ 9. "smitten to whimpers"

______ 10. "loosed my ear"

a. dark landscape

b. wilt and shed leaves

c. experienced

d. sobbing from a beating

e. become depressed

f. lighted window

g. am aware of

h. sad-eyed peering

i. can wonder about

j. rough water

k. stopped listening

l. a teardrop

NAME ____________________ CLASS __________ DATE __________ SCORE __________

UNIT 2: THE ELEMENTS OF POETRY

INTRODUCTION / Understanding Tone

Directions: For each question, place the letter of the best answer in the space provided. *(20 points each)*

1. Tone is difficult to define because it is usually
- **a.** stated
- **b.** implied
- **c.** concealed
- **d.** obvious

1. ______

2. Tone refers to a writer's
- **a.** mood
- **b.** point of view
- **c.** attitude
- **d.** appearance

2. ______

3. In ordinary speech, people use their voices and gestures to indicate
- **a.** symbolism
- **b.** emphasis
- **c.** irony
- **d.** contrast

3. ______

4. When poets indicate tone by choice of words, they are using
- **a.** diction
- **b.** rhyme
- **c.** rhythm
- **d.** imagery

4. ______

5. Other devices that poets use to convey tone are
- **a.** alliteration and onomatopoeia
- **b.** trochees and dactyls
- **c.** iambs and anapests
- **d.** rhythm and rhymes

5. ______

NAME ______________________ CLASS ________ DATE ________ SCORE ________

UNIT 2: THE ELEMENTS OF POETRY

TONE: Revealing an Attitude

A. RECOGNIZING TONE

Directions: For each question, place the letter of the best answer in the space provided. *(6 points each)*

1. In the poems by Kherdian and Marquis, the words of the speakers reflect
a. regret
b. sarcasm
c. curiosity
d. a condescending attitude
1. ______

2. Despite Frost's words, the tone in "Out, Out—" is one of
a. aloof commentary
b. bitter disbelief
c. cruel disinterest
d. suppressed pain
2. ______

3. Compare the tone of "She loved him all her life" and "Lucinda Matlock." Of the two women, Lucinda is clearly
a. weaker
b. stronger
c. kinder
d. more fearful
3. ______

4. The young men in the poems by Wagoner and Trccce sound ironic because
a. they are tired of fighting for what they want
b. they are disillusioned in their assumptions
c. they fail at everything they do
d. taking chances has proven fruitless
4. ______

5. From "Needs" and "Highway: Michigan," you can tell that Ammons and Roethke both have
a. little regard for our dependence on machines
b. great admiration for industrial progress
c. humorous views on our need for speed
d. disdain for technicians
5. ______

B. INTERPRETING POETRY

Directions: In the spaces provided, mark each true statement **T** and each false statement **F**. *(3 points each)*

Part 1. Finding Facts

1. The letter in Kherdian's poem is an apology. **1.** ______

2. In the poem "Out,Out—," the saw seems to have a life of its own. **2.** ______

3. The woman in Alvarez's poem is more concerned with death than love. **3.** ______

4. The title of Roethke's poem is significant because Michigan has numerous traffic accidents. **4.** ______

5. Lucinda Matlock lives in the 1980's. **5.** ______

Part 2. Understanding Moods and Meanings

6. In "The Lesson of the Moth," archy wishes he had more passion. 6. ______

7. Treece is being ironic when he says the dog would "die at last in peace." 7. ______

8. Ammons uses the language of advertising to underline his sarcasm in "Needs." 8. ______

9. The speaker in "Every Good Boy Does Fine" thinks successful people lack an appreciation of poetry. 9. ______

10. Masters' poem is an affirmation of life. 10. ______

Part 3. Writing About Poetry

The following lines are from "Mabel Osborne" by Edgar Lee Masters:

> And I, who had happiness to share
> And longed to share your happiness;
> I who loved you, Spoon River,
> And craved your love,
> Withered before your eyes, Spoon River—
> Thirsting, thirsting,...

Directions: On a separate sheet of paper, write a paragraph comparing the tone of these lines with Masters' poem "Lucinda Matlock." *(10 points)*

C. LEARNING THE LANGUAGE OF POETRY

Directions: Match each poetic phrase in the left-hand column with the best meaning in the right-hand column. Place the letter of the best definition in the space provided. *(3 points each)*

______ 1. "seeming failure"	**a.** make one big effort
______ 2. "lifted eyes"	**b.** sweep out
______ 3. "breeze drew across"	**c.** unsure performance
______ 4. "shoot the roll"	**d.** apparent lack
______ 5. "flutter away"	**e.** gained by effort
______ 6. "wobbly solo"	**f.** jumped up
______ 7. "started up"	**g.** raised eyebrows
______ 8. "tow and sow"	**h.** wind blew
______ 9. "dearly won"	**i.** died peacefully
______ 10. "passed to a sweet repose"	**j.** stop beating
	k. pull and plant
	l. looked up

NAME ______________________ CLASS ________ DATE ________ SCORE ________

UNIT 2: THE ELEMENTS OF POETRY

INTRODUCTION / Understanding Ballads and Lyrics

Directions: For each question, place the letter of the best answer in the space provided. *(20 points each)*

1. The oldest and simplest poetry we know involved
a. dances
b. cave paintings
c. stories
d. musical compositions
1. ______

2. A story told with a lilt or beat that is easily sung or recited from memory is called
a. an epic
b. a fable
c. a lyric
d. a ballad
2. ______

3. A line, phrase, or whole stanza that is repeated exactly, or almost exactly, throughout a song is a
a. lyric
b. refrain
c. ballad
d. narrative
3. ______

4. A poem that expresses feelings instead of telling a story is a
a. lyric
b. ballad
c. riddle
d. epic
4. ______

5. The most prevalent form of poetry written in the Western world is the
a. ballad
b. couplet
c. narrative
d. lyric
5. ______

NAME ______________________ CLASS ________ DATE ________ SCORE ________

UNIT 2: THE ELEMENTS OF POETRY

TWO KINDS OF POETRY: Ballads and Lyrics

A. RECOGNIZING BALLADS AND LYRICS

Directions: For each question, place the letter of the best answer in the space provided. *(6 points each)*

1. The lovers in "The Unquiet Grave" and "The Demon Lover"
a. are both dead
b. have the same purpose
c. differ in their feelings
d. make likely promises
1. ______

2. The ballad "Edward" tells the story of a
a. brave son and an evil mother
b. lying son and a suspicious mother
c. murdering son and an innocent mother
d. remorseful son and a guilty mother
2. ______

3. In "Old Christmas," Lomey Carter visits Sally Anne Barton to
a. repeat some local gossip about a murder
b. let her know that Lomey's husband is dead
c. celebrate the meaning of the season
d. make her face a terrible tragedy
3. ______

4. Linda Pastan's poem expresses
a. hope for communication with unknown readers
b. desire to please her mother
c. a need to reach everyone who reads her work
d. ambition to get a good grade on her work
4. ______

5. Both Dickinson and Hayden express feelings about
a. meaningless hopes
b. missed opportunities
c. unexpressed love
d. untold victories
5. ______

B. INTERPRETING POETRY

Directions: In the spaces provided, mark each true statement **T** and each false statement **F**. *(3 points each)*

Part 1. Finding Facts

1. "The Unquiet Grave" takes place immediately after the young woman's death. **1.** ______

2. In "The Demon Lover," the mariner tricks the woman he has returned to claim. **2.** ______

3. The son in "Edward" will have to leave his family because of his deed. **3.** ______

4. In "Old Christmas," Lomey Carter returns to kill Sally Anne. **4.** ______

5. The father in "Those Winter Sundays" earned a living as a laborer. **5.** ______

Part 2. Understanding Moods and Meanings

6. Pastan suggests that her mother didn't like her poetry. 6. ______

7. Dickinson says that failure creates greater insight into success. 7. ______

8. Hayden's poem wouldn't be so strong if he talked about Mondays. 8. ______

9. The woman in "The Unquiet Grave" suggests that her lover should join her. 9. ______

10. In "Old Christmas," the last word whispered by Lomey Carter's husband concerned revenge. 10. ______

Part 3. Writing About Poetry

Death is an important theme in each of the ballads that you have read. Choose two of the ballads and think carefully about how death is treated in each of them.

Directions: On a separate sheet of paper, write a paragraph comparing how the authors of the two ballads you have chosen present the subject of death. *(10 points)*

C. LEARNING THE LANGUAGE OF POETRY

Directions: Match each poetic phrase in the left-hand column with the best meaning in the right-hand column. Place the letter of the best definition in the space provided. *(3 points each)*

______ 1. "'Tis"

______ 2. "breed sad strife"

______ 3. "four-and-twenty"

______ 4. "fare over the sea"

______ 5. "hungering after your face"

______ 6. "fainting fast"

______ 7. "sharpening his red pencil"

______ 8. "took the flag"

______ 9. "whose forbidden ear"

______ 10. "speaking indifferently"

a. twenty-four

b. wanting to see you

c. won the battle

d. who didn't earn the victory

e. make trouble

f. disappearing quickly

g. stole a banner

h. It is

i. talking without showing appreciation

j. sail away

k. getting ready to mark

l. having a big appetite

NAME ________________ CLASS ________ DATE ________ SCORE ________

UNIT 2: THE ELEMENTS OF POETRY

WORD ANALOGIES / Extending Vocabulary Skills

Directions: In the space provided, write the letter of the pair of words that best describes a *relationship* that is closest to that of the capitalized pair of words. *(5 points each)*

1. STANZA : POEM ::
- **a.** subject : verb
- **b.** paragraph : prose
- **c.** subject : sentence
- **d.** sentence : essay

1. ______

2. POET : FEELINGS ::
- **a.** chef : restaurant
- **b.** teacher : school
- **c.** lawyer : courtroom
- **d.** statistician : numbers

2. ______

3. PIVOT : ROTATE ::
- **a.** revolve : swivel
- **b.** fixed : mobile
- **c.** spin : standing
- **d.** riveted : twirl

3. ______

4. REVELATION : DISCLOSURE ::
- **a.** denial : admission
- **b.** bombshell : cover-up
- **c.** unveiling : confession
- **d.** smokescreen : eyeopener

4. ______

5. TRANSPARENT : CLEAR ::
- **a.** apparent : plain
- **b.** impairment : injury
- **c.** invisible : obvious
- **d.** translucent : opaque

5. ______

6. EMISSARY : REPRESENTATIVE ::
- **a.** missionary : priest
- **b.** president : senator
- **c.** ambassador : messenger
- **d.** religion : government

6. ______

7. CORDIALITY : FRIENDLINESS ::
- **a.** geniality : disagreeableness
- **b.** coldness : warmth
- **c.** insincerity : heartiness
- **d.** amiability : agreeableness

7. ______

8. DEFERRED : POSTPONED ::
- **a.** shaved : trimmed
- **b.** expedited : facilitated
- **c.** advanced : hindered
- **d.** suspended : hanged

8. ______

9. DEGENERATE : IMMORAL ::
- **a.** corrupt : moral
- **b.** virtuous : ethical
- **c.** perverted : upright
- **d.** noble : improper

9. ______

10. INCESSANT : INTERMITTENT ::
- **a.** rare : infrequent
- **b.** unceasing : continual
- **c.** ceaseless : occasional
- **d.** periodic : perpetual

10. ______

11. AWED : ASTONISHED ::
- **a.** flawed : perfect
- **b.** calm : excited
- **c.** expected : unexpected
- **d.** surprised : amazed

11. ______

12. ENVIOUS : JEALOUS ::
- **a.** indifferent : uncaring
- **b.** spiteful : caring
- **c.** neutral : resentful
- **d.** watchful : blind

12. ______

13. SARCASTIC : CONTEMPTUOUS ::
- **a.** complimentary : appreciative
- **b.** healing : cutting
- **c.** silly : ridiculous
- **d.** supportive : antagonistic

13. ______

14. IRONIC : INCONSISTENT ::
- **a.** natural : unnatural
- **b.** surprising : expected
- **c.** unexpected : curious
- **d.** straight : absurd

14. ______

15. NOSTALGIA : ANTICIPATION ::
a. forecast : foresee
b. memory : reminiscence
c. pain : suffering
d. past : future **15.** ______

16. ALLUSION : SUGGESTION ::
a. illusion : reality
b. mention : hint
c. intimate : formal
d. secret : public **16.** ______

17. RENT : TORN ::
a. apartment : lease
b. own : purchase
c. ripped : tattered
d. hire : charter **17.** ______

18. PATRIARCH : MATRIARCH ::
a. child : mother
b. adult : child
c. father : son
d. male : female **18.** ______

19. ETYMOLOGY : WORD ::
a. zoology : animal
b. genealogy : person
c. botany : plant
d. physics : energy **19.** ______

20. TRACK : PATH ::
a. run : trail
b. draw : sketch
c. slight : extreme
d. shortcut : sidewalk **20.** ______

NAME ________________ CLASS________ DATE________ SCORE ________

UNIT 2: THE ELEMENTS OF POETRY

UNIT REVIEW / Applying Skills I

A. READING A POEM

Directions: Read the following poem carefully. Then answer the questions that follow.

Upon Westminster Bridge

Earth has not anything to show more fair:
Dull would he be of soul who could pass by
   A sight so touching in its majesty:
This City now doth like a garment wear
The beauty of the morning; silent, bare 5
   Ships, towers, domes, theatres, and temples lie
   Open unto the fields, and to the sky;
All bright and glittering in the smokeless air.
Never did sun more beautifully steep
   In his first splendour valley, rock, or hill; 10
Ne'er saw I, never felt, a calm so deep!
   The river glideth at his own sweet will:
Dear God! the very houses seem asleep;
   And all that mighty heart is lying still!

—William Wordsworth

B. ANALYZING A POEM

Directions: For each question, place the letter of the best answer in the space provided. *(5 points each)*

1. Wordsworth presents the city as
a. a valley of beautiful rocks
b. someone old and abandoned
c. a sleeping person
d. someone who has just died
1. ______

2. To describe dawn, Wordsworth uses a simile comparing it to
a. something royal
b. a long dress
c. a group of buildings
d. the glittering sunlight
2. ______

3. The tone of Wordsworth's poem is one of
a. acceptance
b. reverence
c. irony
d. sadness
3. ______

4. The rhythm and rhyme schemes of Wordsworth's poem
   a. border on free verse
   b. are quite consistent
   c. allow for no run-on lines
   d. change midway in the poem

4. ______

5. Used so closely together, the words "sun," "steep," and "splendour" provide
   a. internal rhyme
   b. onomatopoeia
   c. approximate rhyme
   d. alliteration

5. ______

C. WRITING ABOUT A POEM

Directions: Carefully read Emily Dickinson's poem below. Then answer the questions that follow. *(10 points each)*

She sweeps with many-colored Brooms—
And leaves the Shreds behind—
Oh Housewife in the Evening West—
Come back, and dust the Pond!

You dropped a Purple Ravelling in—
You dropped an Amber thread—
And now you've littered all the East
With Duds of Emerald!

And still, she plies her spotted Brooms,
And still the Aprons fly,
Till Brooms fade softly into stars—
And then I come away—

1. What particular time of evening is Dickinson describing? How do you know?

____

____

____

____

____

____

____

____

____

____

2. Is the "housewife" in this poem an efficient, orderly person? What clues lead you to your opinion?

____

____

____

____

____

____

____

____

____

____

3. What does Dickinson really see in the pond, and to what does she compare them?

____

____

____

____

____

____

____

____

____

4. In which line of the poem does Dickinson switch to apostrophe? Whom is she personifying in this way?

____

____

____

____

5. What is the tone of Dickinson's poem, and how is it different from the tone in Wordsworth's poem?

D. ANALYZING THE LANGUAGE OF POETRY

Directions: In the spaces provided, mark each true statement **T** and each false statement **F**. *(5 points each)*

1. In the second line of Wordsworth's poem, the word "dull" means "boring". **1.** ______

2. In line 9 of "Upon Westminster Bridge," the word "steep" means "cover." **2.** ______

3. Through the use of the word "his" in lines 10 and 13, Wordsworth personifies the sun and the river. **3.** ______

4. In line 8 of the Dickinson poem, "duds" means "clothes." **4.** ______

5. From the wording of the last line in Dickinson's poem, you can infer that the speaker goes out to the pond. **5.** ______

NAME ______________________ CLASS __________ DATE __________ SCORE __________

UNIT 2: THE ELEMENTS OF POETRY

CRITICAL THINKING AND WRITING / Applying Skills II

A. COMPARING AND CONTRASTING POEMS

Directions: Write *two* paragraphs comparing and contrasting "Flannan Isle" and "Conquerors." In the first paragraph, contrast and compare the settings and moods of the poems. In the second paragraph, contrast and compare the rhythm and other sound effects. (*40 points*)

B. SUMMARIZING THE USES OF PERSONIFICATION

Directions: In *one* paragraph, explain what personification is and how poets use it to make images more vivid. Support the statements in your summary by quoting lines from four different poems in this unit. *(30 points)*

C. RESPONDING TO POETRY

Directions: Choose a poem in this section that expresses a message with which you do not agree. In *one* paragraph explain what the poet's message is, why you do not agree with it, and what you would say in a poem of your own on the same subject. *(30 points)*

NAME ____________________ CLASS ________ DATE ________ SCORE ________

UNIT 3: THE ELEMENTS OF NONFICTION

UNIT INTRODUCTION / Understanding the Elements of Nonfiction

Directions: For each question, place the letter of the best answer in the space provided. *(10 points each)*

1. What distinguishes nonfiction from fiction is that nonfiction is always
- **a.** an example of expository writing
- **b.** based on current happenings
- **c.** based on some sort of fact
- **d.** statistically verifiable

1. ______

2. It is impossible for a writer to tell the whole truth about any experience or event because
- **a.** readers would not accept it
- **b.** the act of writing changes experience
- **c.** writers are not especially good researchers
- **d.** writers seldom get all the facts straight

2. ______

3. In order to write good nonfiction, a writer must
- **a.** be good at inventing plots
- **b.** have a purpose
- **c.** want to persuade the reader to accept his or her view
- **d.** be talented at creating characters

3. ______

4. Dictionary and encyclopedia articles that define, explain, or inform use a type of writing called
- **a.** description
- **b.** exposition
- **c.** narration
- **d.** persuasion

4. ______

5. The method of writing that tells about a series of events, usually in chronological order, is called
- **a.** exposition
- **b.** description
- **c.** persuasion
- **d.** narration

5. ______

6. When a writer selects information to convince you of something, he is writing
- **a.** narration
- **b.** exposition
- **c.** persuasion
- **d.** description

6. ______

7. The writer who uses extensive imagery to create a mood or arouse an emotion is using a type of writing called
   a. description
   b. narration
   c. exposition
   d. persuasion

7. ______

8. In order to interest the reader, the nonfiction writer
   a. must pick up current topics
   b. uses all the techniques of fiction
   c. must do extensive research
   d. should choose the narrative method of writing

8. ______

9. The kind of writing found in reports in which the author is not a presence is known as
   a. personal writing
   b. factual writing
   c. descriptive writing
   d. objective writing

9. ______

10. Writing which reveals feelings and emotions about a subject is
   a. descriptive writing
   b. narrative writing
   c. personal writing
   d. autobiographical writing

10. ______

NAME ______________________ CLASS __________ DATE __________ SCORE __________

UNIT 3: THE ELEMENTS OF NONFICTION

INTRODUCTION / Understanding Personal Essays

Directions: For each question, place the letter of the best answer in the space provided. *(20 points each)*

1. The kind of writing in which writers reveal private feelings and biases is called
a. objective
b. personal
c. scholarly
d. inspirational

1. ______

2. The French word *essais,* or *essays*, means
a. tries
b. trends
c. treason
d. trials

2. ______

3. In addition to its subject, a personal essay also presents
a. historical information
b. statistical data
c. political commentary
d. its writer's personality

3. ______

4. The style of a personal essay is
a. slangy
b. formal
c. conversational
d. exaggerated

4. ______

5. To make an essay seem real to readers, the essayist uses
a. photographs
b. detailed research
c. propaganda techniques
d. all the elements of literature

5. ______

NAME ______________________ CLASS __________ DATE __________ SCORE __________

UNIT 3: THE ELEMENTS OF NONFICTION

THE GIANT WATER BUG **Annie Dillard**

A. RECOGNIZING ELEMENTS OF PERSONAL ESSAYS

Directions: For each question, place the letter of the best answer in the space provided. *(6 points each)*

1. The subject of "The Giant Water Bug" is
- **a.** the death of a frog
- **b.** a frog playing in a pond
- **c.** a water bug biting a person
- **d.** the anatomy of a water bug

1. ______

2. The method of writing used by Annie Dillard is best described as
- **a.** persuasion
- **b.** description
- **c.** narration
- **d.** exposition

2. ______

3. Which of the following statements provides the factual basis for Dillard's essay?
- **a.** She is walking in the woods.
- **b.** She is going for a swim in the lake.
- **c.** She sets out to scare frogs.
- **d.** She is looking for rare birds.

3. ______

4. Dillard personalizes her essay by
- **a.** describing the effect the event has on her life
- **b.** discussing the meaning of the event
- **c.** describing her reaction to what she sees
- **d.** speculating about the outcome had she interfered

4. ______

5. In "The Giant Water Bug," Dillard uses suspense to
- **a.** help you interpret the essay's meaning
- **b.** describe the frog's slow destruction before explaining what caused it
- **c.** describe her reaction to the scene
- **d.** avoid describing the death of the frog until the very end

5. ______

B. INTERPRETING MEANINGS

Part 1. *Directions:* For each question, place the letter of the best answer in the space provided. *(5 points each)*

1. Dillard notices the frog because
- **a.** it is small and green
- **b.** it lies half in and half out of the water and does not jump
- **c.** it utters a loud cry of pain
- **d.** there is a splash as it hops into the water

1. ______

2. While the author is watching, the frog
- **a.** floats far from the shore
- **b.** fights the water bug
- **c.** turns into a frog skin bag
- **d.** eats the water bug

2. ______

3. The water bug kills the frog by
   a. tearing it apart
   b. choking the creature to death
   c. drowning the frog
   d. injecting a poison that dissolves all body parts except the skin

3.______

4. What is Dillard's reaction to the death of the frog?
   a. amusement
   b. horror
   c. confusion
   d. sorrow

4.______

5. The essay begins with the following words

   A couple of summers ago I was walking along the edge of the island to see what I could see in the water, and mainly to scare frogs. Frogs have an inelegant way of taking off from invisible positions on the bank just ahead of your feet, in dire panic, emitting a froggy "Yike!" and splashing into the water. Incredibly, this amused me, and, incredibly, it amuses me still.

   In this passage, you learn that Dillard
   a. knows a great deal about frogs
   b. is a trained scientist
   c. writes poetry
   d. takes a childlike joy in nature

5.______

Part 2. Annie Dillard describes her reaction to the scene she witnessed.

Directions: Explain how your own reaction on seeing this event would have been different from, or similar to, the author's. *(15 points)*

C. DEVELOPING VOCABULARY

Directions: Match each word in the left-hand column with the best meaning in the right-hand column. Place the letter of the best definition in the space provided. *(3 points each)*

______1. dire

______2. schematic

______3. to rumple

______4. taut

______5. scum

______6. to appall

______7. tadpole

______8. to paralyze

______9. enzyme

______10. amphibian

a. tightly stretched

b. to wrinkle or crumple

c. to make powerless or inactive

d. a very young frog or toad

e. organized as a plan

f. uncomfortable

g. any of a class of vertebrates that usually begin life in the water and later develop lungs

h. a substance able to break down food so that it can be digested

i. dreadful, terrible

j. to increase in size

k. to horrify

l. a thin layer of material that rises to the top of a liquid

NAME ______________________ CLASS __________ DATE __________ SCORE __________

UNIT 3: THE ELEMENTS OF NONFICTION

THE NIGHT THE BED FELL **James Thurber**

A. UNDERSTANDING WHAT HAPPENED

Directions: In the spaces provided, mark each true statement **T** and each false statement **F**. *(3 points each)*

1. A bed actually falls on James Thurber's father. **1.** ______

2. The members of Thurber's family have many quirks of character. **2.** ______

3. Thurber's mother doesn't want his father to sleep in the attic because she believes the bed is wobbly and unsafe. **3.** ______

4. Grandfather is attacked by the dog. **4.** ______

5. Sleeping in the Thurber home is a noisy ordeal for many members of the family. **5.** ______

6. Thurber's cot rolls over, trapping him underneath it. **6.** ______

7. Herman is afraid of suffocating in his sleep. **7.** ______

8. Afterwards, Thurber's mother refers to his fall as "the night the bed fell on your father." **8.** ______

9. Father got a splinter from wandering around in his bare feet. **9.** ______

10. When Mother sees Father is unharmed, she begins to weep. **10.** ______

B. RECOGNIZING ELEMENTS OF PERSONAL ESSAYS

Directions: For each question, place the letter of the best answer in the space provided. *(8 points each)*

1. According to the author, "The Night the Bed Fell" is more effective when read aloud. Why?
a. It includes rhymes.
b. Its humor is related to the different sounds of the incident.
c. Thurber believes all literature should be read aloud.
d. The barking dog plays a major role in the piece. **1.** ______

2. The method of writing used by Thurber is an example of
a. persuasion **c.** description
b. exposition **d.** narration **2.** ______

3. The tone of the essay indicates that Thurber regards his family and childhood
a. with affection and humor
b. tragically
c. objectively
d. as difficult and trying **3.** ______

4. The event that triggers the confusion in the Thurber household occurs when
   a. Rex begins to bark
   b. Mother becomes hysterical
   c. the narrator's bed rolls over
   d. Briggs Beall believes he is suffocating

4. ______

5. The principal irony of the comic situation related by Thurber is that
   a. the family members' ideas of the cause of the commotion reflect their own fears and concerns
   b. the narrator is the only one who does not wake up when he falls out of bed
   c. the narrator's relatives are eccentric
   d. there are no bad results, despite everyone's fears

5. ______

C. DEVELOPING VOCABULARY

Directions: Match each word in the left-hand column with the best meaning in the right-hand column. Place the letter of the best definition in the space provided. *(3 points each)*

______ 1. passel
______ 2. premonition
______ 3. calamity
______ 4. fortitude
______ 5. canopy
______ 6. deluge
______ 7. pungent
______ 8. culprit
______ 9. ominous
______ 10. uncanny

a. innocent person
b. threatening
c. flood
d. a large number or amount
e. courage to endure pain, hardship, or danger
f. a person guilty of fault or crime
g. cheerful or pleasant
h. covering hung over a bed or entrance way
i. great misfortune, disaster
j. producing a sharp sensation of smell or taste
k. a feeling that something will happen
l. so remarkable or unusual as to seem supernatural

NAME ________________ CLASS ________ DATE ________ SCORE ________

UNIT 3: THE ELEMENTS OF NONFICTION

THE WASHWOMAN **Isaac Bashevis Singer**

A. UNDERSTANDING WHAT HAPPENED

Directions: In the spaces provided, mark each true statement **T** and each false statement **F**. *(4 points each)*

1. This essay concerns events that took place in Poland. 1. ______
2. The washwoman is Jewish. 2. ______
3. The old washwoman continues to work because she does not wish to be a burden. 3. ______
4. The old woman is invited to her son's wedding. 4. ______
5. Singer's mother admires the washwoman's son. 5. ______
6. The old woman appears even in the bitter cold of winter. 6. ______
7. The Singer family worries and mourns for the woman when she does not show up. 7. ______
8. When the washwoman returns, she seems healthy. 8. ______
9. The old woman thanks Singer's mother for her blessing. 9. ______
10. The washwoman cannot die until she finishes her work. 10. ______

B. RECOGNIZING ELEMENTS OF PERSONAL ESSAYS

Directions: For each question, place the letter of the best answer in the space provided. *(6 points each)*

1. In "The Washwoman," Isaac Bashevis Singer's purpose is to
   a. explain circumstances
   b. create a special mood
   c. persuade you to believe certain facts
   d. relate a series of events and stir emotion 1. ______

2. The method of writing used in "The Washwoman" is
   a. persuasion
   b. narration
   c. exposition
   d. description 2. ______

3. Singer uses all of the following techniques of fiction *except*
   a. characters
   b. dialogue
   c. humor
   d. suspense 3. ______

4. The washwoman's explanation, "The wash would not let me die," reveals her
   a. devotion to laundering
   b. commitment to tasks she has undertaken
   c. desire to earn money for her son
   d. loyalty to her family

4. ______

5. Singer's portrait of the washwoman reflects the view that
   a. goodness is found among all people regardless of their religion
   b. Poles are extraordinary people
   c. Jewish people are very spiritual
   d. virtue is its own reward

5. ______

C. DEVELOPING VOCABULARY

Directions: Match each word in the left-hand column with the best meaning in the right-hand column. Place the letter of the best definition in the space provided. *(3 points each)*

______ 1. rancor	a. an idle wanderer
______ 2. affront	b. living at the expense of others
______ 3. institution	c. to repay
______ 4. atonement	d. deep hate or ill will
______ 5. parasitic	e. extraordinary disaster or misfortune
______ 6. dear	f. to review
______ 7. vagrant	g. amends made for wrongdoing
______ 8. catastrophe	h. an open, intentional insult
______ 9. benediction	i. a fragment
______ 10. to recompense	j. an established law or custom
	k. expensive
	l. a blessing

NAME ____________________ CLASS ________ DATE ________ SCORE ________

UNIT 3: THE ELEMENTS OF NONFICTION

CHARLEY IN YELLOWSTONE **John Steinbeck**

A. RECOGNIZING ELEMENTS OF PERSONAL ESSAYS

Directions: For each question, place the letter of the best answer in the space provided. *(6 points each)*

1. The subject of "Charley in Yellowstone" is
a. the beauty of national parks
b. the dangers of wild animals
c. travel in the West
d. a dog's reaction to a bear
1. ______

2. John Steinbeck's account is an example of
a. objective reporting **b.** a personal essay **c.** history **d.** biography
2. ______

3. In recounting his journey with his poodle, the author uses
a. dialogue **b.** character **c.** suspense **d.** all of the above
3. ______

4. When Steinbeck explains his dog's personality to the park guard, he is using a technique called
a. irony **b.** conflict **c.** suspense **d.** mood
4. ______

5. Steinbeck strives to convince you that the emotions of animals are not simple. This method of writing is
a. description **b.** exposition **c.** persuasion **d.** narration
5. ______

B. INTERPRETING MEANINGS

Part 1. *Directions:* For each question, place the letter of the best answer in the space provided. *(5 points each)*

1. Steinbeck's main experience in Yellowstone is his
a. admiration of the beautiful scenery
b. discovery about his dog's nature
c. trouble with his camper
d. amusement over the park bears
1. ______

2. When Steinbeck says, "This is a unique dog," he is referring to Charley's
a. fierceness
b. courage
c. lack of aggressiveness
d. many tricks
2. ______

3. The park guard worries that
a. Charley will attack the bears
b. Steinbeck will leave food behind
c. the bears will attack Charley
d. Charley has no leash
3. ______

4. How does Steinbeck let you know that his real subject is the behavior of his dog?
a. He omits detailed descriptions of Yellowstone Park.
b. He tells you so at the end of the second paragraph.
c. He argues with the park guard.
d. He moves Charley into the house behind the cab.
4. ______

5. Toward the beginning of the essay, the author writes:

> ...To the best of my knowledge Charley had never seen a bear and in his whole history had showed great tolerance for every living thing. Besides all this, Charley is a coward, so deep-seated a coward that he has developed a technique for concealing it. And yet he showed every evidence of wanting to get out and murder a bear that outweighed him a thousand to one. I don't understand it.

From this passage, it can be inferred that
a. Charley is a coward
b. Charley had always showed great tolerance for every living thing
c. Charley wanted to get out and attack a bear
d. Steinbeck doesn't know as much about Charley as he thought he did **5.** ______

Part 2. At the end of the selection, Steinbeck says, "I wonder why we think the thoughts and emotions of animals are simple."

Directions: On a separate sheet of paper, write a paragraph explaining why you think Steinbeck makes this statement. How has he misjudged Charley's thoughts and emotions during the course of the day? *(15 points)*

C. DEVELOPING VOCABULARY

Directions: For each of the following, place the letter of the best answer in the space provided. (*3 points each*)

1. tranquillity
a. thoughtfulness **b.** calmness **c.** coldness **d.** anxiety **1.** ______

2. to amble
a. to jump **b.** to speed **c.** to walk at a leisurely pace **d.** to sing **2.** ______

3. cuff
a. a slap **b.** a pair of trousers **c.** a type of dog **d.** a cliff **3.** ______

4. palpable
a. able to be understood **c.** able to float
b. able to be touched, felt, or handled **d.** extremely anxious **4.** ______

5. to rant
a. to fight **b.** to submerge **c.** to discourage **d.** to speak wildly **5.** ______

6. mania
a. craze **b.** depression **c.** physical exertion **d.** emptiness **6.** ______

7. to scuttle
a. to argue **b.** to move quickly, scamper **c.** to wander **d.** to fight **7.** ______

8. to deplete
a. to increase **b.** to cheat **c.** to empty or exhaust **d.** to avenge **8.** ______

9. pandemonium
a. scene of wild disorder **b.** circus **c.** type of sailboat **d.** well-being **9.** ______

10. to belch
a. to curse **b.** to gush or spurt **c.** to skim **d.** to guard **10.** ______

NAME ______________________ CLASS __________ DATE __________ SCORE __________

UNIT 3: THE ELEMENTS OF NONFICTION

INTRODUCTION / Understanding Reports on People and Events

Directions: For each question, place the letter of the best answer in the space provided. *(20 points each)*

1. An expository essay that presents interesting information on some object or event is called a
a. biography
b. report
c. memoir
d. memo
1. ______

2. A reporter's language uses images to
a. make people and places seem immediate and real
b. force personal values upon others
c. exaggerate situations
d. create fantasy
2. ______

3. A story with details showing how an event affects ordinary human lives is known as
a. character study
b. human interest
c. self-help
d. how-to
3. ______

4. A well-written report is
a. emotional and imaginative
b. accurate and objective
c. scholarly and critical
d. cheerful and optimistic
4. ______

5. Distorting facts in order to influence readers' thinking is called
a. irony
b. imagery
c. propaganda
d. plot development
5. ______

NAME ____________ CLASS ____________ DATE ____________ SCORE ____________

UNIT 3: THE ELEMENTS OF NONFICTION

FROM **COMING INTO THE COUNTRY** **John McPhee**

A. UNDERSTANDING WHAT HAPPENED

Directions: In the spaces provided, mark each true statement **T** and each false statement **F.** *(3 points each)*

1. The plane crashes in Alaska. **1.** ______

2. Leon Crane survives because he has had previous experience in the wilderness. **2.** ______

3. John McPhee feels the government should restrict cabin-building on federal land. **3.** ______

4. Crane starts a fire with his father's letter to keep warm. **4.** ______

5. At first, Crane believes that he will be rescued. **5.** ______

6. Before Crane finds the cabin, he gives up all hope of survival. **6.** ______

7. The supplies in the cabin enable Crane to regain his strength. **7.** ______

8. Leon Crane bandages his hands with melted candle wax. **8.** ______

9. When he realizes there is insufficient food, Crane panics and leaves the cabin. **9.** ______

10. At the end of his ordeal, Crane believes that there is a reason for his survival, but does not know what it is. **10.** ______

B. RECOGNIZING ELEMENTS OF REPORTS

Directions: For each question, place the letter of the best answer in the space provided. *(6 points each)*

1. John McPhee describes his story as
- **a.** an adventure story
- **b.** an account of unusual death
- **c.** a story of a death postponed
- **d.** a backwoods tale

1. ______

2. McPhee best demonstrates traditional reporting skills when he
- **a.** describes the Alaskan scenery
- **b.** tracks down Leon Crane
- **c.** explains federal land policies
- **d.** describes his first meeting with Crane

2. ______

3. The central mystery of the story involves
- **a.** how Crane survived
- **b.** why Crane survived
- **c.** how government regulations change the wilderness
- **d.** how McPhee found Crane

3. ______

4. Narration and storytelling are best demonstrated in the description of
   a. Crane's ordeal
   b. the Alaskan scenery
   c. Alaskan customs
   d. Crane's reaction to his ordeal
   4. ______

5. In describing Crane's endurance, McPhee's style is
   a. heightened by details of the survivor's bravery
   b. exaggerated by descriptions of Alaska's winter and terrain
   c. weakened by descriptions of Crane's war heroics
   d. low-key in describing Crane's survival tactics
   5. ______

C. DEVELOPING VOCABULARY

Directions: Match each word in the left-hand column with the best meaning in the right-hand column. Place the letter of the best definition in the space provided. *(4 points each)*

______ 1. sarcophagus
______ 2. promontory
______ 3. exodus
______ 4. oblique
______ 5. refurbishment
______ 6. tundra
______ 7. oblivion
______ 8. mukluk
______ 9. williwaw
______ 10. to abrade

a. a high waterproof boot
b. to wear down by rubbing
c. waterproof cloth used as covering
d. a stone coffin
e. a departure
f. slanting, not straightforward
g. the state of being completely forgotten
h. a vast treeless plain in the Arctic region
i. a violent gust of wind
j. pertaining to mountain conditions
k. renovation
l. a peak of high land that juts out into a body of water

NAME ______________________ CLASS__________ DATE__________ SCORE__________

UNIT 3: THE ELEMENTS OF NONFICTION

EVERYTHING IN ITS PATH **Kai Erickson**

A. UNDERSTANDING WHAT HAPPENED

Directions: In the spaces provided, mark each true statement **T** and each false statement **F**. *(3 points each)*

1. The disaster takes place in Appalachia. **1.** ______

2. The residents in the area were among the poorest in the region. **2.** ______

3. The Buffalo Mining Company was dumping its waste in Middle Fork. **3.** ______

4. The company tries to warn the residents of possible disaster. **4.** ______

5. The disaster is caused by excessive precipitation. **5.** ______

6. The flood carries away everything in the village of Saunders. **6.** ______

7. As the flood progresses, houses and buildings from villages that had been hit earlier also are washed away. **7.** ______

8. After the flood, dazed survivors search for missing relatives. **8.** ______

9. Most of the organized relief activity is handled by the inhabitants of Buffalo Creek. **9.** ______

10. HUD's relief work is not entirely successful in the long run. **10.** ______

B. RECOGNIZING ELEMENTS OF REPORTS

Directions: For each question, place the letter of the best answer in the space provided. *(6 points each)*

1. The type of writing used at the beginning of "Everything in Its Path" is best described as

a. exposition
b. description
c. narration
d. persuasion **1.** ______

2. The impact of "Everything in Its Path" is heightened by Erickson's use of

a. dialogue
b. legal documentation
c. vivid similes and metaphors
d. the victim's medical reports **2.** ______

3. "Everything in Its Path" differs from the essay by John McPhee in that Kai Erickson
   a. interviews others
   b. uses figures of speech
   c. does not appear in the report
   d. expresses sympathy for his subject   3. ______

4. The effect of having different speakers offer personal recollections is to
   a. increase the sense of devastation through an accumulation of impressions
   b. give greater variety to the causes of the catastrophe
   c. demonstrate different points of view about the nature of the disaster
   d. indicate the extent of the research involved   4. ______

5. Erickson's point of view regarding the disaster is
   a. belief that the Buffalo Mining Company acted responsibly
   b. concern for the victims of an unnecessary tragedy
   c. feeling that the villages failed to protect themselves sufficiently
   d. suspicion that the tragedy was an act of God   5. ______

C. DEVELOPING VOCABULARY

Directions: Match each word in the left-hand column with the best meaning in the right-hand column. Place the letter of the best definition in the space provided. *(4 points each)*

______ 1. affluent
______ 2. impoverished
______ 3. impoundment
______ 4. slag
______ 5. viscous
______ 6. to clamber
______ 7. to accentuate
______ 8. precarious
______ 9. carnage
______ 10. disconsolate

a. to emphasize or stress
b. to shout loudly
c. rich, wealthy
d. risky, uncertain, insecure
e. poor
f. full of sadness or despair
g. bloody or extensive slaughter
h. flowing smoothly
i. to climb using both hands and feet
j. an enclosure to gather water for irrigation
k. a mixture of mine dust, shale, and other impurities
l. having a sticky, fluid consistency

NAME ________________ CLASS ________ DATE ________ SCORE ________

UNIT 3: THE ELEMENTS OF NONFICTION

ANNAPURNA **Maurice Herzog**

A. RECOGNIZING ELEMENTS OF REPORTS

Directions: In the spaces provided, mark each true statement **T** and each false statement **F**. *(6 points each)*

1. "Annapurna" is an example of
a. persuasion **b.** exposition **c.** criticism **d.** biography — **1.** ______

2. At the beginning of the excerpt, the author writes, "It is said that mountaineers have a sixth sense that warns them of danger..." The effect that Herzog is trying to create here is called
a. human interest **b.** a hook **c.** a distraction **d.** suspense — **2.** ______

3. In accurately reporting the facts about the Annapurna expedition, Herzog was being
a. objective **b.** fictional **c.** manipulative **d.** inspirational — **3.** ______

4. The unusual feature of Herzog's best-selling account is his use of
a. unconventional writing style
b. personal recollections
c. vivid details
d. interesting characters — **4.** ______

5. The "hook" that captures reader interest in "Annapurna" can best be described as
a. the title of the book
b. literary technique
c. the dangerous challenge of the climb
d. Herzog's vow to conquer the mountain — **5.** ______

B. INTERPRETING MEANINGS

Part 1. *Directions:* For each question, place the letter of the best answer in the space provided. *(5 points each)*

1. Herzog fears the abnormal heat because it will cause
a. overwhelming discomfort
b. deteriorating frostbite
c. an avalanche
d. irritability — **1.** ______

2. Herzog's concern about the Sherpas' slow descent reveals
a. irritability **b.** disorientation **c.** prejudice **d.** egotism — **2.** ______

3. What does the author mean when he says, "Setting this limit somehow cheered me on"?
a. He knew that rescue was imminent.
b. He knew he would recover shortly.
c. The idea of being able to rest in one hour enabled him to keep going.
d. Sarki and Aila cheered him by promising him sleep within one hour — **3.** ______

4. Herzog's concern about his injured hands evokes feelings in him of
a. anger and fear of permanent damage to his hands
b. self-pity and dismay about his future
c. panic and fatalism about whether his hands will heal
d. revulsion and hope that his hands will not be injured beyond repair — **4.** ______

5. This paragraph appears early in Herzog's account:

> Conscious of a shadow, as from a passing cloud, I looked up instinctively, and lo and behold! Two scared black faces were framed against the circle of blue sky. Aila and Sarki! They were safe and sound and at once set to work to rescue me. I was incapable of giving them the slightest advice. Aila disappeared, leaving Sarki alone at the edge of the hole; they began to pull on the rope, slowly, so as not to hurt me, and I was hauled up with a power and steadiness that gave me fresh courage. At last I was out. I collapsed on the snow.

In this passage the author lets you know that
a. his injuries have incapacitated him
b. he has temporary amnesia
c. the Sherpas have saved his life with tremendous difficulty
d. he was expecting to be rescued
5. ______

Part 2. What, do you think, is the attitude of Maurice Herzog toward the other mountaineers? Does he view the Sherpas differently from the others?

Directions: On a separate sheet of paper, write a paragraph explaining your point of view and citing portions of the report that indicate the author's feelings about the climbers. *(15 points)*

C. DEVELOPING VOCABULARY

Directions: For each of the following, place the letter of the best answer in the space provided. (*3 points each*)

1. to sap
a. to hit **b.** to weaken **c.** to lose **d.** to struggle
1. ______

2. to rouse
a. to stir up **b.** to sleep **c.** to ascend **d.** to frolic
2. ______

3. to linger
a. to lessen
b. to scale a mountain
c. to yearn for
d. to stay because of reluctance to leave
3. ______

4. chaos
a. serenity **b.** complete disorder **c.** freedom **d.** genuineness
4. ______

5. to wrench
a. to wield a tool
b. to hold
c. to pull or twist jerkily
d. to move toward something
5. ______

6. frenzy
a. a type of rope
b. an outburst of activity of feeling
c. a sense of calm
d. a loud sound
6. ______

7. instinctively
a. loudly **b.** boisterously **c.** fiercely **d.** naturally
7. ______

8. couloir
a. a deep gorge
b. the crest of a mountain
c. an avalanche
d. a mountaineer's rope
8. ______

9. to diminish
a. to increase **b.** to lessen **c.** to explode **d.** to deflate
9. ______

10. to hurtle
a. to hurl
b. to hustle
c. to move with great speed or force
d. to hurdle
10. ______

NAME ____________________ CLASS__________ DATE__________ SCORE__________

UNIT 3: THE ELEMENTS OF NONFICTION

INTRODUCTION / Understanding Biography and Autobiography

Directions: For each question, place the letter of the best answer in the space provided. *(20 points each)*

1. A biography is
a. a fictionalized tale about a writer
b. the written story of a life
c. the written story of the writer's own life
d. a study of a famous literary character
1. ______

2. Biographies are based on
a. imagination
b. study and research
c. memory
d. hearsay
2. ______

3. The written story of the writer's own life is called
a. a short story
b. a novel
c. an autobiography
d. science fiction
3. ______

4. Writing objectively requires
a. extensive statistics
b. an unbiased account of the subject
c. a flattering account of the subject
d. psychological analysis
4. ______

5. Subjectivity, or the inside story, is usually found in
a. autobiography
b. biography
c. fiction
d. poetry
5. ______

NAME ____________ CLASS ________ DATE ________ SCORE ________

UNIT 3: THE ELEMENTS OF NONFICTION

"ANNIE" **Joseph P. Lash**

A. RECOGNIZING ELEMENTS OF BIOGRAPHY

Directions: For each question, place the letter of the best answer in the space provided. *(4 points each)*

1. The *primary* method of writing used by Lash is
a. exposition **b.** persuasion **c.** description **d.** narration — **1.** ______

2. The author's use of Annie's own words increases interest in her life by
a. enabling you to understand better the period in which she lived
b. helping you to understand better how she reacted and felt about her experience
c. providing descriptions of her family
d. explaining the importance of the Irish famine — **2.** ______

3. Joseph P. Lash's viewpoint toward Annie Sullivan can be described as
a. cool detachment
b. warm admiration
c. strict objectivity
d. hostility — **3.** ______

4. Which of the following episodes reveals that Joseph Lash has done historical research on the period of Annie's life?
a. the death of Jimmie
b. the description of Tewksbury during Annie's stay there
c. the death of Annie's mother
d. Annie's return to Tewksbury years later — **4.** ______

5. The author's quotation of Annie's father's heavy Irish brogue adds to this account by
a. relating old Irish folktales
b. giving you a vivid impression of Annie's father
c. supplying an example of his use of the English language
d. illustrating Irish humor — **5.** ______

B. INTERPRETING MEANINGS

Part 1. *Directions:* For each question, place the letter of the best answer in the space provided. *(4 points each)*

1. Annie Sullivan was greatly influenced by
a. primary school
b. college
c. her Irish-Catholic upbringing
d. the accomplishments of her father — **1.** ______

2. When Annie says, "I knew very little about my parents," she means that
a. they died right after her birth
b. she was separated from them shortly after birth
c. she knew little about their background
d. she could not understand them at all — **2.** ______

3. Although Annie's father was sometimes brutal, Annie remembers fondly his
   a. love for his mother
   b. affection for Irish lore
   c. help to their neighbors
   d. devotion to religion
   3.______

4. The central emotional experience of Annie's young life is
   a. the death of her mother
   b. the death of her brother Jimmie
   c. the fact that she is almost blind
   d. the unhappiness at Tewksbury
   4.______

5. The following paragraph occurs near the end of this selection:

   "Very much of what I remember about Tewksbury is indecent, cruel, melancholy," she told Nella Braddy fifty years later, "gruesome in the light of grown-up experience; but nothing corresponding with my present understanding of these ideas entered my child mind. Everything interested me. I was not shocked, pained, grieved, or troubled by what happened. Such things happened. People behaved like that—that was all that there was to it. It was all the life I knew. Things impressed themselves upon me because I had a receptive mind. Curiosity kept me alert and keen to know everything...."

   In this passage, Annie recalls her experience in order to explain
   a. her hope that no one else will experience anything similar
   b. the terrible cruelties of her early life
   c. how she gained insight as a result of her experiences
   d. that her experiences were bearable because they seemed natural
   5.______

Part 2. According to Joseph Lash, "a sense that she was different" enabled Annie to keep alive her ambition to attend school. Why would this be important at Tewksbury?

Directions: On a separate sheet of paper, write a paragraph explaining how Annie's belief in herself enabled her to go to school. Cite examples from the selection that illustrate Annie's strength. *(20 points)*

C. DEVELOPING VOCABULARY

Directions: Match each word in the left-hand column with the best meaning in the right-hand column. Place the letter of the best definition in the space provided. *(4 points each)*

______1. destitution
______2. desolate
______3. illiterate
______4. to defray
______5. dilapidated
______6. to relent
______7. manic
______8. penance
______9. melancholy
______10. mortality

a. to become less severe, harsh, or strict
b. sadness
c. destruction
d. lonely, joyless, sorrowful
e. to anger
f. suggestive of madness
g. abject poverty
h. death
i. unable to read or write
j. to pay or furnish the money for
k. punishment borne to show sorrow or remorse for a wrong done
l. falling into disrepair

NAME ________________ CLASS ________ DATE ________ SCORE ________

UNIT 3: THE ELEMENTS OF NONFICTION

BARRIO BOY **Ernesto Galarza**

A. UNDERSTANDING WHAT HAPPENED

Directions: In the spaces provided, mark each true statement **T** and each false statement **F**. *(3 points each)*

1. Ernesto Galarza goes to a school where only Spanish is spoken. **1.** ______

2. The principal of the school is very stern when she first meets Ernesto. **2.** ______

3. In Miss Ryan's class, the children speak many foreign languages. **3.** ______

4. Some children in the class receive special private lessons. **4.** ______

5. In the first-grade class, Ernesto learns to read English. **5.** ______

6. The students never exchange ethnic insults. **6.** ______

7. As Ernesto becomes Americanized, he feels ashamed of being Mexican. **7.** ______

8. Ernesto loses the class election by two votes. **8.** ______

9. Miss Hopley stops the singing of "My Country 'Tis of Thee" because she sees two gentlemen with their hats on. **9.** ______

10. Ernesto leaves Lincoln School after first grade. **10.** ______

B. RECOGNIZING ELEMENTS OF AUTOBIOGRAPHY

Directions: For each question, place the letter of the best answer in the space provided. *(6 points each)*

1. Ernesto Galarza's feelings about his childhood differ from those of Annie Sullivan because
- **a.** Galarza comes from another country
- **b.** he recollects his youth with affection
- **c.** he enjoys school
- **d.** Galarza disliked the United States

1. ______

2. The selection deals primarily with Galarza's
- **a.** life in California
- **b.** experiences with prejudice in California
- **c.** Americanization through school experiences
- **d.** relationship with his family

2. ______

3. The author's metaphor for his experience of Americanization at the Lincoln School is a
   a. melting pot
   b. salad
   c. griddle
   d. cauldron

3.______

4. Galarza's attitude toward his Mexican heritage can be described as
   a. shame
   b. anger
   c. indifference
   d. pride

4.______

5. By comparing Lincoln School with the governor's mansion, Ernesto Galarza is identifying the school as
   a. playing governmental role in the children's lives
   b. a central part of their lives
   c. an imposing building
   d. a symbol of power

5.______

C. DEVELOPING VOCABULARY

Directions: Match each word in the left-hand column with the best meaning in the right-hand column. Place the letter of the best definition in the space provided. *(4 points each)*

______ **1.** contraption	**a.** to answer
______ **2.** barrio	**b.** to look over
______ **3.** to flank	**c.** small
______ **4.** benchmark	**d.** having a full, deep sound
______ **5.** gringo	**e.** a device or gadget
______ **6.** buxom	**f.** misunderstood
______ **7.** to survey	**g.** plump
______ **8.** runty	**h.** a Spanish community
______ **9.** to wither	**i.** a Spanish term for an American
______ **10.** resonant	**j.** to cause to feel small, as by a scornful glance
	k. to be at the side of
	l. a turning point, a significant change in direction

NAME ______________________ CLASS ________ DATE ________ SCORE ________

UNIT 3: THE ELEMENTS OF NONFICTION

THE PHANTOM OF YAZOO **Willie Morris**

A. RECOGNIZING ELEMENTS OF AUTOBIOGRAPHY

Directions: For each question, place the letter of the best answer in the space provided. *(6 points each)*

1. Willie Morris shows you the small town of Yazoo from
a. many points of view **c.** a third-person point of view
b. his own point of view **d.** the point of view of the Old Scotchman **1.** ______

2. As a youth, Morris's attitude toward most of his neighbors was one of
a. puzzlement **b.** hatred **c.** superiority **d.** fear **2.** ______

3. Willie Morris is writing the story of his own life. A similar type of writing was done by
a. Kai Erickson in "Everything in Its Path"
b. Ernesto Galarza in "Barrio Boy"
c. John McPhee in "Coming into the Country"
d. Isaac Bashevis Singer in "The Washwoman" **3.** ______

4. The author's main purpose is to
a. tell a good story **c.** examine youthful influences
b. describe the town of Yazoo **d.** solve a mystery **4.** ______

5. In "The Phantom of Yazoo," the techniques utilized are mainly
a. comparison and contrast **c.** direct and indirect characterization
b. external and internal conflict **d.** description and narration **5.** ______

B. INTERPRETING MEANINGS

Part 1. *Directions:* For each question, place the letter of the best answer in the space provided. *(5 points each)*

1. What does Morris mean when he calls Gentleman Joe's training techniques "soul-strengthening rituals"?
a. The training strengthens each member of the team.
b. The routine supplies the discipline champions need.
c. The training makes Morris feel good.
d. Training regimes strengthen the feet. **1.** ______

2. Morris's experience with the baseball quiz program and his role of Phantom tells you that he
a. is a baseball expert **c.** craves money
b. enjoys playing a joke on people **d.** needs approval **2.** ______

3. The town of Yazoo is described as
a. bustling **b.** beautiful **c.** uneventful **d.** exotic **3.** ______

4. What is Bozo's reaction when he learns that the Old Scotchman recreates the descriptions of the games?
   a. He admires the Old Scotchman's ingenuity.
   b. He feels angry and deceived.
   c. He is disappointed that the broadcast is made up.
   d. It isn't important to him. 4.______

5. Morris describes his discovery about the Scotchman as follows:

   > ...The Old Scotchman, for all his wondrous expressions, was not only several innings behind every game he described but was no doubt sitting in some air-conditioned studio in the hinterland, where he got the happenings of the game by news ticker; sound effects accounted for the crack of the bat and the crowd noises. Instead of being disappointed in the Scotchman, I was all the more pleased by his genius, for he made pristine facts more actual than actuality, a valuable lesson when the day finally came that I started reading literature. I must add, however, that this appreciation did not obscure the realization that I had at my disposal a weapon of unimaginable dimensions.

   In this passage, Morris acknowledges his debt to the Old Scotchman by
   a. praising his idea of sitting in an air-conditioned studio
   b. extolling his cleverness in using sound effects
   c. appreciating his objective, factual reporting
   d. recognizing his mastery of dramatic embellishment 5.______

Part 2. After Morris is exposed as the Phantom, he goes back to listening to the Old Scotchman rather to than the more up-to-date baseball news on the shortwave radio. Would you make such a choice?

Directions: On a separate sheet of paper, write a paragraph explaining your point of view. Cite examples from Morris's account of both styles of reporting. *(15 points)*

C. DEVELOPING VOCABULARY

Directions: For each of the following, place the letter of the best answer in the space provided. (*5 points each*)

1. seer
   a. a prophet **b.** a protector **c.** a viewer **d.** a baseball expert 1.______

2. acute
   a. loud **b.** tiny **c.** prolonged **d.** severe and sharp 2.______

3. tortuous
   a. torture **b.** bottomless **c.** twisting and turning **d.** exciting 3.______

4. gyration
   a. an agreement **c.** a union
   b. the act of whirling about **d.** a better argument 4.______

5. cryptic
   a. extremely dry **c.** pertaining to puzzles
   b. having a hidden or unclear meaning **d.** public knowledge 5.______

6. somnolence
   a. laziness or drowsiness **c.** great wisdom
   b. obesity **d.** the spirit of a people 6.______

NAME ______________________ CLASS __________ DATE __________ SCORE __________

UNIT 3: THE ELEMENTS OF NONFICTION

I KNOW WHY THE CAGED BIRD SINGS Maya Angelou

A. UNDERSTANDING WHAT HAPPENED

Directions: In the spaces provided, mark each true statement **T** and each false statement **F**. *(4 points each)*

1. Maya Angelou travels to Arkansas with her entire family. 1. ______
2. The community immediately embraces Maya and Bailey. 2. ______
3. Maya soon regards her grandmother as a mother. 3. ______
4. The Store is the center for much of the black life in Stamps. 4. ______
5. Most of the black inhabitants of Stamps are successful cotton pickers. 5. ______
6. Maya and Bailey get some of their early schooling at home. 6. ______
7. Uncle Willie is crippled from birth. 7. ______
8. The family stove both attracts and repels Maya. 8. ______
9. Uncle Willie is often the butt of jokes because of his disability. 9. ______
10. Maya is ashamed of Uncle Willie's attempt to hide his lameness from the visiting teachers. 10. ______

B. RECOGNIZING ELEMENTS OF AUTOBIOGRAPHY

Directions: For each question, place the letter of the best answer in the space provided. *(6 points each)*

1. The subject of this selection from Maya Angelou's autobiography is
   a. the most important episode in her early life
   b. a character portrait of her grandmother, Uncle Willie, and the townspeople of Stamps
   c. her relationship with Bailey
   d. her resentment toward her parents 1. ______

2. Maya Angelou uses irony in her account of the trip to Stamps when she
   a. explains why she left California
   b. explains the role of the porter in her trip
   c. states that her early travel experience was not unique
   d. describes reaching the segregated southern part of the journey 2. ______

3. Maya Angelou's attitude toward her subject is
   a. warm and respectful
   b. aloof and objective
   c. pitying
   d. disillusioned 3.______

4. Angelou uses contrasting imagery for morning and evening to underscore her description of the cotton pickers' lives. She does this by
   a. linking the fatigue of the workers in the morning to the intense heat of late afternoon
   b. contrasting the joking and bragging in the soft morning light to the disappointment and frustration in the harshness of late afternoon
   c. stressing the role of sunlight in helping people to remain optimistic
   d. illustrating that people are happiest when they rise early 4.______

5. Angelou attempts to conquer personal fear when she
   a. takes the train trip to Stamps
   b. jumps at the stove
   c. meets the teachers from Little Rock
   d. works at the Store 5.______

C. DEVELOPING VOCABULARY

Directions: Match each word in the left-hand column with the best meaning in the right-hand column. Place the letter of the best definition in the space provided. *(3 points each)*

______ **1.** segregated **a.** supplies of food, provisions

______ **2.** paranoia **b.** to fail to honor a promise or commitment

______ **3.** to renege **c.** bitter hatred or ill will

______ **4.** staple **d.** to employ

______ **5.** inordinate **e.** ability

______ **6.** to wince **f.** separated or set apart

______ **7.** vittles **g.** to draw back suddenly, to flinch

______ **8.** to thwart **h.** to frustrate

______ **9.** capacity **i.** feelings of being victimized

______ **10.** rancor **j.** a principal article of trade

k. ownership

l. lacking restraint or moderation

NAME ____________________ CLASS ________ DATE ________ SCORE ________

UNIT 3: THE ELEMENTS OF NONFICTION

LIFE ON THE MISSISSIPPI **Mark Twain** 

A. RECOGNIZING ELEMENTS OF AUTOBIOGRAPHY

Directions: For each question, place the letter of the best answer in the space provided. *(6 points each)*

1. The method of writing Mark Twain uses in the opening paragraph of "I Take a Few Extra Lessons" is
a. exposition **b.** description **c.** narration **d.** persuasion — **1.** ______

2. When Twain writes, "This was simply *bound to* be a success," to refer to his rounding the boat, the literary device he uses is
a. exaggeration **b.** metaphor **c.** simile **d.** human interest — **2.** ______

3. In "The Catastrophe," Twain's writing differs from that in his earlier chapters in that he no longer makes major use of
a. exaggeration **b.** irony **c.** metaphor **d.** simile — **3.** ______

4. In the dialogue with the captain following Twain's fight with Brown, the mood is primarily
a. tragic **b.** sad **c.** angry **d.** comic — **4.** ______

5. It is ironic that the chief mate survives because
a. he had been carried to the "death room" three times
b. the doctor and his assistants said he was doomed
c. the priest reads him last rites
d. he is the least competent crewman aboard — **5.** ______

B. INTERPRETING MEANINGS

Part 1. *Directions:* For each question, place the letter of the best answer in the space provided. *(5 points each)*

1. Twain is able to cope with the intolerable situation involving Brown by using
a. physical strength
b. mental superiority
c. trickery
d. the power of imagination — **1.** ______

2. Twain breaks the ship's rules by fighting Brown. During the battle he feels
a. guilty **b.** indignant **c.** afraid **d.** satisfied — **2.** ______

3. The catastrophe that Twain describes was caused by
a. the tyrannical pilot, Brown
b. collision with the wood-flat
c. the explosion of four boilers
d. Captain Klinefelter — **3.** ______

4. In Twain's account of his brother's death, his literary technique can best be described as
a. exaggeration
b. objective reporting
c. dramatization
d. hyperbole — **4.** ______

5. In this chapter on the steamboat accident, Twain writes as follows:

> The night before the *Pennsylvania* left, Henry and I sat chatting on a freight pile on the levee till midnight. The subject of the chat, mainly, was one which I think we had not exploited before—steamboat disasters. One was then on its way to us, little as we suspected it; the water which was to make the steam which should cause it was washing past some point fifteen hundred miles up the river while we talked—but it would arrive at the right time and the right place. We doubted if persons not clothed with authority were of much use in cases of disaster and attendant panic, still they might be of *some* use; so we decided that if a disaster ever fell within our experience we would at least stick to the boat and give such minor service as chance might throw in the way. Henry remembered this, afterward, when the disaster came, and acted accordingly.

In this passage Twain heightens the impact of Henry's death and reveals his belief about

a. God and religion **c.** man's fate
b. need for safety laws **d.** correct action 5.______

Part 2. Mark Twain does not state any opinions about organized religion, but the selection contains hints as to his attitude.

Directions: Write a paragraph explaining how you feel about Twain's views on religion. Cite parts of the story that influence your decision. *(15 points)*

C. DEVELOPING VOCABULARY

Directions: For each of the following, place the letter of the best synonym in the space provided. (*3 points each*)

1. malicious
a. angry **b.** fearful **c.** evil **d.** spiteful 1.______

2. to obliterate
a. to erase **b.** to spend **c.** to exhume **d.** to postpone 2.______

3. contemptuously
a. sorrowfully **b.** scornfully **c.** cantankerously **d.** suspiciously 3.______

4. to facilitate
a. to utilize **b.** to conserve **c.** to ease **d.** to strengthen 4.______

5. to ejaculate
a. to exclaim **b.** to rebound **c.** to catapult **d.** to scream 5.______

6. pretext
a. encyclopedia **b.** labor **c.** excuse **d.** expense 6.______

7. furtive
a. furious **b.** sneaky **c.** famous **d.** smoky 7.______

8. intimation
a. hint **b.** beginning **c.** finale **d.** closeness 8.______

9. solicitude
a. spite **b.** youth **c.** pity **d.** concern 9.______

10. supplication
a. plea **b.** license **c.** cheer **d.** intention 10.______

NAME ______________________ CLASS __________ DATE __________ SCORE __________

UNIT 3: THE ELEMENTS OF NONFICTION

WORD ANALOGIES / Extending Vocabulary Skills

Directions: In the space provided, write the letter of the pair of words that best describes a *relationship* that is closest to that of the capitalized words. (*5 points each*)

1. VIVACITY : ZEST ::
   a. liveliness : indolence
   b. ardor : stupor
   c. somnolence : torpor
   d. active : passive
   1. ______

2. DESTITUTE : AFFLUENT ::
   a. impoverished : enriched
   b. indigent : needy
   c. full : empty
   d. wealthy : prosperous
   2. ______

3. VITUPERATION : SCOLDING ::
   a. abuse : praising
   b. neglect : flattering
   c. solicitude : caring
   d. harmful : hurting
   3. ______

4. BENEDICTION : MALEDICTION ::
   a. ban : prohibition
   b. contradiction : denial
   c. prayer : grace
   d. blessing : curse
   4. ______

5. IRREDEEMABLE : IRREVOCABLE ::
   a. irrecoverable : irreplaceable
   b. reversible : changeable
   c. irregular : irresponsible
   d. alterable : final
   5. ______

6. SARCOPHAGUS : BODY ::
   a. grave : gravestone
   b. cache : food
   c. funeral : cremation
   d. carcass : corpse
   6. ______

7. CONSECRATE : DESECRATE ::
   a. deceive : trick
   b. conserve : save
   c. dedicate : violate
   d. conspire : plan
   7. ______

8. CRYPTIC : OBVIOUS ::
   a. grave : corpse
   b. ambiguous : uncertain
   c. mysterious : evident
   d. apparent : transparent
   8. ______

9. ILLITERATE : SKILLS
   a. ignorant : knowledge
   b. reiterate : information
   c. illegible : handwriting
   d. recognize : images
   9. ______

10. CONTEMPTUOUS : RESPECTFUL ::
    a. arrogant : pompous
    b. civil : disrespectful
    c. obliging : humble
    d. disdainful : gracious
    10. ______

11. PALPABLE : NOTICEABLE ::
    a. apparent : obvious
    b. clear : dim
    c. indistinct : visible
    d. intangible : perceptible
    11. ______

12. PRECARIOUS : INSECURE ::
    a. shaky : sure
    b. perilous : risky
    c. dubious : dependable
    d. uncontrolled : reliable
    12. ______

13. STORM : ABATES ::
    a. tornado : twists
    b. army : attacks
    c. mob : disperses
    d. person : relents
    13. ______

14. INSIDIOUS : TREACHEROUS ::
    a. truthful : honest
    b. fair : foul
    c. outspoken : sincere
    d. murder : theft
    14. ______

15. RESPLENDENT : DILAPIDATED ::
a. old : new
b. bright : shabby
c. decay : damage
d. ablaze : aglow **15.** ______

16. FACILITATE : SIMPLIFY ::
a. understand : recognize
b. difficult : easy
c. obstruct : help
d. hinder : complicate **16.** ______

17. INORDINATE : EXCESSIVE ::
a. outrageous : reasonable
b. unreasonable : surplus
c. moderate : extravagant
d. equitable : unequal **17.** ______

18. VERISIMILITUDE : PLAUSIBILITY ::
a. truth : falsity
b. actual : probable
c. genuineness : authenticity
d. imaginary : reality **18.** ______

19. ESTRANGE : UNITE ::
a. alienate : reconcile
b. strange : common
c. reunite : antagonize
d. establish : create **19.** ______

20. SINISTER : WICKED ::
a. noble : evil
b. fair : dishonest
c. sinful : virtuous
d. honorable : upright **20.** ______

NAME ______________________ CLASS __________ DATE __________ SCORE __________

UNIT 3: THE ELEMENTS OF NONFICTION

UNIT REVIEW / Applying Skills I

A. READING NONFICTION

Directions: Read the following passage carefully. Then answer the questions that follow.

Then comes Sir Walter Scott with his enchantments, and by his single might checks this wave of progress, and even turns it back; sets the world in love with dreams and phantoms; with decayed and swinish forms of religion; with the sillinesses and emptinesses, sham grandeurs, sham gauds, and sham chivalries of a brainless and worthless long-vanished society. He did measureless harm; more real and lasting harm, perhaps, than any other individual that ever wrote. Most of the world has now outlived good part of these harms, though by no means all of them; but in our South they flourish pretty forcefully still. Not so forcefully as half a generation ago, perhaps, but still forcefully. There, the genuine and wholesome civilization of the nineteenth century is curiously confused and commingled with the Walter Scott Middle Age sham civilization and so you have practical, common-sense, progressive ideas, and progressive works, mixed up with the duel, the inflated speech, and the jejune romanticism of an absurd past that is dead, and out of charity ought to be buried. But for the Sir Walter disease, the character of the Southerner—or Southron, according to Sir Walter's starchier way of phrasing it—would be wholly modern, in place of modern and medieval mixed, and the South would be fully a generation further advanced than it is. It was Sir Walter who made every gentleman in the South a Major or a Colonel, or a General or a Judge, before the war; and it was he, also, who made these gentlemen value these bogus decorations. For it was he that created rank and caste down there, and also reverence for rank and caste, and pride and pleasure in them. Enough is laid on slavery, without fathering upon it these creations and contributions of Sir Walter.

Sir Walter had so large a hand in making Southern character, as it existed before the war, that he is in great measure responsible for the war. It seems a little harsh toward a dead man to say that we never should have had any war but for Sir Walter; and yet something of a plausible argument might, perhaps, be made in support of that wild proposition. The Southerner of the American revolution owned slaves; so did the Southerner of the Civil War: but the former resembles the latter as an Englishman resembles a Frenchman. The change of character can be traced rather more easily to Sir Walter's influence than to that of any other thing or person.

One may observe, by one or two signs, how deeply that influence penetrated, and how strongly it holds. If one take up a Northern or Southern literary periodical of forty, or fifty years ago, he will find it filled with wordy, windy, flowery "eloquence," romanticism, sentimentality—all imitated from Sir Walter, and sufficiently badly done, too—innocent travesties of his style and methods, in fact. This sort of literature being the fashion in both sections of the country, there was opportunity for the fairest competition; and as a consequence, the South was able to show as many well-known literary names, proportioned to population, as the North could.

But a change has come, and there is no opportunity now for a fair competition between North and South. For the North has thrown out that old inflated style, whereas the Southern writer still clings to it—clings to it and has a restricted market for his wares, as a consequence. There is as much literary talent in the South, now, as ever there was, of course; but its work can gain but slight currency under present conditions; the authors write for the past, not the present; they use obsolete forms, and a dead language. But when a Southerner of genius writes modern English, his book goes upon crutches no longer, but upon wings; and they carry it swiftly all about America and England, and through the great English reprint publishing houses of Germany—as witness the experience of Mr. Cable and Uncle Remus, two of the very few Southern authors who do not write in the southern style. Instead of three or four widely known literary names, the South ought to have a dozen or two—and will have them when Sir Walter's time is out.

FROM *Life on the Mississippi* by Mark Twain

B. ANALYZING NONFICTION

Directions: For each question, place the letter of the best answer in the space provided. *(5 points each)*

1. The method of writing used by Mark Twain in this selection is
a. description
b. persuasion
c. exposition
d. narration

1. ______

2. In the range of topics included under nonfiction, this selection would serve as an example of
a. politics
b. travel
c. biography
d. science

2. ______

3. Twain's attitude toward his subject is
a. hostile
b. favorable
c. warm
d. amused

3. ______

4. Twain's use of the word "enchantments" to describe Scott's writing is meant
a. humorously
b. realistically
c. ironically
d. truthfully

4. ______

NAME ________________ CLASS ________ DATE ________ SCORE ________

5. You can infer from this excerpt that Twain believes that literature
   a. can have a great effect upon society
   b. is important to an individual's fantasy life
   c. can be educational
   d. is not essential to understanding a society

5. ______

6. The tone, or mood, of the selection is
   a. fearful
   b. angry
   c. comic
   d. tragic

6. ______

7. In his description of the Middle Ages, Twain uses
   a. repetition
   b. alliteration
   c. exaggeration
   d. all of the above

7. ______

8. Twain helps to prove his point by contrasting
   a. East and West
   b. Englishmen and Frenchmen
   c. Mr. Cable and Uncle Remus
   d. slavery and chivalry

8. ______

9. Twain makes clear his opinion of Scott's writing style by his
   a. criticism of its effects on other writers
   b. example of Scott's prose
   c. direct statement of opinion
   d. imitation of Scott's style

9. ______

10. The "Sir Walter disease" is
   a. the physical disease from which Scott suffered
   b. a special disease found among Southerners
   c. blind worship of rank, caste, and the past
   d. hypocrisy and slavery

10. ______

C. WRITING ABOUT NONFICTION

Judging from Twain's criticism of Scott's writing, what do you think Twain's idea of good writing must be? How can you tell? What evidence in the excerpt supports your opinion?

Directions: Using the evidence from the excerpt, write *one* paragraph, perhaps beginning with a statement such as: "Mark Twain believes good writing should be ________. This is clear because ________." *(25 points)*

____

____

____

____

D. ANALYZING LANGUAGE AND DEVELOPING VOCABULARY

Directions: In the spaces provided, mark each true statement **T** and each false statement **F**. *(5 points each)*

1. In the first sentence, Twain uses alliteration. **1.** ______

2. Judging from the context, the meaning of *sham* (paragraph 1) is "false." **2.** ______

3. Judging from the context, *jejune* (paragraph 1) probably refers to practical activity. **3.** ______

4. The word *travesties* (paragraph 3) helps the reader to understand Twain's style of writing. **4.** ______

5. Paragraph 4 contains an example of personification. **5.** ______

NAME ________________________ CLASS __________ DATE __________ SCORE __________

UNIT 3: THE ELEMENTS OF NONFICTION

CRITICAL THINKING AND WRITING / Applying Skills II

A. SUMMARIZING A REPORT

Directions: In *one* paragraph, summarize the objective information in the text selection "Everything in Its Path." Be sure to organize your information in time sequence (that is, list events in the order they occurred) and to avoid personal opinions. *(40 points)*

____

____

____

____

____

____

____

____

____

____

B. COMPARING AND CONTRASTING HUMOR IN NONFICTION

Directions: Write *two* paragraphs comparing and contrasting the use of humor in the two essays, "Charley in Yellowstone" and "The Night the Bed Fell." In the first paragraph, explain similarities in the authors' use of humor. In the second paragraph, describe different comic techniques used by Steinbeck and Thurber. *(30 points)*

____

____

____

____

____

____

____

C. RESPONDING TO NONFICTION

Directions: Write *one* paragraph to describe your response to any *two of* the following autobiographical accounts: "The Washwoman," "Barrio Boy," and "I Know Why the Caged Bird Sings."

Begin your paragraph by stating which account you like better. Follow this with details that compare the two accounts and support your opinion. You might wish to comment on elements of the autobiographical accounts, such as each author's point of view and attitude toward his or her early life. *(30 points)*

NAME ______________________ CLASS ________ DATE ________ SCORE ________

UNIT 4: THE ELEMENTS OF DRAMA

UNIT INTRODUCTION / Understanding the Elements of Drama

Directions: For each question, place the letter of the best answer in the space provided. *(10 points each)*

1. Playwright Eugene O'Neill said that a play should reveal "the most intense basic human interrelationships." Perhaps this is why so many playwrights write about
a. war
b. families
c. royalty
d. religion
1. ______

2. The introduction of the characters and basic situation of a play is called the
a. conflict
b. exposition
c. stage directions
d. situation
2. ______

3. The protagonist of a play is likely to be
a. the person with the most speeches
b. the person the audience likes best
c. the person who has something to achieve or overcome
d. the first person to appear on stage
3. ______

4. In a play, when the protagonist encounters an obstacle,
a. conflict occurs
b. the exposition begins
c. the climax begins
d. the denouement occurs
4. ______

5. The basic dramatic question is:
a. Will the play end happily?
b. Is the play a comedy or tragedy?
c. Will the protagonist achieve his or her goal?
d. Will the main character receive the most applause?
5. ______

6. The tension and emotions of a play reach their peak during the
a. exposition
b. denouement
c. climax
d. resolution
6. ______

7. During the course of a play, the relationships between characters
a. change
b. remain the same
c. usually become more intimate
d. usually grow more hostile
7. ______

8. Audiences generally respond best to a play in which the characters
   a. are unique and bizarre
   b. represent types of people the audience recognizes
   c. are foreigners
   d. are comic or tragic

8. ______

9. Obstacles can be based upon differences in
   a. race
   b. social position
   c. religion
   d. all of these

9. ______

10. The difference between activity and action in a play is that
   a. activity is any simple movement on stage; action is a meaningful activity that advances the plot or develops character
   b. activity is any simple movement on stage; action is more dramatic and bolder
   c. activity develops character; action advances the plot
   d. activity is added by a director; action is written by the playwright

10. ______

NAME ____________________ CLASS __________ DATE __________ SCORE __________

UNIT 4: THE ELEMENTS OF DRAMA

THE MIRACLE WORKER, Act One **William Gibson**

A. UNDERSTANDING WHAT HAPPENED

Directions: In the spaces provided, mark each true statement **T** and each false statement **F**. *(3 points each)*

1. Helen is born blind and deaf. **1.** ______

2. While playing with other children, Helen becomes fascinated by their lip movements. **2.** ______

3. Captain Keller feels more optimistic about Helen's future than his wife does. **3.** ______

4. The Kellers refuse to discipline Helen because they pity her. **4.** ______

5. Annie Sullivan's sight has been restored after numerous operations. **5.** ______

6. Annie is an experienced teacher. **6.** ______

7. Dr. Howe has taught many deaf-blind children to communicate as well as normal children. **7.** ______

8. Annie realizes that Helen is bright when she teaches her the manual alphabet. **8.** ______

9. Helen locks Annie in the room because Annie has tried to discipline her. **9.** ______

10. James respects Annie and her desire to help Helen. **10.** ______

B. RECOGNIZING ELEMENTS OF DRAMA

Directions: For each question, place the letter of the best answer in the space provided. *(6 points each)*

1. In Act One, the protagonist is
a. James
b. Helen
c. Captain Keller
d. Annie **1.** ______

2. From Annie's first appearance onstage, her character comes across as
a. girlish and light-hearted
b. knowledgeable but immature
c. strong-willed and determined
d. temperamental **2.** ______

3. The basic dramatic question posed in Scene 3 is whether
a. Helen is retarded
b. Helen needs more discipline
c. the family should put Helen in an institution
d. the Captain will write to an oculist **3.** ______

4. Annie begins to realize the intense conflict that lies ahead with her pupil
   a. when she steps off the train
   b. after Helen strikes her
   c. after meeting Captain Keller
   d. when James laughs at Annie

4. ______

5. Annie's climb onto Captain Keller's shoulders at the end of Act One is an example of
   a. crisis
   b. activity
   c. suspense
   d. comedy

5. ______

C. DEVELOPING VOCABULARY

Directions: Match each word in the left-hand column with the best meaning in the right-hand column. Place the letter of the best definition in the space provided. *(4 points each)*

______ 1. acute	a. unable to express oneself fully or clearly
______ 2. vivacious	b. arrogant, proud
______ 3. oculist	c. severe, intense
______ 4. inarticulate	d. a sleeveless, apron-like garment
______ 5. intimations	e. suggestions, hints
______ 6. pinafore	f. sharpness of temper
______ 7. voluminous	g. very lively
______ 8. imperious	h. an exaggerated portrait
______ 9. caricature	i. eye doctor
______ 10. asperity	j. very large or bulky
	k. slow and lazy
	l. inflammation of the ears

NAME ______________________ CLASS __________ DATE __________ SCORE __________

UNIT 4: THE ELEMENTS OF DRAMA

THE MIRACLE WORKER, Act Two **William Gibson** 

A. RECOGNIZING ELEMENTS OF DRAMA

Directions: For each question, place the letter of the best answer in the space provided. *(6 points each)*

1. Throughout Act Two, Annie's distress about her brother's death is suggested by the use of
- **a.** flashbacks
- **b.** exposition
- **c.** stereotypes
- **d.** choreography

1. ______

2. The most important conflict at the breakfast table in Scene 2 is between
- **a.** Keller and James arguing about the war
- **b.** Annie and the Kellers over how to treat Helen
- **c.** Kate and Viney over the breakfast
- **d.** Annie and Kate over Helen's love

2. ______

3. Annie's struggle to force Helen to eat with a spoon in Scene 3 is an example of
- **a.** comedy
- **b.** melodrama
- **c.** suspense
- **d.** action

3. ______

4. Annie's decision to pack her suitcase in Scene 5 can best be described as
- **a.** farce
- **b.** reversal
- **c.** realism
- **d.** conflict

4. ______

5. William Gibson's purpose in using flashbacks to reveal Annie's childhood is to
- **a.** make you feel sorry for Annie
- **b.** help you understand her motivation for helping Helen
- **c.** make clear why she is so tough
- **d.** provide a contrast to Helen's pampered life

5. ______

B. INTERPRETING MEANINGS

Part 1. *Directions:* For each question, place the letter of the best answer in the space provided. *(5 points each)*

1. One of Annie's strongest motivations for helping Helen is
- **a.** the fact that other teachers helped her
- **b.** her belief that Helen wants to learn
- **c.** her desire to prove that she is a good teacher
- **d.** her need to show the Kellers that she is right and they are wrong

1. ______

2. Flashbacks are used to suggest Annie's inner conflict. That conflict deals with
   a. uncertainty whether she can work with Helen
   b. disloyalty to the Perkins Institution
   c. anger toward God
   d. remorse about failing her brother

2. ______

3. In Annie's opinion, Helen's greatest handicap is
   a. blindness b. deafness c. temper d. her family's pity

3. ______

4. The Kellers allow Annie and Helen to live alone for two weeks because they
   a. understand that their interference is not desirable
   b. trust Annie
   c. need peace and quiet for a change
   d. fear Helen will have to enter an institution

4. ______

5. Annie says, "I must teach her one word. Everything." What does she mean?
   a. She wants to teach Helen all words.
   b. She has to teach her the word *everything*.
   c. She doubts Helen can learn language.
   d. Once Helen learns to connect a word and an object, she will understand that all words have meaning.

5. ______

Part 2. William Gibson makes clear that several of the characters are beginning to change their attitudes by the end of Act Two. What changes do you notice in Captain Keller, Kate Keller, and James Keller?

Directions: On a separate sheet of paper, write a paragraph explaining your point of view and citing parts of the story that influence your opinion. *(15 points)*

C. DEVELOPING VOCABULARY

Directions: Match each word in the left-hand column with the best meaning in the right-hand column. Place the letter of the best definition in the space provided. *(3 points each)*

______ 1. impassively	a. spasm
______ 2. temperance	b. to remove from a grave
______ 3. nonplussed	c. self-restraint
______ 4. feigned	d. angry look
______ 5. compunction	e. perplexed
______ 6. glower	f. irritated
______ 7. to disinter	g. stubbornly
______ 8. nettled	h. faked
______ 9. paroxysm	i. regret
______ 10. intractably	j. without emotion
	k. excited
	l. happily

NAME ______________________ CLASS __________ DATE __________ SCORE __________

UNIT 4: THE ELEMENTS OF DRAMA

THE MIRACLE WORKER, Act Three **William Gibson**

A. UNDERSTANDING WHAT HAPPENED

Directions: In the spaces provided, mark each true statement **T** and each false statement **F**. *(3 points each)*

1. Helen's changed appearance at the start of this act indicates that she is learning to obey Annie. **1.** ______

2. James's problem focuses on his growing dislike of Annie. **2.** ______

3. Annie wants to be alone with Helen for another week to teach her language. **3.** ______

4. Captain Keller believes that Helen lacks the intelligence to learn language. **4.** ______

5. Helen misbehaves at the dinner table because she is over-stimulated. **5.** ______

6. James comes to Annie's aid by learning to finger-spell. **6.** ______

7. When Annie says, "God owes me a resurrection," she is referring to the hard life she's led. **7.** ______

8. Helen finally understands the meaning of *water* because she dimly remembers the word from babyhood. **8.** ______

9. At the end of the play, Helen is reborn because she has learned to communicate with people. **9.** ______

10. Although Annie is able to work a miracle, she cannot learn to love Helen. **10.** ______

B. RECOGNIZING ELEMENTS OF DRAMA

Directions: For each question, place the letter of the best answer in the space provided. *(6 points each)*

1. Which of the following descriptive words best sums up Annie's situation as Act Three opens?
a. amazement
b. frustration
c. serenity
d. defeat **1.** ______

2. In the subplot, the conflict between James and his father appears likely to be resolved when
a. Keller tells James his opinions are worthless
b. James insults Annie
c. James stands up to his father
d. Kate overcomes her resentment of James **2.** ______

3. Which of the following techniques does William Gibson use to tell viewers about Annie Sullivan's life?
   a. linear style
   b. interior monologue
   c. minimal scenery
   d. dream sequences

3. ______

4. When the miracle finally happens, the action of the scene is primarily
   a. verbal
   b. physical
   c. realistic
   d. expressionistic

4. ______

5. The climax of *The Miracle Worker* occurs when
   a. Annie subdues Helen in the garden house
   b. the Kellers agree to give Annie and Helen the garden house
   c. Helen recognizes her father
   d. Helen understands the sign for *water*

5. ______

C. DEVELOPING VOCABULARY

Directions: Match each word in the left-hand column with the best meaning in the right-hand column. Place the letter of the best definition in the space provided. *(4 points each)*

______ 1. audible	a. motionless with awe
______ 2. to manipulate	b. fearful uncertainty, anxiety
______ 3. simultaneously	c. to make less in amount or degree
______ 4. trepidation	d. occurring at the same time
______ 5. consummately	e. loud enough to be heard
______ 6. transfixed	f. a return to life from the dead
______ 7. to grope	g. to feel about with the hands
______ 8. afflicted	h. to handle, operate, or manage skillfully
______ 9. resurrection	i. completely
______ 10. to abate	j. suffering, having an illness or disability
	k. to strike forcefully
	l. repaired

NAME ________________________ CLASS __________ DATE __________ SCORE __________

UNIT 4: THE ELEMENTS OF DRAMA

VISITOR FROM FOREST HILLS **Neil Simon**

A. UNDERSTANDING WHAT HAPPENED

Directions: In the spaces provided, mark each true statement **T** and each false statement **F**. *(3 points each)*

1. Mimsey has locked herself in the bathroom because she doesn't love Borden. **1.** ______

2. Norma Hubley tries to hide the problem from Borden's parents. **2.** ______

3. Roy Hubley blames his wife for Mimsey's behavior. **3.** ______

4. Roy enters the bathroom through the window. **4.** ______

5. Time is important in this play because the guests are waiting for the wedding to begin. **5.** ______

6. Roy thinks that anger and sternness will bring Mimsey out of the bathroom. **6.** ______

7. Mimsey has never been eager to marry Borden. **7.** ______

8. Mimsey fears she and Borden will become like Roy and Norma. **8.** ______

9. Borden is very understanding about Mimsey's fears. **9.** ______

10. Norma finally succeeds in coaxing Mimsey to come out of the bathroom. **10.** ______

B. RECOGNIZING ELEMENTS OF DRAMA

Directions: For each question, place the letter of the best answer in the space provided. *(6 points each)*

1. Which of the following events is an example of farce?
a. Roy Hubley yells at his wife.
b. Norma Hubley rips her stockings.
c. Roy steps onto the window ledge in his tuxedo.
d. Mimsey Hubley plays with her false eyelashes. **1.** ______

2. In this play the Jack-in-the-box character is represented by
a. Mimsey
b. Roy
c. Norma
d. Borden Eisler **2.** ______

3. Norma Hubley can be described as a stereotype because she
a. behaves like a typical mother
b. is concerned about Mimsey's feelings
c. values what other people think
d. is a scatterbrained wife **3.** ______

4. Roy's chief character flaw is
   a. his domineering manner
   b. miserliness
   c. a tendency to spoil his daughter
   d. sarcasm — 4. ______

5. A serious moment in Neil Simon's comedy occurs when
   a. Roy tells Mimsey how much the wedding costs
   b. Roy realizes that he and his wife have presented a poor model of marriage for their daughter
   c. Norma fights with her husband
   d. Norma speaks to Borden's father on the telephone — 5. ______

C. DEVELOPING VOCABULARY

Directions: Match each word in the left-hand column with the best meaning in the right-hand column. Place the letter of the best definition in the space provided. *(4 points each)*

______ 1. farce
______ 2. stereotype
______ 3. squabbling
______ 4. incredulously
______ 5. to barricade
______ 6. to brandish
______ 7. interminable
______ 8. gargoyle
______ 9. vehemence
______ 10. despondent

a. a waterspout on a building in the form of a fantastic creature
b. doubtingly
c. hopeless, dejected
d. a play with ridiculous situations
e. petty quarreling
f. an unfair, inaccurate idea about people or things
g. to wave something in a menacing way
h. very strong expression of feeling
i. seemingly endless
j. to shut in or keep out with a barrier
k. a cloth made of synthetic fibers
l. to behave insincerely

NAME ______________________ CLASS __________ DATE __________ SCORE __________

UNIT 4: THE ELEMENTS OF DRAMA

THE MOTHER **Paddy Chayefsky**

A. RECOGNIZING ELEMENTS OF DRAMA

Directions: For each question, place the letter of the best answer in the space provided. *(6 points each)*

1. A television play differs from a stage play in that
a. a stage play supplies more depth
b. a stage play runs longer
c. television playwrights are more skillful
d. a camera allows the action to move easily from one setting to another **1.** ______

2. The main conflict in *The Mother* takes place between
a. Annie and her husband over whether her mother should live with them
b. Annie and Marie for their mother's love
c. Annie and her mother over the latter's need for independence
d. the mother and the boss **2.** ______

3. Annie's true motive for wanting to take care of her mother is her
a. need for her mother's love
b. desire to do her duty
c. eagerness to show up her sister and brother
d. need to have her own way **3.** ______

4. In the climax of the play, the mother
a. loses her job
b. arrives to live with Annie
c. wins the job
d. decides to return to her own apartment and continue looking for work **4.** ______

5. The resolution occurs when
a. the mother comes to live with Annie
b. the daughter learns to admire her mother's determination and pride
c. the husband and wife decide to go on vacation
d. the mother loses her job **5.** ______

B. INTERPRETING MEANINGS

Part 1. *Directions:* For each question, place the letter of the best answer in the space provided. *(5 points each)*

1. The mother has trouble holding sewing jobs because
a. she can't remember the necessary skills
b. there's no money in it
c. she is too slow
d. she cannot concentrate **1.** ______

2. Annie's stated objections to her mother's return to work include
   a. old age and poor health
   b. no need for money
   c. dangerous working conditions
   d. an opportunity to travel
   2. ______

3. The boss fires the mother
   a. after she shows up late
   b. after she sews the sleeves wrong
   c. following complaints from co-workers
   d. at the bookkeeper's insistence
   3. ______

4. According to Marie, her mother's favorite has always been
   a. Marie
   b. Annie
   c. Frank
   d. George
   4. ______

5. The prospect of giving away her furniture causes the mother to feel
   a. sad
   b. angry
   c. lighthearted
   d. serene
   5. ______

Part 2. Paddy Chayefsky concludes his play with the mother's decision to continue her job search. Is Chayefsky's ending convincing? Why would someone past retirement age make such a decision?

Directions: On a separate sheet of paper, explain why you think the mother changes her mind. *(15 points)*

C. DEVELOPING VOCABULARY

Directions: Match each word in the left-hand column with the best meaning in the right-hand column. Place the letter of the best definition in the space provided. *(3 points each)*

______ 1. fluidity
______ 2. foyer
______ 3. petulant
______ 4. lenient
______ 5. montage
______ 6. apprehensive
______ 7. covert
______ 8. staccato
______ 9. meticulousness
______ 10. valise

a. a small, soft-bound suitcase
b. smooth, liquid-like motion
c. hidden, concealed
d. great attention to detail
e. a set of images combined for one effect
f. a rapid series of short, sharp sounds
g. entrance hall
h. worried
i. a dance step
j. ill-humored
k. patient and forgiving
l. faithful

NAME ______________________ CLASS__________ DATE__________ SCORE__________

UNIT 4: THE ELEMENTS OF DRAMA

WORD ANALOGIES / Extending Vocabulary Skills

Directions: In the space provided, write of the pair of words that best describes a *relationship* that is closest to that of the capitalized pair of words. *(5 points each)*

1. COVERT : IMPERCEPTIBLE ::
   - **a.** concealed : obvious
   - **b.** surreptitious : unnoticeable
   - **c.** hidden : noticeable
   - **d.** disguised : clear

   1. ______

2. ALLAY : AGGRAVATE ::
   - **a.** contrive : endeavor
   - **b.** feign : pretend
   - **c.** anger : irritate
   - **d.** reduce : intensify

   2. ______

3. HUMILIATE : EMBARRASS ::
   - **a.** belittle : humble
   - **b.** honor : shame
   - **c.** humor : comedy
   - **d.** degrade : elevate

   3. ______

4. INDULGENCE : LENIENCY ::
   - **a.** punishment : kindness
   - **b.** defiance : cooperation
   - **c.** patience : roughness
   - **d.** denial : repression

   4. ______

5. BEMOAN : AFFLICTION ::
   - **a.** sound : silence
   - **b.** lament : hardship
   - **c.** scowl : grimace
   - **d.** wish : intention

   5. ______

6. ASPERITY : FEROCITY ::
   - **a.** aspiration : desire
   - **b.** perspire : sweat
   - **c.** crossness : cruelty
   - **d.** anxiety : serenity

   6. ______

7. CONTENTION : INTIMATION ::
   - **a.** declaration : hint
   - **b.** deny : restate
   - **c.** confrontation : intervention
   - **d.** illusion : dream

   7. ______

8. DESPONDENT : DEPRESSED ::
   - **a.** dehydrated : desiccated
   - **b.** desperate : dangerous
   - **c.** description : depiction
   - **d.** discouraged : dejected

   8. ______

9. TREPIDATION : RESOLUTE ::
   - **a.** deliberate : cautious
   - **b.** nervousness : confident
   - **c.** confession : guilt
   - **d.** appraisal : value

   9. ______

10. FACETIOUS : STOLID ::
    - **a.** humorous : unexcitable
    - **b.** passive : active
    - **c.** weak : solid
    - **d.** serious : unemotional

    10. ______

11. DEFERENTIAL : YIELDING ::
    - **a.** uncertain : irresolute
    - **b.** emphatic : forceful
    - **c.** decisive : submissive
    - **d.** flexible : firm

    11. ______

12. INDOLENT : VIGOROUS ::
    - **a.** surly : sullen
    - **b.** explosive : volatile
    - **c.** irate : impassive
    - **d.** idle : energetic

    12. ______

13. PROFOUND : SHALLOW ::
    - **a.** informed : know
    - **b.** wise : foolish
    - **c.** thoughtful : complete
    - **d.** deep : superficial

    13. ______

14. APPORTION : ALLOCATE ::
    - **a.** divide : distribute
    - **b.** part : whole
    - **c.** collect : receive
    - **d.** assemble : separate

    14. ______

15. COMPUNCTION : REGRET ::
   a. certainty : hesitation
   b. remorse : joy
   c. scruple : uneasiness
   d. honest : dishonest

15. ______

16. IMMUNE : VULNERABLE ::
   a. invulnerable : resistant
   b. protected : unprotected
   c. susceptible : sheltered
   d. endangered : safe

16. ______

17. LABORIOUS : RIGOROUS ::
   a. strenuous : simple
   b. toilsome : effortless
   c. difficult : challenging
   d. hard : soft

17. ______

18. IMPERTINENT : BRASH ::
   a. disrespectful : impudent
   b. discourteous : mannerly
   c. deferential : smart alecky
   d. polite : rude

18. ______

19. REQUISITE : NECESSARY ::
   a. unessential : prerequisite
   b. wanted : needed
   c. essential : required
   d. unnecessary : indispensable

19. ______

20. CONFRONT : OPPOSE ::
   a. face : challenge
   b. brave : avoid
   c. counter : yield
   d. attack : retreat

20. ______

NAME ______________________ CLASS__________ DATE__________ SCORE__________

UNIT 4: THE ELEMENTS OF DRAMA

UNIT REVIEW / Applying Skills I

A. READING A PLAY

Directions: Read the following excerpt from the first scene of Neil Simon's autobiographical play, *Brighton Beach Memoirs,* and then answer the questions that follow. As the scene opens, Eugene is outside playing with his baseball. His mother Kate, sister Laurie, and Aunt Blanche are in the kitchen. Eugene is talking to the audience about his sister.

EUGENE *(Turns to the audience again)* She gets all this special treatment because the doctors say she has kind of a flutter in her heart...I got hit with a baseball right in the back of the skull, I saw two of everything for a week and I still had to carry a block of ice home every afternoon...Girls are treated like queens. Maybe that's what I should have been born—an Italian girl...

KATE *(Picks up a sweat sock from the floor)* EUGENE!!

EUGENE *What??*

KATE How many times have I told you not to leave your things around the house?

EUGENE A hundred and nine.

KATE What?

EUGENE You said yesterday, "I told you a hundred and nine times not to leave your things around the house."

BLANCHE DON'T BE FRESH TO YOUR MOTHER, GENE!

EUGENE *(To the audience)* Was I fresh? I swear to God, that's what she said to me yesterday...One day I'm going to put all this in a book or a play. I'm going to be a writer like Ring Lardner or somebody— that's if things don't work out first with the Yankees, or the Cubs, or the Red Sox, or maybe possibly the Tigers...If I get down to the St. Louis Browns, then I'll definitely be a writer.

LAURIE Mom, can I have a glass of lemonade?

BLANCHE It'll spoil your dinner, darling.

KATE A small glass, it couldn't hurt her.

BLANCHE All right. In a minute, angel.

KATE I'll get it. I'm in the kitchen anyway.

EUGENE *(To the audience)* Can you believe that? She'd better have a bad heart or I'm going to kill her one day...*(He gets up to walk into the house, then stops on the porch steps and turns to the audience again...confidentially)* Listen, I hope you don't repeat this to anybody...What I'm telling you are my secret memoirs. It's called, "The Unbelievable, Fantastic and Completely Private Thoughts of I, Eugene Morris Jerome, in this, the fifteenth year of his life, in the year nineteen hundred and thirty-seven, in the community of Brighton Beach, Borough of Brooklyn, Kings Country, City of New York, Empire State of the American Nation—"

KATE *(Comes out of the kitchen with a glass of lemonade and one roller skate)* A roller skate? On my kitchen floor? Do you want me dead, is that what you want?

EUGENE *(Rushes into the house)* I didn't leave it there.

KATE No? Then who? Laurie? Aunt Blanche? Did you ever see them on skates? *(She holds out the skate)* Take this upstairs...Come here!

EUGENE *(Approaches, holding the back of his head)* Don't hit my skull, I have a concussion.

KATE *(Handing the glass to* LAURIE*)* What would you tell your father if he came home and I was dead on the kitchen floor?

EUGENE I'd say, "Don't go in the kitchen, Pa!"

KATE *(Swings at him, he ducks and she misses)* Gct upstairs! And don't come down with dirty hands.

EUGENE *(Goes up the stairs. He turns to the audience)* You see why I want to write all this down? In case I grow up all twisted and warped, the world will know why.

BLANCHE *(Still sewing)* He's a boy. He's young. You should be glad he's healthy and active. Before the doctors found out what Laurie had, she was the same way.

KATE Never. Girls are different. When you and I were girls, we kept the house spotless. It was Ben and Ezra who drove Momma crazy. *(We see* EUGENE, *upstairs, enter his room and take out a notebook and pencil and lie down on his bed, making a new entry in his "memoirs")*...I've always been like that. I have to have things clean. Just like Momma. The day they packed up and left the house in Russia, she cleaned the place from top to bottom. She said, "No matter what the Cossacks did to us, when they broke into our house, they would have respect for the Jews."

LAURIE Who were the Cossacks?

KATE The same filthy bunch as live across the street.

LAURIE Across the street? You mean the Murphys?

KATE *All* of them.

LAURIE The Murphys are Russian?

BLANCHE The mother is nice. She's been very sweet to me.

KATE Her windows are so filthy, I thought she had black curtains hanging inside.

BLANCHE I was in their house. It was very neat. *Nobody* could be as clean as you.

KATE What business did you have in their house?

BLANCHE She invited me for tea.

KATE To meet that drunken son of hers?

BLANCHE No. Just the two of us.

KATE I'm living here seven years, she never invited *me* for tea. Because she knows your situation. I know their kind. Remember what Momma used to tell us. "Stay on your own side of the street. That's what they have gutters for."

(She goes back into the kitchen)

B. ANALYZING A PLAY

Directions: For each question, place the letter of the best answer in the space provided. *(5 points each)*

1. This excerpt presents the
a. exposition of the play
b. major conflict
c. minor characters
d. climax
1. ______

2. The protagonist of this play is
a. Kate
b. Laurie
c. Eugene
d. Blanche
2. ______

3. The character of Kate is shown by
a. her actions and dialogue
b. interior conflict
c. reversals
d. the shock of recognition
3. ______

4. Eugene's line, "One day I am going to put all this down in a book or a play," is
a. an attempt to win over the audience
b. idle talk, because a boy cannot know his future
c. untrue, because Eugene really wants to be a baseball player
d. foreshadowing, because the real "Eugene," Neil Simon, did just that
4. ______

5. In Eugene's first speech in this excerpt,
a. he is foreshadowing the conflict
b. he is talking to the audience
c. he reveals that he has always wanted to be a girl
d. he describes his father
5. ______

6. From this excerpt, you might expect the play's main conflict to arise between
a. Blanche and Laurie
b. Kate and Laurie
c. Eugene and his family
d. Eugene and the Murphys
6. ______

7. The discussion between Blanche and Kate about the Murphys is an example of
a. the dramatic question
b. symbolism
c. dramatic irony
d. flashback
7. ______

8. Eugene's line, "She'd better have a bad heart or I'm going to kill her one day," implies that
   a. Eugene wants to murder Laurie
   b. Eugene is insensitive
   c. Eugene is jealous of Laurie
   d. Eugene thinks Laurie's heart ailment is a fraud — 8. ______

9. Blanche's line, "You should be glad he's healthy and active. Before the doctors found out what Laurie had, she was the same way," implies that
   a. coddling Laurie has affected her behavior
   b. Eugene is going to get sick
   c. Blanche does not like Laurie
   d. Laurie is going to die — 9. ______

10. The title of the play implies that
   a. the play takes place on the seashore
   b. the play takes place in summer
   c. the play takes place before World War II
   d. elements of the play come from the author's past — 10. ______

C. WRITING ABOUT A PLAY

Directions: Using the character information from this excerpt, write a short scene between Eugene and Laurie in which the two are dividing the household chores. Remember that Laurie has a supposed heart ailment and that Eugene is skeptical about her illness. *(25 points)*

D. ANALYZING LANGUAGE AND DEVELOPING VOCABULARY

Directions: In the spaces provided, mark each true statement **T** and each false statement **F**. *(5 points each)*

1. During the scene, Eugene is wearing a baseball glove and playing with a baseball. These items are symbols. — 1. ______

2. Judging from the title, the plot of *Brighton Beach Memoirs* centers around Eugene. The relationship between Blanche and the Murphys is a subplot. — 2. ______

3. During the scene, Eugene argues with his mother. Kate is an obstacle, or antagonist. — 3. ______

4. Kate's line, "Stay on your own side of the street. That's what they have gutters for," is an example of foreshadowing. — 4. ______

5. From the context, you can gather that Cossacks were bloodthirsty terrorists. — 5. ______

NAME ________________ CLASS ________ DATE ________ SCORE ________

UNIT 4: THE ELEMENTS OF DRAMA

CRITICAL THINKING AND WRITING / Applying Skills II

A. COMPARING/CONTRASTING EXPOSITION

Directions: In *three* short paragraphs, compare or contrast the ways in which the basic situation, or exposition, is introduced in each of the three plays, *The Miracle Worker, The Visitor from Forest Hills,* and *The Mother*. *(40 points)*

B. ANALYZING CHARACTER

Directions: In *one* paragraph, describe the character of Boss in *The Mother*. What pressures cause him to dismiss the Mother? Do you think he would have fired her on a less stressful day? *(30 points)*

C. ANALYZING A SCENE

Directions: Reread Act Two, Scene 2 of *The Miracle Worker*. Write *one* paragraph to describe the problem, the conflict, and the resolution of the scene. *(30 points)*

NAME ____________________ CLASS__________ DATE__________ SCORE__________

UNIT 5: WILLIAM SHAKESPEARE

UNIT INTRODUCTION / Understanding Shakespeare

Directions: For each question, place the letter of the best answer in the space provided. *(10 points each)*

1. The theatrical group, The King's Men, was so named because
a. all of the members were royalty
b. the king selected the participants
c. the company was supported by the king
d. the company traveled with the king
1. ______

2. Shakespeare called his theater a "wooden O"
a. in honor of the wooden horse with which the Greeks invaded Troy
b. because he disliked it
c. because it was round and made of wood
d. because it was always empty
2. ______

3. In the Globe Theater, the lighting was provided by
a. candles
b. kerosene lamps
c. gas lamps
d. daylight
3. ______

4. Theatrical scenery in Shakespeare's time
a. was suggested by the language of the play
b. was usually made of straw
c. is often reproduced in modern productions
d. was documented by the artist Burbage
4. ______

5. The groundlings in Shakespearean theaters
a. illuminated the stage
b. were hung like banners around the stage
c. secured the stage to the floor
d. stood and watched the play for a penny
5. ______

6. All of Shakespeare's women characters
a. contain a tragic element
b. speak in rhyming couplets
c. originally were played by men and boys
d. were historical characters
6. ______

7. Shakespeare would have called a proscenium stage
a. an inner stage
b. the yard
c. a balcony stage
d. the Globe
7. ______

8. On a thrust stage,
a. the actors must remain onstage once they have entered
b. the audience sits on three sides
c. the actors walk into the audience
d. comedies are always performed

8. ______

9. Most of the topics for Shakespeare's plays were
a. created by the actors in the company
b. written by the king
c. based on poems
d. well known to the audience before they appeared in the plays

9. ______

10. Shakespeare wrote his plays
a. in iambic pentameter and blank verse
b. in London
c. for his wife
d. in order to have good acting parts to perform

10. ______

NAME ________________ CLASS ________ DATE ________ SCORE ________

UNIT 5: WILLIAM SHAKESPEARE

THE TRAGEDY OF ROMEO AND JULIET, Act I **William Shakespeare**

A. UNDERSTANDING WHAT HAPPENED

Directions: In the spaces provided, mark each true statement **T** and each false statement **F**. *(3 points each)*

1. Tybalt tries to stop the fighting between the servants of the Montagues and the servants of the Capulets. **1.** ______

2. The Prince warns the feuding families that another riot will result in a death sentence. **2.** ______

3. Romeo is lovesick over Rosaline. **3.** ______

4. Juliet is always falling in love. **4.** ______

5. Juliet wishes to marry Paris. **5.** ______

6. Benvolio urges Romeo to go to Capulet's feast to recover from his love of Rosaline. **6.** ______

7. Mercutio has a charming personality. **7.** ______

8. Lord Capulet is unaware that Romeo is at the party. **8.** ______

9. Juliet knows that Romeo is a Montague when she first kisses him. **9.** ______

10. Both Romeo and Juliet realize that their love will bring them trouble and sorrow. **10.** ______

B. RECOGNIZING ELEMENTS OF DRAMA

Directions: For each question, place the letter of the best answer in the space provided. *(6 points each)*

1. Shakespeare uses a prologue to inform the audience that
a. Juliet is a widow
b. Romeo is a fugitive
c. the lovers from the long-feuding families will die
d. Romeo is a Montague and Juliet a Capulet **1.** ______

2. Mercutio can be described as a foil to Romeo because
a. they come from different social classes
b. Romeo is much younger than Mercutio
c. Romeo is a Montague and Mercutio a Capulet
d. Romeo takes love seriously while Mercutio does not **2.** ______

3. The following quotation occurs in Act I, Scene 1: *Capulet.* "What noise is this? Give me my long sword, ho!" These lines are an illustration of
   a. alliteration
   b. blank verse
   c. a couplet
   d. prose
   3.______

4. All of the following are examples of archaic words *except*
   a. coz
   b. good-den
   c. halt
   d. Marry!
   4.______

5. Shakespeare uses foreshadowing in the following passage:
   Romeo.

   ...my mind misgives
   Some consequence yet having in the stars
   Shall bitterly begin his fearful date
   With this night's revels and expire the term
   Of a despisèd life, closed in my breast,
   By some vile forfeit of untimely death.

   What events does this quotation predict?
   a. a renewal of an old feud
   b. Romeo's death
   c. the beginning of a new love for Romeo
   d. an accident at the ball
   5.______

C. DEVELOPING VOCABULARY

Directions: Match each word in the left-hand column with the best meaning in the right-hand column. Place the letter of the best definition in the space provided. *(4 points each)*

______**1.** Anon!
______**2.** Good-den
______**3.** hap
______**4.** humor
______**5.** to mark
______**6.** to owe
______**7.** shrift
______**8.** Soft!
______**9.** withal
______**10.** to wot

a. to listen
b. Coming!
c. mood
d. with that, with
e. Good evening
f. Quiet!
g. to own
h. luck
i. to know
j. forgiveness for sins confessed to a priest
k. Congratulations!
l. to celebrate

NAME ____________________ CLASS __________ DATE __________ SCORE __________

UNIT 5: WILLIAM SHAKESPEARE

THE TRAGEDY OF ROMEO AND JULIET, ACT II — William Shakespeare

A. RECOGNIZING ELEMENTS OF DRAMA

Directions: For each question, place the letter of the best answer in the space provided. *(6 points each)*

1. In the balcony scene, several of Juliet's speeches convey a sense of foreboding. Which one of the following fears is *not* mentioned?
a. their love is moving too swiftly
b. Romeo will be discovered
c. this love will result in her death
d. Romeo could prove faithless
1. ______

2. The purpose of the humor arising from the nurse's comic character is to
a. furnish relief from the tragedy
b. display Shakespeare's wit
c. suggest that love has its funny side
d. indicate that the servants are foolish
2. ______

3. When Friar Laurence agrees to marry the couple, his chief motive is to
a. please the lovers
b. prove that Romeo is sincere
c. prevent an elopement
d. end the feud between their families
3. ______

4. Shakespeare creates suspense in Scene 4 when you learn that Tybalt
a. plans to challenge Romeo to a duel
b. insults Mercutio
c. refuses to make peace with the Montagues
d. tries to talk Juliet out of the marriage
4. ______

5. Scene 6 opens with the following lines:

"So smile the heavens upon this holy act
That after hours with sorrow chide us not!"

This quotation is an example of
a. iambic pentameter
b. a couplet
c. personification
d. a sonnet
5. ______

B. INTERPRETING MEANINGS

Part 1. *Directions:* For each question, place the letter of the best answer in the space provided. *(5 points each)*

1. In the balcony scene, Juliet says:

What's Montague? It is nor hand, nor foot,
Nor arm, nor face....
What's in a name? That which we call a rose
By any other word would smell as sweet.

What does she mean?
a. Montague is an unimportant name in Verona.
b. Romeo should take her last name when they marry.
c. Romeo's name is an accident of birth, not an essential part of himself.
d. It is wrong to fall in love with a Montague.
1. ______

2. Juliet quickly admits her love to Romeo because
   a. she wants to marry him
   b. she is sure his love is true
   c. she is not a flirt
   d. he overhears her musing about her love for him — 2. ______

3. Juliet says, "Parting is such sweet sorrow/ That I shall say goodnight till it be morrow." By this she means
   a. Romeo should stay till morning
   b. Romeo should leave immediately
   c. short goodbyes are less painful than long ones
   d. parting is painful but still so enjoyable that she wants to prolong it — 3. ______

4. Shakespeare reveals the hour at which the balcony scene and the scene in Friar Laurence's cell take place by using
   a. characters to describe the time of day
   b. colorful scenery
   c. realistic lighting
   d. a chorus to announce the time — 4. ______

5. Friar Laurence rebukes Romeo because
   a. Romeo is causing trouble by wooing Juliet
   b. Romeo is so changeable in love
   c. Juliet is too young to marry
   d. Romeo is unfaithful to Rosaline — 5. ______

Part 2. In Act II, Shakespeare uses a technique called *foreshadowing* to suggest that the marriage of Romeo and Juliet will end in their deaths.

Directions: Find two examples of lines in Scene 6 that foreshadow trouble for the young lovers. *(15 points)*

C. DEVELOPING VOCABULARY

Directions: Match each word in the left-hand column with the best meaning in the right-hand column. Place the letter of the best definition in the space provided. *(3 points each)*

______ 1. to discourse — a. to be armored or protected against
______ 2. counsel — b. favor
______ 3. to be proof — c. private thoughts
______ 4. to discover — d. to speak
______ 5. bounty — e. a trinket or cheap jewel
______ 6. baleful — f. to reveal
______ 7. grace — g. Wait!
______ 8. bauble — h. evil or poisonous
______ 9. Stay! — i. to destroy
______ 10. to confound — j. capacity for giving
k. to run
l. Quiet!

NAME ______________________________ CLASS__________ DATE__________ SCORE__________

UNIT 5: WILLIAM SHAKESPEARE

THE TRAGEDY OF ROMEO AND JULIET, ACT III — William Shakespeare

A. UNDERSTANDING WHAT HAPPENED

Directions: In the spaces provided, mark each true statement **T** and each false statement **F**. *(3 points each)*

1. Tybalt and Mercutio fight because Mercutio seeks to protect Romeo's honor. 1. ______
2. Mercutio is killed because Tybalt is a better swordsman. 2. ______
3. The Prince punishes Romeo for killing Tybalt by sentencing him to death. 3. ______
4. Juliet thinks Romeo is dead because the nurse tells her so. 4. ______
5. Romeo threatens to kill himself because death is preferable to living without Juliet. 5. ______
6. In his speech to Romeo, Friar Laurence convinces Romeo that he will be reunited with Juliet. 6. ______
7. The lovers' plan to reunite is ruined when Romeo must leave for Mantua. 7. ______
8. Juliet's parents treat her with love and understanding. 8. ______
9. Juliet's nurse advises her to marry Paris. 9. ______
10. At the close of Act III, Juliet decides to ask Friar Laurence's advice. 10. ______

B. RECOGNIZING ELEMENTS OF DRAMA

Directions: For each question, place the letter of the best answer in the space provided. *(6 points each)*

1. In Scene 1, Mercutio speaks the following line and then pauses: "Tybalt, you ratcatcher, will you walk?" This type of line is called
   a. run-on
   b. simile
   c. end-stopped
   d. soliloquy
   1. ______

2. Tybalt's sudden stabbing and killing of Mercutio illustrates a technique called
   a. reversal
   b. shock of recognition
   c. conflict
   d. stereotype
   2. ______

3. The turning point of the play occurs when
   a. Romeo and Juliet marry
   b. Mercutio is killed
   c. Romeo kills Tybalt
   d. Juliet's parents insist on her marriage to Paris
   3. ______

4. Why is the following passage an example of dramatic irony?

Lady Capulet.
Well, well, thou has a careful father, child:
One who, to put thee from thy heaviness,
Hath sorted out a sudden day of joy
That thou expects not nor I looked not for.
Juliet.
Madam, in happy time! What day is that?
Lady Capulet.
Marry, my child, early next Thursday morn
The gallant, young, and noble gentleman,
The County Paris, at Saint Peter's Church,
Shall happily make thee there a joyful bride.

a. Its tone is sarcastic.
b. Juliet is presented with a way out of her dilemma.
c. Juliet's mother makes a dramatic announcement.
d. Lady Capulet is unaware that her daughter is already married. **4.**______

5. Lord and Lady Capulet are similar to Mimsey's parents in Neil Simon's *Visitor from Forest Hills*. The two pairs illustrate
a. flashbacks
b. the battle of the sexes
c. theater-in-the-round
d. Jack-in-the-box characters **5.**______

C. DEVELOPING VOCABULARY

Directions: Match each word in the left-hand column with the best meaning in the right-hand column. Place the letter of the best definition in the space provided. *(4 points each)*

______ **1.** doublet
______ **2.** dissemble
______ **3.** strange
______ **4.** sack
______ **5.** entertained
______ **6.** civil
______ **7.** fain
______ **8.** fond
______ **9.** spleen
______ **10.** estate

a. lie
b. thought of
c. willingly
d. foolish
e. plunder and destroy
f. anger
g. well-behaved
h. situation
i. unfamiliar
j. stupid
k. thrusts
l. jacket

NAME ____________________ CLASS__________ DATE__________ SCORE __________

UNIT 5: WILLIAM SHAKESPEARE

THE TRAGEDY OF ROMEO AND JULIET, ACT IV — William Shakespeare

A. UNDERSTANDING WHAT HAPPENED

Directions: In the spaces provided, mark each true statement **T** and each false statement **F**. *(3 points each)*

1. Juliet tells Paris that she will marry him. **1.** ______

2. Juliet tells Friar Laurence that she would rather kill herself than marry Paris. **2.** ______

3. Friar Laurence proposes that Juliet use a sleeping potion and pretend to be dead on her wedding day. **3.** ______

4. Friar Laurence promises that he and Romeo will be in the tomb when Juliet wakes up. **4.** ______

5. Lord Capulet changes the wedding day from Thursday to Wednesday. **5.** ______

6. Juliet fears that Romeo will never come to claim her in the tomb. **6.** ______

7. Juliet is sure that the drug will work. **7.** ______

8. The Capulets regret their treatment of Juliet when they discover her dead. **8.** ______

9. The Nurse feels little grief over Juliet's death. **9.** ______

10. At the end of Act IV, there is still hope that Romeo and Juliet may be reunited. **10.** ______

B. RECOGNIZING ELEMENTS OF DRAMA

Directions: For each question, place the letter of the best answer in the space provided. *(6 points each)*

1. In Scene 1, the playwright presents insight into Juliet's developing character through
a. her response to Paris's passion
b. her remarks to Friar Laurence
c. the conversation between Paris and Friar Laurence
d. Juliet's anger toward her parents **1.** ______

2. Lord Capulet's insistence that the wedding take place one day earlier than originally planned is an example of
a. dramatic irony
b. a complication in the plot
c. a soliloquy
d. foreshadowing **2.** ______

3. Before taking the sleeping potion, Juliet expresses her fears and doubts in a speech best identified as
   a. dramatic irony
   b. a complication in the plot
   c. a soliloquy
   d. comic relief

3.______

4. Because the audience knows that Juliet is alive, the scene in which the Capulets, the Nurse, and Paris bemoan her death is an illustration of
   a. dramatic irony
   b. a complication in the plot
   c. a soliloquy
   d. comic relief

4.______

5. At the end of Act IV, the scene between Peter and the musicians provides
   a. foreshadowing of important events
   b. a plot complication
   c. a soliloquy
   d. comic relief

5.______

C. DEVELOPING VOCABULARY

Directions: Match each word in the left-hand column with the best meaning in the right-hand column. Place the letter of the best definition in the space provided. *(4 points each)*

______1. God shield	a. skillful
______2. drift	b. where bones from old graves are kept
______3. cunning	c. prayers
______4. closet	d. frown
______5. orisons	e. beg your pardon
______6. rosemary	f. God forbid
______7. lower	g. intentions
______8. fond nature	h. private quarters
______9. carry	i. foolish human nature
______10. cry you mercy	j. Good evening
	k. endure
	l. an herb that stands for remembrance

NAME ______________________ CLASS __________ DATE __________ SCORE __________

UNIT 5: WILLIAM SHAKESPEARE

THE TRAGEDY OF ROMEO AND JULIET, ACT V — William Shakespeare

A. RECOGNIZING ELEMENTS OF DRAMA

Directions: For each question, place the letter of the best answer in the space provided. *(6 points each)*

1. When Romeo hears that Juliet is dead, the dramatic irony lies in the fact that
a. Juliet is already wed to Paris
b. Romeo feels deep grief
c. the audience knows Juliet is alive
d. Juliet lies in the Capulet tomb
1. ______

2. As Friar Laurence's plan begins to go wrong in Scenes 1 and 2, there is a buildup in
a. conflict
b. comic relief
c. exposition
d. suspense
2. ______

3. In Scene 3, the grief-stricken Romeo refers to Juliet's tomb as a "mouth." This speech makes use of a
a. metaphor
b. simile
c. pun
d. riddle
3. ______

4. The climax of *Romeo and Juliet* occurs when
a. Paris is killed
b. Juliet stabs herself and dies
c. Romeo takes his life
d. Romeo is killed
4. ______

5. At the close of the play, Shakespeare underscores the tragedy by means of
a. flashbacks to Juliet as a young child
b. mournful music
c. stage directions showing the lovers' deaths
d. a return of the Prologue chorus
5. ______

B. INTERPRETING MEANINGS

Part 1. *Directions:* Place the letter of the best answer in the space provided. *(5 points each)*

1. During the course of the play, we see Juliet change as she
a. falls more and more deeply in love
b. becomes extremely confused
c. clashes with her parents
d. gains the courage and maturity to fight for her love for Romeo
1. ______

2. Friar Laurence makes a deadly mistake when he
a. urges the two lovers to marry without telling their parents
b. sends the letter to Mantua
c. fails to tell Paris that Juliet is married
d. neglects to stop the feud himself
2. ______

3. Romeo and Juliet act destructively when they
   a. go against their parents' wishes
   b. marry in haste without considering the consequences
   c. offend the Prince
   d. trust Friar Laurence

3. ______

4. How does "heaven" or fate punish the Capulets and Montagues for their feud?
   a. The Prince becomes angry at the two families.
   b. Their children fall in love but lose their lives as a result of the feud.
   c. Their children keep secrets from their parents.
   d. Both families fall into disgrace.

4. ______

5. The important lesson that the deaths of Romeo and Juliet teach their families is that
   a. fate can be cruel
   b. love cannot be tampered with
   c. children should be supervised more closely
   d. feuds are a waste of human life

5. ______

Part 2. Describe how the story of Romeo and Juliet might take place today. What two feuding groups might Romeo and Juliet belong to? How might the same kind of tragedy occur again?

Directions: On a separate sheet of paper, write a paragraph explaining your point of view and citing parts of the story that influence your opinion. *(15 points)*

C. DEVELOPING VOCABULARY

Directions: Match each word in the left-hand column with the best meaning in the right-hand column. Place the letter of the best definition in the space provided. *(3 points each)*

______ 1. presage	a. to summon
______ 2. beseech	b. cause
______ 3. penury	c. mouth
______ 4. loathsome	d. flag, signal
______ 5. obsequies	e. happenings
______ 6. ensign	f. poverty
______ 7. maw	g. foretell
______ 8. morsel	h. a rough bed or mattress
______ 9. ground	i. beg
______ 10. pallet	j. funeral rites
	k. small piece
	l. detestable, repulsive

NAME ________________________ CLASS ________ DATE ________ SCORE ________

UNIT 5: WILLIAM SHAKESPEARE

WORD ANALOGIES / Extending Vocabulary Skills

Directions: In the space provided, write the letter of the pair of words that best describes a *relationship* that is closest to that of the capitalized pair of words. (*5 points each*)

1. BLESSED : CURSED ::
a. fortunate : lucky
b. lost : found
c. favored : condemned
d. unfortunate : ill-starred
1. ______

2. UNDERLING : SUBORDINATE ::
a. vassal : serf
b. executive : flunky
c. employer : employee
d. inferior : superior
2. ______

3. CRAVE : DESIRE ::
a. covet : detest
b. loathe : yearn for
c. reject : spurn
d. aspire to : despise
3. ______

4. GRUDGE : ILL WILL ::
a. resentment : benevolence
b. friendliness : spite
c. goodwill : hard feelings
d. malice : animosity
4. ______

5. STRIFE : CONFLICT ::
a. accord : unrest
b. discord : turmoil
c. disharmony : harmony
d. peace : upheaval
5. ______

6. ATTEND : HEED ::
a. pay attention : ignore
b. listen to : harken to
c. disregard : consider
d. note : miss
6. ______

7. MISSHAPEN : MALFORMED ::
a. unimpaired : deformed
b. distorted : flawless
c. contorted : twisted
d. exquisite : grotesque
7. ______

8. CIVIL : AMIABLE ::
a. rude : ill-mannered
b. political : religious
c. war : revolution
d. non-military : civilian
8. ______

9. GRAVE : SOBER ::
a. spirited : boisterous
b. quick : dead
c. eat : drink
d. serious : lighthearted
9. ______

10. COUNSEL : ADVICE ::
a. urge : advise
b. instruct : learn
c. council : assembly
d. admonish : warning
10. ______

11. VEX : ANNOY ::
a. please : delight
b. exasperate : pacify
c. hex : curse
d. quiet : provoke
11. ______

12. DISCREET : PRUDENT ::
a. thoughtful : thoughtless
b. impolite : rude
c. impetuous : rash
d. infectious : disease
12. ______

13. DESPAIR : ANGUISH ::
a. misery : ease
b. anxiety : happiness
c. hopelessness : confidence
d. solace : consolation
13. ______

14. EXQUISITE : MEDIOCRE ::
a. inferior : superior
b. superb : ordinary
c. question : answer
d. common : usual
14. ______

15. DEVOUT : ARDENT ::
a. devour : consume
b. passive : indifferent
c. intense : bright
d. fervent : cool

15. ______

16. PRODIGIOUS : IMMENSE ::
a. minute : far-reaching
b. overwhelming : trivial
c. trifling : vast
d. negligible : insignificant

16. ______

17. CONJURE : GHOST ::
a. frighten : children
b. raise : spirit
c. connect : parts
d. cast : spell

17. ______

18. DISCOURSE : SPEAK ::
a. follow : lead
b. scathe : hurt
c. heed : listen
d. yield : conquer

18. ______

19. BALEFUL : SINISTER ::
a. threatening : malicious
b. spiteful : favorable
c. friendly : evil
d. beneficial : venomous

19. ______

20. PENURY : POVERTY ::
a. comfort : misery
b. abundance : privation
c. pennilessness : wealth
d. prosperity : affluence

20. ______

NAME ______________________________ CLASS__________ DATE__________ SCORE__________

UNIT 5: WILLIAM SHAKESPEARE

UNIT REVIEW / Applying Skills I

A. READING A SHAKESPEAREAN PLAY

Directions: Read the following excerpt from Act IV, Scene 3, of Shakespeare's *Othello*. Othello has been convinced by Emilia's husband, Iago, that his wife, Desdemona, is unfaithful to him. Desdemona, innocent of the charge, seeks solace from Emilia.

Emil. How goes it now? He looks gentler than he did.
Des. He says he will return incontinent.
He hath commanded me to go to bed,
And bid me to dismiss you. 15
Emil. Dismiss me?
Des. It was his bidding. Therefore, good Emilia,
Give me my nightly wearing, and adieu.
We must not now displease him.
Emil. I would you had never seen him! 20
Des. So would not I. My love doth so approve him
That even his stubbornness, his checks, his frowns
(Prithee unpin me) have grace and favor in them.
Emil. I have laid those sheets you bade me on the bed.
Des. All's one. Good faith, how foolish are our minds! 25
If I do die before thee, prithee shroud me
In one of those same sheets.
Emil. Come, come! You talk.
Des. My mother had a maid called Barbary.
She was in love; and he she loved proved mad 30
And did forsake her. She had a song of "Willow."
And old thing 'twas; but it expressed her fortune,
And she died singing it. That song tonight
Will not go from my mind. I have much to do
But to go hang my head all at one side 35
And sing it like poor Barbary. Prithee dispatch.
Emil. Shall I go fetch your nightgown?
Des. No, unpin me here.
This Lodovico is a proper man.
Emil. A very handsome man. 40
Des. He speaks well.
Emil. I know a lady in Venice would have walked
barefoot to Palestine for a touch of his nether lip.
Des. *(Sings)*
The poor soul sat sighing by a sycamore
tree, 45
Sing all a green willow:
Her hand on her bosom, her head on her
knee,
Sing willow, willow, willow.
The fresh streams ran by her and mur- 50
mured her moans;

Sing willow, willow, willow;
Her salt tears fell from her, and soft'ned
the stones.
Sing willow— 55

Lay by these.
willow, willow;
Prithee hie thee; he'll come anon.

Sing all a green willow must be my garland.
Let nobody blame him; his scorn I approve— 60

Nay, that's not next. Hark! who is't that knocks?
Emil. It is the wind.
Des.
I called my love false love; but what said
he then?
Sing willow, willow, willow: 65
If I court mo women, you'll couch with
mo men.

So, get thee gone; good night. Mine eyes do itch.
Doth that bode weeping?
Emil. 'Tis neither here nor there. 70
Des. I have heard it said so. O, these men, these men!
Dost thou in conscience think—tell me, Emilia—
That there be women do abuse their husbands
In such gross kind?
Emil. There be some such, no question. 75
Des. Wouldst thou do such a deed for all the world?
Emil. Why, would not you?
Des. No, by this heavenly light!
Emil. Nor I neither by this heavenly light.
I might do't as well i' the dark. 80
Des. Wouldst thou do such a deed for all the world?
Emil. The world's a huge thing. It is a great price for
a small vice.
Des. In troth, I think thou wouldst not.
Emil. In troth, I think I should; and undo't when I 85
had done it. Marry, I would not do such a thing for a
joint-ring, nor for measures of lawn, nor for gowns, petti-
coats, nor caps, nor any petty exhibition; but, for all the
whole world—'Ud's pity! who would not make her hus-
band a cuckold to make him a monarch? I should venture 90
purgatory for't.
Des. Beshrew me if I would do such a wrong
For the whole world.
Emil. Why, the wrong is but a wrong i' the world;
and having the world for your labor, 'tis a wrong in your 95
own world, and you might quickly make it right.
Des. I do not think there is any such woman.
Emil. Yes, a dozen; and as many to the vantage as
would store the world they played for.
But I do think it is their husbands' faults 100
If wives do fall. Say that they slack their duties
And pour our treasures into foreign laps;
Or else break out in peevish jealousies,
Throwing restraint upon us; or say they strike us,

Or scant our former having in despite— 105
Why, we have galls; and though we have some grace,
Yet have we some revenge. Let husbands know
Their wives have sense like them. They see, and smell,
And have their palates both for sweet and sour,
As husbands have. What is it that they do 110
When they change us for others? Is it sport?
I think it is. And doth affection breed it?
I think it doth. Is't frailty that thus errs?
It is so too. And have not we affections,
Desires for sport, and frailty, as men have? 115
Then let them use us well; else let them know,
The ills we do, their ills instruct us so.
Des. Good night, good night. Heaven me such uses
send,
Not to pick bad from bad, but by bad mend! 120
Exeunt.

B. ANALYZING A SHAKESPEAREAN PLAY

Directions: For each question, place the letter of the correct answer in the space provided. *(5 points each)*

1. Judging from the excerpt, Desdemona appears to be
a. an honest and loving wife
b. guilty of the charge of infidelity
c. a cynical person
d. unkind to Emilia
1. ______

2. The activity that occurs during the scene is
a. Emilia's lesson about men
b. a singing lesson
c. Desdemona's preparations for bed
d. a bath
2. ______

3. Unknown to Desdemona, Emilia has aided her husband Iago in his attempts to convince Othello of Desdemona's faithlessness. This results in
a. Emilia's confession during the scene
b. Iago's happiness
c. Othello trusting Emilia
d. dramatic irony during the scene
3. ______

4. Desdemona's line, "If I do die before thee, prithee shroud me/In one of those same sheets," is an example of
a. foreshadowing
b. exposition
c. verbal irony
d. a rhyming couplet
4. ______

5. Emilia blames the infidelities of wives on their
a. hearty appetites
b. husbands' inattention and abuse
c. desire for change
d. galls and spleens
5. ______

6. When Desdemona says that she would not deceive her husband, Emilia replies: "Nor I neither by this heavenly light/I might do't as well in the dark." This means that
   a. she is unfaithful
   b. heaven watches the world only in daylight
   c. she can deceive her husband by day or night
   d. she would take care that her husband did not discover her infidelities — 6. ______

7. According to what she says, Emilia would go to Purgatory to
   a. make her husband a king
   b. have an affair
   c. get attention from her husband
   d. avoid hell — 7. ______

8. The line, "Then let them use us well; else let them know / The ills we do, their ills instruct us so," is an example of
   a. metaphor
   b. simile
   c. rhyming couplet
   d. internal conflict — 8. ______

9. Desdemona's "nightly wearing" (line 18) is
   a. her nightgown
   b. an evening dress
   c. a symbol
   d. netting for her hair — 9. ______

10. The "willow song" creates dramatic irony because
   a. the song is so sad
   b. willow trees are "weeping" willows
   c. the song is so well known
   d. the audience connects the song with Desdemona's situation — 10. ______

C. UPDATING A SCENE

Directions: Imagine that you are writing for a television soap opera, and rewrite the scene in contemporary language. Set the scene in Desdemona's house, and omit the song. *(25 points)*

D. ANALYZING LANGUAGE AND DEVELOPING VOCABULARY

Directions: In the spaces provided, mark each true statement **T** and each false statement **F**. *(5 points each)*

1. Most of the scene is written in *blank verse.* — 1. ______

2. In this scene, Emilia is a *foil* to Desdemona. — 2. ______

3. The "willow song" is an example of *personification.* — 3. ______

4. Emilia's speech, beginning on line 100, is written in *iambic pentameter.* — 4. ______

5. Desdemona's last speech is an example of a *rhyming couplet.* — 5. ______

NAME ______________________ CLASS __________ DATE __________ SCORE __________

UNIT 5: WILLIAM SHAKESPEARE

CRITICAL THINKING AND WRITING / Applying Skills II

A. SUMMARIZING THE EXPOSITION

Directions: In *one* paragraph, summarize the exposition of *Romeo and Juliet*. Remember to include all of the main characters and the basic situation. *(40 points)*

____

____

____

____

____

____

____

____

____

____

____

____

____

B. RESPONDING TO A CHARACTER'S ACTIONS

Directions: Throughout most of the play, the Nurse is Juliet's friend and confidante. Yet, she advises Juliet to marry Paris against her will. Write *one* paragraph to analyze the Nurse's behavior in this situation. *(30 points)*

____

____

____

____

____

____

C. TESTING A HYPOTHESIS

Directions: Write *one* paragraph in which you support or refute the following statement. "Paris is an innocent victim." Remember to support your thesis with specific points from the play. *(30 points)*

NAME ______________________ CLASS __________ DATE __________ SCORE __________

UNIT 6: THE ELEMENTS OF THE EPIC

UNIT INTRODUCTION / Understanding the Elements of an Epic

Directions: For each question, place the letter of the best answer in the space provided. *(10 points each)*

1. An epic is best described as a
- **a.** long story about an important person
- **b.** story that relates events in the Bible
- **c.** long narrative poem about a hero
- **d.** lyric poem about an historical figure

1. ______

2. The hero of an epic always
- **a.** embodies the values of his day
- **b.** rescues someone from danger
- **c.** tells the truth
- **d.** speaks in rhyme

2. ______

3. The epic that serves as our primary model for the epic of a long journey is Homer's
- **a.** *Iliad*
- **b.** *Odyssey*
- **c.** *Aeneid*
- **d.** *Song of Roland*

3. ______

4. In Homer's time, heroes were considered to be
- **a.** unlucky, ordinary men
- **b.** the equivalent of the gods, except for their mortality
- **c.** the loneliest of men
- **d.** aristocrats, placed between the gods and ordinary men

4. ______

5. A story that is told in chronological order
- **a.** uses flashbacks to tell the story
- **b.** describes events in the order in which they occur
- **c.** relates events out of order
- **d.** presents events in order of importance

5. ______

6. Myths are
- **a.** stories that use fantasy to express difficult ideas
- **b.** long poems that describe the adventures of heroes
- **c.** stories about imaginary animals
- **d.** stories about the lives of kings and queens

6. ______

7. The *rhapsodes*, or "singers of tales," were
- **a.** historians, entertainers, and myth-makers
- **b.** priests
- **c.** kings and queens
- **d.** merchants

7. ______

8. The oral tradition of reciting epic poems
a. is still used today
b. was used in ancient Greece
c. arose before people could read
d. all of the above **8.** ______

9. The *rhapsodes* used suspense
a. infrequently
b. to ensure that their audience would return
c. in place of facts
d. to make the story more demanding **9.** ______

10. An example of *Homeric* or *heroic simile* might be:
a. Her voice brushed my ear like the wind tickling a leaf.
b. The child skipped as lightly as a breeze.
c. He lifted the mighty stone as easily as a child lifts a toy.
d. He looked like a tiger. **10.** ______

NAME ______________________ CLASS __________ DATE __________ SCORE __________

UNIT 6: THE ELEMENTS OF THE EPIC

THE ODYSSEY, Books 1–4 **Homer**

A. RECOGNIZING ELEMENTS OF THE EPIC

Directions: For each question, place the letter of the best answer in the space provided. *(6 points each)*

1. The *Odyssey* has served as the basic model for which one of the following types of epics?
a. the coming-of-age epic
b. the war epic
c. the epic of the broken heart
d. the epic of the long journey
1. ______

2. The source of the *Odyssey* and the *Iliad* is thought to be
a. Sumerian hieroglyphics
b. a combination of legend and history
c. Homer's imagination
d. historical fact
2. ______

3. The type of literary form that Homer used to describe relationships between humans and the gods is called
a. myth **b.** irony **c.** allegory **d.** biography
3. ______

4. Odysseus's wife tricks her suitors by unraveling the shroud at night. In the character of Penelope, Homer embodies the Greek virtue of
a. cunning **b.** hard work **c.** loyalty **d.** thrift
4. ______

5. The problem between Telemachus and his mother's suitors provides the plot element known as
a. the hook of curiosity **b.** conflict **c.** climax **d.** resolution
5. ______

B. INTERPRETING MEANINGS

Part 1. *Directions:* For each question, place the letter of the best answer in the space provided. *(5 points each)*

1. Athena fails to tell Telemachus that his father is alive because
a. Zeus has forbidden her to do so
b. she wants him to kill the suitors first
c. she wants him to prove himself by finding Odysseus
d. she is afraid he will reveal the secret to his mother
1. ______

2. What action suggests the character of the people of Pylos?
a. demanding courtesy for their king
b. paying homage to Athena
c. welcoming the visitors and inviting them to the feast
d. sending men to help Telemachus find his father
2. ______

3. It is clear that Nestor does not know who Athena is because
   a. Nestor cannot see her
   b. Nestor speaks of her as if she were not present
   c. Athena conceals herself
   d. Nestor calls her by another name — 3.______

4. Helen's regrets over her role in the war are indicated by
   a. her sorrow for having caused Telemachus to lose his father
   b. her lack of control over her feelings
   c. her attempt to conceal her feelings
   d. her reference to herself as "the wanton that I was" — 4.______

5. The following passage begins with line 210:

   > At this gray-eyed Athena broke in, saying: "What strange talk you permit yourself, Telemachus. A god could save the man by simply wishing it—from the farthest shore in the world."

   Athena's purpose in saying this is to
   a. warn Telemachus that he depends on her help
   b. chide Telemachus for doubting the gods' power
   c. remind Telemachus that he cannot fail
   d. reveal her identity to Nestor — 5.______

Part 2. You gather from the introduction that a god can be the alter ego of a character. Athena, the goddess of wisdom, accompanies Telemachus and helps him make decisions. Does she do anything in this section that he could not do, or decide, for himself?

Directions: On a separate sheet of paper, write a paragraph explaining your point of view. Cite parts of the epic that influence your decision. *(15 points)*

C. DEVELOPING VOCABULARY

Directions: Match each word in the left-hand column with the best meaning in the right-hand column. Place the letter of the best definition in the space provided. *(3 points each)*

______ **1.** to contend	**a.** using careful planning and good judgment
______ **2.** din	**b.** clear, easily understood
______ **3.** to disperse	**c.** to mention for the first time, to introduce
______ **4.** to lavish	**d.** to scatter
______ **5.** insolent	**e.** respectful
______ **6.** lucid	**f.** to consider, to think over
______ **7.** to broach	**g.** to fight, to dispute
______ **8.** prudently	**h.** disrespectful, deliberately rude
______ **9.** to ponder	**i.** to pass across or over
______ **10.** host	**j.** to give or spend very freely
	k. a large number, a multitude
	l. a loud, confused noise

NAME ______________________ CLASS __________ DATE __________ SCORE __________

UNIT 6: THE ELEMENTS OF THE EPIC

THE ODYSSEY, Book 5 **Homer**

A. UNDERSTANDING WHAT HAPPENED

Directions: In the spaces provided, mark each true statement **T** and each false statement **F**. *(3 points each)*

1. Odysseus is being held prisoner by Calypso. **1.** ______

2. Zeus sends Hermes to secure Odysseus's release. **2.** ______

3. When Hermes arrives at Calypso's island, he finds her working at her loom. **3.** ______

4. Hermes is indifferent to the beauty of Calypso's home. **4.** ______

5. Calypso refuses to obey Zeus. **5.** ______

6. Odysseus pines for his home and family. **6.** ______

7. To give Odysseus strength for his journey, Calypso feeds him the food of the gods. **7.** ______

8. Calypso is jealous of Penelope. **8.** ______

9. Still angry at Odysseus, the sea god Poseidon destroys Odysseus's raft. **9.** ______

10. With Athena's help, Odysseus arrives on the island of Sheria, home of the Phaeacians. **10.** ______

B. RECOGNIZING ELEMENTS OF THE EPIC

Directions: For each question, place the letter of the best answer in the space provided. *(6 points each)*

1. Homer uses an epic simile comparing Hermes' journey with
a. a bird in flight
b. a gull catching fish
c. the whitecaps cresting the waves
d. a fisherman with his nets **1.** ______

2. Homer describes Calypso's home by using the sensory imagery of
a. smell, sight, and hearing
b. sight, hearing, and touch
c. sight and hearing
d. smell and sight **2.** ______

3. Odysseus is first seen looking out to sea and weeping. Why is this scene ironic?
a. He is widely known as a courageous man of action.
b. He has good reason to weep.
c. He should be enjoying his stay with Calypso.
d. Athena is helping him. **3.** ______

4. A plot complication is introduced when
   a. Hermes straps on his sandals
   b. Calypso and Hermes meet
   c. Calypso gives Odysseus a raft
   d. Poseidon takes revenge on Odysseus

4. ______

5. Which of the following metaphors is used to describe Odysseus's actions when he arrives on Scheria?
   a. a leaf dropping from a tree
   b. a spark in a dying fire
   c. a burning stick temporarily buried in embers
   d. a flower washed away in a rainstorm

5. ______

C. DEVELOPING VOCABULARY

Directions: Match each word in the left-hand column with the best meaning in the right-hand column. Place the letter of the best definition in the space provided. *(4 points each)*

______ **1.** to veer

______ **2.** to douse

______ **3.** mandate

______ **4.** forlorn

______ **5.** victuals

______ **6.** versatile

______ **7.** adversity

______ **8.** to pine

______ **9.** strategist

______ **10.** shade

a. one skilled in careful, clever planning to achieve a goal

b. misfortune, suffering, affliction

c. a phantom or ghost

d. to change direction, to turn or swing around

e. victorious

f. food supplies, provisions

g. to long for, to yearn

h. to plunge into water, throw liquid on

i. competent in, having many uses

j. to cut down trees

k. an order or command

l. sad and lonely because of desertion or isolation

NAME ______________________ CLASS __________ DATE __________ SCORE __________

UNIT 6: THE ELEMENTS OF THE EPIC

THE ODYSSEY, Books 6–8 **Homer**

A. RECOGNIZING ELEMENTS OF THE EPIC

Directions: For each question, place the letter of the best answer in the space provided. *(6 points each)*

1. Homer frequently uses similes. When Odysseus *first* appears before Nausicaa and her maids, he is compared to
a. a beggar
b. a mountain lion
c. a mountain nymph
d. an olive tree
1. ______

2. Which of the following metaphors does Homer use to describe Odysseus *after* he has taken his bath?
a. sea creature
b. a craftsman
c. a work of art made of gold and silver
d. a golden flask
2. ______

3. Which of the following religious principles causes Nausicaa to help Odysseus?
a. Hardships are sent by the gods.
b. Soldiers deserve respect.
c. Strangers and beggars are protected by Zeus.
d. Kings are favorites of the gods.
3. ______

4. Nausicaa's reason for sending Odysseus into the city alone (lines 615-618) is an example of
a. social values
b. Homer's values
c. heroic simile
d. religious values
4. ______

5. Odysseus, hearing the minstrel's song, is as moved as
a. a wife mourning for her lord
b. a volcano
c. a defeated warrior
d. a wounded soldier
5. ______

B. INTERPRETING MEANINGS

Part 1. *Directions:* For each question, place the letter of the best answer in the space provided. *(6 points each)*

1. Nausicaa is depicted as self-reliant in that she
a. goes off without her parents' permission
b. drives the cart and horse herself
c. launders the family's clothes
d. prepares for her wedding
1. ______

2. Nausicaa exhibits courage when she
a. goes to the river with her maids
b. disobeys her father's warning
c. stands her ground and speaks to Odysseus
d. escorts Odysseus to the palace
2. ______

3. The Phaeacians are protected from attack by
   a. a powerful navy
   b. their reputation for cruelty
   c. Poseidon
   d. distance from other lands and the gods' favor

3.______

4. The minstrel's song reminds Odysseus of
   a. friends killed in battle
   b. his horse
   c. his son
   d. his wife

4.______

5. King Alcinous asks Odysseus to
   a. recite a story
   b. make his home on Scheria
   c. reveal his name
   d. marry his daughter

5.______

Part 2. In Book 6, Homer first describes how Odysseus adapts to a new situation. What virtues and qualities does he demonstrate in this book?

Directions: On a separate sheet of paper, write a paragraph presenting your view of Odysseus. Cite parts of Book 6 that influence your opinion. *(10 points)*

C. DEVELOPING VOCABULARY

Directions: Match each word in the left-hand column with the best meaning in the right-hand column. Place the letter of the best definition in the space provided. *(3 points each)*

______ 1. oblivion
______ 2. honeyed
______ 3. apparel
______ 4. to prowl
______ 5. toil
______ 6. harmonious
______ 7. serenity
______ 8. to infuse
______ 9. averse
______ 10. uncouth

a. unwilling, reluctant
b. to understand
c. clothing
d. uncultured, crude, boorish
e. to move about quietly and in secret
f. calmness, peacefulness
g. hard work, tiring labor
h. a state of being forgotten, forgetting
i. moving upward from
j. sweetened, flattering
k. to put one thing into another so as to affect it throughout
l. agreement in feelings, ideas, or actions

NAME ______________________ CLASS __________ DATE __________ SCORE __________

UNIT 6: THE ELEMENTS OF THE EPIC

THE ODYSSEY, Book 9 **Homer**

A. UNDERSTANDING WHAT HAPPENED

Directions: In the spaces provided, mark each true statement **T** and each false statement **F**. *(3 points each)*

1. Three of Odysseus's men ate the lotus plant. **1.** ______

2. Odysseus tells Polyphemus that his ship was wrecked so that the Cyclops won't find it and destroy it. **2.** ______

3. Odysseus does not kill the Cyclops because his men are unable to move the stone blocking the cave entrance. **3.** ______

4. On the second night, Odysseus tricks Polyphemus into bringing the rams inside the cave. **4.** ______

5. In return for Odysseus's gift of wine, the Cyclops promises to devour Odysseus last. **5.** ______

6. The other Cyclops fail to respond to Polyphemus's bellows and roars. **6.** ______

7. Odysseus and his men escape by clinging to the bellies of the monster's sheep. **7.** ______

8. Once offshore, Odysseus does not hesitate to tell Polyphemus his real name. **8.** ______

9. Odysseus's crewmen urge him to hurl insults at the Cyclops. **9.** ______

10. Poseidon is the father of Polyphemus and therefore the enemy of Odysseus. **10.** ______

B. RECOGNIZING ELEMENTS OF THE EPIC

Directions: For each question, place the letter of the best answer in the space provided. *(6 points each)*

1. When Odysseus describes his reputation for guile to Alcinous, he is revealing
a. internal conflict
b. character
c. external conflict
d. irony
1. ______

2. By making the Cyclops refuse Odysseus's request for hospitality, Homer increases
a. realism
b. symbolism
c. vivid characterization
d. suspense
2. ______

3. The gory details describing the Cyclops's cannibalism shows Homer's skill at
   a. fascinating audiences
   b. establishing character
   c. depicting setting
   d. creating realistic plots

3. ______

4. Homer heightens suspense when
   a. the Cyclops drinks Odysseus's wine
   b. the rams bleat
   c. the Cyclops milks his ewes
   d. the Cyclops stops Odysseus's ram

4. ______

5. The Cyclops's curse is an example of
   a. simile
   b. imagery
   c. foreshadowing
   d. alliteration

5. ______

C. DEVELOPING VOCABULARY

Directions: Match each word in the left-hand with the best meaning in the right-hand column. Place the letter of the best definition in the space provided. *(4 points each)*

______ 1. formidable
______ 2. guile
______ 3. to muster
______ 4. to ravage
______ 5. gale
______ 6. to dismember
______ 7. ninny
______ 8. sage
______ 9. to bolt
______ 10. meditation

a. a strong wind
b. to destroy violently, to devastate
c. to assemble, to gather together
d. curious, inquisitive
e. inspiring awe, wonder, or dread
f. impulsive, reckless
g. to dash off, to run away
h. the use of cunning or trickery
i. a fool
j. thought, contemplation
k. wise, showing good judgment
l. to separate or divide into parts

NAME ______________________ CLASS __________ DATE __________ SCORE __________

UNIT 6: THE ELEMENTS OF THE EPIC

THE ODYSSEY, Books 10–11 **Homer**

A. RECOGNIZING ELEMENTS OF THE EPIC

Directions: For each question, place the letter of the best answer in the space provided. *(6 points each)*

1. Which of the following details about Circe is the most curious?
a. her lovely voice
b. the silent woods
c. the tame wolves and lions
d. her enchanting house
1. ______

2. When Odysseus compares his fear of Hades to "a weight like stone within me," he is using
a. colloquialism
b. suspense
c. vivid narration
d. simile
2. ______

3. By having Odysseus narrate portions of his journey, Homer shifts the point of view to
a. first-person narration
b. third-person limited
c. third-person omniscient
d. second-person limited
3. ______

4. Teiresias's warning to avoid Helios's cattle (line 1113) is an example of
a. conflict
b. foreshadowing
c. characterization
d. irony
4. ______

5. In creating a picture of life after death, Homer relies on
a. characterization
b. vivid language
c. rhyme
d. myth
5. ______

B. INTERPRETING MEANINGS

Part 1. *Directions:* For each question, place the letter of the best answer in the space provided. *(5 points each)*

1. Circe turns Odysseus's men into
a. wild animals
b. cloth
c. nuts and berries
d. pigs
1. ______

2. While waiting for Teiresias, Odysseus fends off the dead souls with
a. fire
b. his sword
c. curses
d. blood
2. ______

3. "The god who thunders on the land" (line 1104) is
a. Zeus
b. Poseidon
c. Helios
d. Hermes
3. ______

4. When Odysseus meets the ghost of his mother, he
a. faints
b. kneels
c. tries to embrace her
d. cries
4. ______

5. Teiresias's prophecy ends with these lines, followed by Odysseus's response to h

" ...Then a seaborne death
soft as this hand of mist will come upon you
when you are wearied our with rich old age,
your country folk in blessed peace around you.
And all this shall be just as I foretell.'
When he had done, I said at once,
'Teiresias,
my life runs on then as the gods have spun it"

Odysseus's reply indicates
a. happiness
b. acceptance of his fate
c. despair
d. disbelief

5. ______

Part 2. The incident with Circe marks the second time that Odysseus and his men have been threatened by a drug. Based on evidence from *The Odyssey*, do you think Homer was opposed to drugs?

Directions: On a separate sheet of paper, write a paragraph explaining your point of view. Cite parts of the epic that influence your decision. *(15 points)*

C. DEVELOPING VOCABULARY

Directions: Match each word in the left-hand column with the best meaning in the right-hand column. Place the letter of the best definition in the space provided. *(3 points each)*

______ 1. to fawn
______ 2. beguiling
______ 3. flitting
______ 4. stealth
______ 5. snare
______ 6. rancor
______ 7. bereft
______ 8. to atone
______ 9. impalpable
______ 10. twinge

a. moving quickly from one place to another
b. pleasing or deceiving by the use of charm
c. uncapable of being felt by
d. to make up for a wrongdoing, to make amends
e. something that traps, tricks, or entangles in difficulties
f. to beat with the fists
g. deep hate or ill will
h. deprived of
i. jagged, sharp
j. a sudden, sharp stab of pain
k. to seek favor by flattery
l. proceeding in a secret, furtive manner

NAME ______________________ CLASS __________ DATE __________ SCORE __________

UNIT 6: THE ELEMENTS OF THE EPIC

THE ODYSSEY, Book 12 **Homer**

A. UNDERSTANDING WHAT HAPPENED

Directions: In the spaces provided, mark each true statement **T** and each false statement **F**. *(3 points each)*

1. Circe warns Odysseus that the Sirens' voices are irresistible. **1.** ______

2. Scylla is a huge dog that lives on the cliffs. **2.** ______

3. Scylla eats six men from every ship that passes by. **3.** ______

4. Charybdis is a wild fig tree that snares men in its branches. **4.** ______

5. Circe advises Odysseus to avoid Scylla and steer toward the cliff where Charybdis lives. **5.** ______

6. Odysseus tells his men all the details of Circe's warning. **6.** ______

7. Odysseus follows Circe's instructions on how to guard against the Sirens. **7.** ______

8. As the ship approaches Scylla and Charybdis, Odysseus exhibits the qualities of a good leader. **8.** ______

9. Odysseus hides from Scylla because he knows that she is dangerous. **9.** ______

10. All of Odysseus's men drown. **10.** ______

B. RECOGNIZING ELEMENTS OF THE EPIC

Directions: For each question, place the letter of the best answer in the space provided. *(6 points each)*

1. Scylla and Charybdis are often referred to as a metaphor for any difficult choice. The alternatives faced by Odysseus are difficult because of
a. high stakes
b. insufficient information
c. a "can't-win" situation
d. the necessity for great skill **1.** ______

2. Circe's detailed instructions for avoiding the perils of Scylla and Charybdis create
a. point of view
b. internal conflict
c. mood
d. suspense **2.** ______

3. The main dramatic conflict of Book 12 involves
a. Odysseus's decision to follow Circe's instructions
b. the sailors' disobedience
c. Zeus's indecision about helping Odysseus
d. Odysseus's skill in escaping the dangers around Circe's island **3.** ______

4. In Book 9, Odysseus refers to his "guile in peace and war." How does he use trickery in Book 12?
   a. He persuades the crew to tie him up so that he can hear the Sirens without endangering himself.
   b. He tells Circe that he will follow her instructions in exchange for his freedom.
   c. He convinces his men that he alone should listen to the Sirens.
   d. He fails to tell his men that Scylla will capture some of them. **4.** ______

5. Odysseus's choosing of Scylla over Charybdis reveals him to be
   a. unselfish
   b. courageous
   c. determined to sacrifice some men in order to save others
   d. inconsiderate of others **5.** ______

C. DEVELOPING VOCABULARY

Directions: Match each word in the left-hand column with the best meaning in the right-hand column. Place the letter of the best definition in the space provided. *(4 points each)*

______	**1.** haunting	**a.**	to become disabled and sink
______	**2.** to knead	**b.**	causing disgust or hatred, detestable
______	**3.** abominably	**c.**	to discover
______	**4.** promontory	**d.**	a noisy commotion, an uproar
______	**5.** to muffle	**e.**	emotional warmth, passion
______	**6.** to baffle	**f.**	to steer a boat
______	**7.** ardor	**g.**	to confuse, prevent, or defeat
______	**8.** tumult	**h.**	a peak of high land that juts out into a body of water
______	**9.** to founder	**i.**	a great or turbulent whirlpool
______	**10.** maelstrom	**j.**	difficult to forget
		k.	to soften or deaden the sound of
		l.	to form or shape by pressing with the hands

NAME ______________________ CLASS ________ DATE ________ SCORE ________

UNIT 6: THE ELEMENTS OF THE EPIC

THE ODYSSEY, Books 16–17 **Homer** 

A. RECOGNIZING ELEMENTS OF THE EPIC

Directions: For each question, place the letter of the best answer in the space provided. *(6 points each)*

1. The reunion of father and son relies for its intense dramatic effect upon
a. irony **b.** suspense **c.** conflict **d.** persuasion — **1.** ______

2. A class of society introduced by Homer as an important character in the epic was the
a. servant class **b.** church **c.** merchant class **d.** nobility — **2.** ______

3. Telemachus's refusal to take the beggar's seat is an example of
a. exposition **b.** dramatic irony **c.** epithet **d.** realism — **3.** ______

4. When Odysseus's disguise is removed, Telemachus cries out:

"I swear you were in rags and old,
and here you stand like one of the immortals."

This passage contains an example of — **4.** ______
a. myth **b.** suspense **c.** simile **d.** heroic quest

5. In relating the story of Odysseus's homecoming, Homer makes use of
a. chronological order **b.** flashback **c.** denouement **d.** exposition — **5.** ______

B. INTERPRETING MEANINGS

Part 1. *Directions:* For each question, place the letter of the best answer in the space provided. *(5 points each)*

1. We are led to believe that Odysseus withholds his identity from Eumaeus because of
a. lack of trust in his old servant
b. shyness after his long absence
c. weariness after his many ordeals — **1.** ______
d. concern that Eumaeus, overjoyed to see his old master, might reveal his identity

2. Telemachus refuses at first to believe that Odysseus is his father because
a. he thinks he is being tricked
b. only a god could transform himself so magnificently
c. the man standing before him appears youthful and handsome — **2.** ______
d. the man claiming to be his father looks like one of Penelope's suitors

3. At first, Telemachus reacts to Odysseus's transformation with
a. anger
b. fear
c. happiness
d. sorrow — **3.** ______

4. By asking Eumaeus why Argos is "left here on the dung pile," Odysseus
   a. insults the dog
   b. finds out what has happened in his absence
   c. prevents Argos from revealing his identity
   d. expresses his grief

4. ______

5. The following passage begins with line 1504:

   "...His owner died abroad,
   and here the woman slaves will take no care of him.
   You know how servants are: without a master
   they have no will to labor, or excel.
   For Zeus who views the wide world takes away
   half the manhood of a man, that day
   he goes into captivity and slavery."

   The principal message in these lines is that
   a. servants must be carefully supervised
   b. Zeus intends slaves to be humble
   c. slavery destroys human beings
   d. slaves cannot think for themselves

5. ______

Part 2. The disguised Odysseus has been discovering what has happened to his household in his absence. What has he learned so far, and how do you think he feels about it?

Directions: On a separate sheet of paper, write a paragraph giving your opinion and citing parts of the epic that support it. *(15 points)*

C. DEVELOPING VOCABULARY

Directions: Match each word in the left-hand column with the best meaning in the right-hand column. Place the letter of the best definition in the space provided. *(3 points each)*

______ 1. to sniffle	a. having claws
______ 2. candor	b. roaming, examining
______ 3. ruddy	c. in the center of
______ 4. sweep	d. a baby bird
______ 5. uncomprehending	e. to breathe noisily
______ 6. meddling	f. not understanding
______ 7. ranging	g. honesty, frankness
______ 8. taloned	h. to notice
______ 9. nestling	i. having a healthy reddish color
______ 10. abroad	j. the range or area covered by something
	k. interfering, tampering with
	l. away from one's own country

NAME ______________________ CLASS __________ DATE __________ SCORE ________

UNIT 6: THE ELEMENTS OF THE EPIC

THE ODYSSEY, Book 19 **Homer**

A. UNDERSTANDING WHAT HAPPENED

Directions: In the spaces provided, mark each true statement **T** and each false statement **F**. *(3 points each)*

1. Odysseus first evades Penelope's questions by flattering her. **1.** ______

2. When Penelope persists, Odysseus pretends to be drunk. **2.** ______

3. Penelope feels she has lost her beauty. **3.** ______

4. Penelope says that both her parents and her son wish her to remarry. **4.** ______

5. Odysseus convinces Penelope that her husband is still alive. **5.** ______

6. When Penelope asks for proof, Odysseus describes his clothing and brooch. **6.** ______

7. Penelope remarks that the beggar resembles Odysseus. **7.** ______

8. The "beggar" gives Penelope hope that she may soon see Odysseus. **8.** ______

9. Eurycleia recognizes Odysseus by a scar on his leg. **9.** ______

10. After Eurycleia identifies Odysseus, Penelope finally recognizes him. **10.** ______

B. RECOGNIZING ELEMENTS OF THE EPIC

Directions: For each question, place the letter of the best answer in the space provided. *(6 points each)*

1. The main dramatic event in Book 19 takes place between
a. Odysseus and Penelope
b. Odysseus and Telemachus
c. Penelope and Athena
d. Odysseus and Eurycleia **1.** ______

2. Odysseus's lies to his wife show him to be
a. reckless
b. kindhearted
c. jealous
d. suspicious **2.** ______

3. When Penelope begins to weep, Homer reveals the expression on her face by his use of
a. persuasion
b. exposition
c. description
d. narration **3.** ______

4. Which of the following is Odysseus using when he says that his tunic fit "like dry onion skin"?
   a. simile
   b. metaphor
   c. characterization
   d. symbolism

4. ______

5. In Book 19, Homer prolongs the suspense by
   a. questioning Odysseus's motives
   b. creating sympathy for Penelope
   c. questioning Eurycleia's loyalty
   d. postponing Penelope's recognition of her husband

5. ______

C. DEVELOPING VOCABULARY

Directions: Match each word in the left-hand column with the best meaning in the right-hand column. Place the letter of the best definition in the space provided. *(4 points each)*

______ 1. laden	a. a person who makes a humble request
______ 2. to suffice	b. to pay close attention to
______ 3. maudlin	c. to transport
______ 4. carriage	d. to be enough
______ 5. renowned	e. shaken or agitated with violent movements
______ 6. to heed	f. made like new again
______ 7. suppliant	g. foolishly and tearfully sentimental
______ 8. realm	h. weighed down, burdened
______ 9. to endow	i. to equip, provide, or furnish with
______ 10. convulsed	j. famous
	k. kingdom
	l. posture, bearing

NAME ______________________ CLASS __________ DATE __________ SCORE __________

UNIT 6: THE ELEMENTS OF THE EPIC

THE ODYSSEY, Book 21 **Homer**

A. RECOGNIZING ELEMENTS OF THE EPIC

Directions: For each question, place the letter of the best answer in the space provided. *(6 points each)*

1. Which of the following characterizations are examples of epithets?
a. "Father Zeus" **c.** "the prince Telemachus"
b. "crooked-minded Cronus" **d.** all of the above **1.** ______

2. Lines 1652-53 "...on her shoulder hung/the quiver spiked with coughing death" foreshadow future events by suggesting
a. Odysseus's brave deeds **c.** the fate of the suitors
b. Odysseus's lost companions **d.** Penelope's test **2.** ______

3. The suitors' scornful remarks about Odysseus's bow are intended as
a. epithet **b.** exaggeration **c.** heroic simile **d.** humor **3.** ______

4. Homer describes the way Odysseus strings the bow by using a metaphor comparing him to
a. a craftsman **b.** an archer **c.** a singing bird **d.** a harp-player **4.** ______

5. Telemachus's actions at the end of Book 21 increase the sense of drama by indicating that
a. he is loyal to his father
b. at last Ulysses will confront the suitors
c. the suitors will attack Odysseus
d. the suitors have treated Telemachus badly **5.** ______

B. INTERPRETING MEANINGS

Part 1. *Directions:* For each question, place the letter of the best answer in the space provided. *(5 points each)*

1. Who does Penelope expect to win the contest?
a. Antinous **b.** the beggar **c.** Odysseus **d.** no one **1.** ______

2. Odysseus questions the swineherd and cowherd because he wants to test their
a. skill as fighters
b. loyalty to him
c. patriotism
d. ability to recognize him **2.** ______

3. The clap of thunder when Odysseus strings the bow indicates that
a. Zeus has helped Odysseus
b. Athena is watching over him
c. Zeus blesses his endeavors
d. Zeus is angry with the suitors **3.** ______

4. What two feasts does Odysseus refer to at the end of Book 21?
   a. Penelope's feast and the one he prepares for the suitors
   b. the punishment of the suitors and the celebration of his return
   c. cooking the lords' mutton and appointing Telemachus as his successor
   d. a "supper by daylight" and an evening songfest

4. ______

5. In the passage beginning with line 1695, Odysseus says:

   "...Prayers I never heard
   except your own that I might come again.
   So now what is in store for you I'll tell you:
   If Zeus brings down the suitors by my hand
   I promise marriages to both, and cattle,
   and houses built near mine...."

   In this passage, Homer lets you know that Odysseus
   a. believes he needs the gods' help to succeed
   b. needs the help of his servants
   c. has mistreated his servants in the past
   d. has the support of his household

5. ______

Part 2. Odysseus was renowned as a military commander. How does he show his thoroughness in planning for battle in Book 21?

Directions: On a separate sheet of paper, list the preparations Odysseus makes. Write a paragraph explaining why he does each of these things. *(15 points)*

C. DEVELOPING VOCABULARY

Directions: Match each word in the left-hand column with the best meaning in the right-hand column. Place the letter of the best definition in the space provided. *(3 points each)*

______ 1. justification	a. the time between two events
______ 2. courier	b. to want greatly
______ 3. adversity	c. to give a correct answer
______ 4. to long for	d. to strike or hit very hard
______ 5. interval	e. a messenger
______ 6. disdainful	f. heaviness, weight
______ 7. heft	g. to break out of
______ 8. to vibrate	h. scornful, filled with contempt
______ 9. to smite	i. an acceptable excuse or defense
______ 10. to adorn	j. to decorate
	k. to move back and forth very rapidly, to quiver
	l. hardship, misfortune

NAME ______________________ CLASS __________ DATE __________ SCORE __________

UNIT 6: THE ELEMENTS OF THE EPIC

THE ODYSSEY, Book 22 **Homer**

A. UNDERSTANDING WHAT HAPPENED

Directions: In the spaces provided, mark each true statement **T** and each false statement **F**. *(3 points each)*

1. Odysseus warns Antinous to be on his guard. **1.** ______

2. The suitors take up their weapons to defend themselves. **2.** ______

3. When they see his remarkable shot kill Antinous, the suitors recognize Odysseus. **3.** ______

4. Eurymachus tries to blame his crimes on Antinous. **4.** ______

5. Eurymachus says Antinous wanted to become king of Ithaca. **5.** ______

6. Eurymachus offers to pay Odysseus to spare his life. **6.** ______

7. Odysseus gives thc suitors a choice: fight or flight. **7.** ______

8. The suitors strongly resist Odysseus. **8.** ______

9. Zeus sends a sign that he supports Odysseus. **9.** ______

10. The maids clean the hall after the battle and then help prepare the feast. **10.** ______

B. RECOGNIZING ELEMENTS OF THE EPIC

Directions: For each question, place the letter of the best answer in the space provided. *(6 points each)*

1. The scene in which Odysseus kills Penelope's suitors presents the epic's
a. final complication
b. climax
c. resolution
d. theme **1.** ______

2. To describe Antinous's fatal wound, Homer wrote: "...Like pipes his nostrils jetted/ crimson runnels, a river of mortal red...." This line contains
a. metaphor
b. simile
c. both metaphor and simile
d. irony **2.** ______

3. Which of the following metaphors does Homer use to describe the suitors' reaction when they recognize Odysseus?
   a. "yellow dogs"
   b. "contempt for the gods"
   c. "you die in blood"
   d. "sickly green fear/pulled at their entrails"

3.______

4. Eurymachus misjudges Odysseus's character by thinking he
   a. fears fighting so many men
   b. is not angry
   c. can be reasoned with and bribed
   d. may be lying

4.______

5. What simile does Homer use to describe Odysseus and his allies as they slaughter the suitors?
   a. like farmers watching hunters
   b. like flies attacking cattle
   c. like eagles catching other birds
   d. like jackals devouring rabbits

5.______

C. DEVELOPING VOCABULARY

Directions: Match each word in the left-hand column with the best meaning in the right-hand column. Place the letter of the best definition in the space provided. *(4 points each)*

______1. wily
______2. revelry
______3. to jostle
______4. to crane
______5. restitution
______6. to glower
______7. ringleader
______8. aloft
______9. to shimmer
______10. to veer

a. leader of a group in mischief or unlawful activity
b. to stare angrily
c. to bring down, to lower
d. to push or crowd against
e. high up
f. noisy merrymaking
g. narrow
h. crafty, cunning
i. to shine with an unsteady, glimmering light
j. to change direction, to turn or swing around
k. to stretch one's neck in an attempt to see something
l. repayment for loss or damage

NAME ________________ CLASS ________ DATE ________ SCORE ________

UNIT 6: THE ELEMENTS OF THE EPIC

THE ODYSSEY, Book 23 **Homer**

A. RECOGNIZING ELEMENTS OF THE EPIC

Directions: For each question, place the letter of the best answer in the space provided. *(6 points each)*

1. Which one of the following qualities does Penelope embody, especially in the reunion scene?
   a. kindness **b.** humor **c.** faithfulness **d.** pride — 1. ______

2. Telemachus tells his mother that she is
   a. silent **b.** skeptical **c.** critical **d.** cold — 2. ______

3. Penelope's insistence to her son that she will recognize Odysseus by "secret signs" is an example of
   a. scene setting **b.** simile **c.** the hook of curiosity **d.** irony — 3. ______

4. By showing Odysseus's pride in the craftsmanship of the bed, Homer reveals
   a. setting **b.** complication **c.** character **d.** point of view — 4. ______

5. Homer uses a simile to describe Odysseus's longing for Penelope (lines 1961-1967). How is this simile expanded into a metaphor for Odysseus's long journey?
   a. Like a shipwrecked sailor, he has kept alive and now crawls onto the beach.
   b. Like a powerful swimmer, he has completed the race.
   c. Like the sunwarmed earth, Penelope has always been prized.
   d. Like a lost ship, he has found his home port. — 5. ______

B. INTERPRETING MEANINGS

Part 1. *Directions:* For each question, place the letter of the best answer in the space provided. *(5 points each)*

1. Odysseus is understanding when his wife fails to welcome him because
   a. new situations have always scared her
   b. his appearance obviously has changed
   c. she resisted Antinous
   d. being with her is enough — 1. ______

2. Penelope's final test to prove her husband's identity is to
   a. order their bed moved
   b. request a bath be prepared
   c. change her gown
   d. call on the gods for help — 2. ______

3. Odysseus believes that only a god could have moved his bed because
   a. no one is allowed to touch it
   b. he made the bed from a tree trunk
   c. Penelope guards it around the clock
   d. it weighs too much for a mere mortal — 3. ______

4. Penelope compares her actions with those of Odysseus by saying
   a. "I armed myself long ago against the frauds of men."
   b. "I could not welcome you with love on sight."
   c. "No one ever matched your caution."
   d. "Think what difficulty the gods gave."

4. ______

5. In the following passage, beginning with line 1944, Penelope says:

"...Think
what difficulty the gods gave: they denied us
life together in our prime and flowering years,
kept us from crossing into age together.
Forgive me, don't be angry. I could not
welcome you with love on sight! I armed myself
long ago against the frauds of men,
imposters who might come—and all those many
whose underhanded ways bring evil on!...
But here and now, what sign could be so clear
as this of our own bed?
No other man has ever laid eyes on it—
only my own slave, Actoris, that my father
sent with me as a gift—she kept our door."

In these lines, Homer shows that Penelope truly loves Odysseus by
   a. pointing out that the gods made them both suffer
   b. explaining the reason for her caution
   c. referring to her difficulties while Odysseus was away
   d. emphasizing her loyalty

5. ______

Part 2. Both Telemachus and Odysseus criticize Penelope for being slow to welcome Odysseus. Do you agree with them?

Directions: On a separate sheet of paper, write a paragraph explaining your point of view. Cite parts of the epic that influence your opinion. *(15 points)*

C. DEVELOPING VOCABULARY

Directions: Match each word in the left-hand column with the best meaning in the right-hand column. Place the letter of the best definition in the space provided. *(3 points each)*

______ 1. to shun	a. easily bent
______ 2. tatters	b. reserved and cool, distant
______ 3. tunic	c. to pause
______ 4. to lavish	d. to keep away from, to avoid
______ 5. aloof	e. trembling, quivering
______ 6. to lop	f. torn shreds of cloth, rags
______ 7. pliant	g. thickened and dried, stiffened
______ 8. tremulous	h. a medicinal drink
______ 9. impostor	i. to cut off
______ 10. clotted	j. a knee-length garment that covers the upper body
	k. one who pretends to be what he or she is not
	l. to give freely

NAME ______________________ CLASS __________ DATE __________ SCORE __________

UNIT 6: THE ELEMENTS OF THE EPIC

THE ODYSSEY, Book 24 Homer

A. UNDERSTANDING WHAT HAPPENED

Directions: In the spaces provided, mark each true statement **T** and each false statement **F**. *(3 points each)*

1. Odysseus invents a story that pains his father. 1. ______

2. Odysseus's "good news" is that he has killed Penelope's suitors. 2. ______

3. Laertes asks for proof that the stranger is indeed Odysseus. 3. ______

4. Laertes asks Odysseus to describe the gift he gave him when he was a child. 4. ______

5. Laertes interprets the death of the suitors as a sign from Zeus. 5. ______

6. Athena makes Odysseus appear godlike to his father. 6. ______

7. Zeus wants peace restored to Ithaca. 7. ______

8. Zeus drops a thunderbolt at Odysseus's feet. 8. ______

9. The townspeople flee because they fear Odysseus. 9. ______

10. Athena commands Odysseus to call off the battle. 10. ______

B. RECOGNIZING ELEMENTS OF THE EPIC

Directions: For each question, place the letter of the best answer in the space provided. *(6 points each)*

1. Laertes' gesture of covering his head with dust is symbolic of
a. vanity
b. grief
c. death
d. rebirth
1. ______

2. Which of the following metaphors does Homer use to describe Laertes' feelings?
a. a heart that bleeds
b. a silent tree
c. a cloud of pain
d. a speechless harp
2. ______

3. It is ironic that the families of the dead suitors arm themselves against Odysseus because they
a. are all scholarly people
b. have just returned from war
c. cannot possibly win this battle
d. have never been in combat before
3. ______

4. Homer brings the *Odyssey* to an end by giving the final words to
   a. the humans
   b. the gods
   c. the dead
   d. nature

4. ______

5. The resolution of the story occurs when
   a. peace is established
   b. Odysseus flees
   c. Odysseus becomes a tyrant
   d. the gods take pity on Odysseus

5. ______

C. DEVELOPING VOCABULARY

Directions: Match each word in the left-hand column with the best meaning in the right-hand column. Place the letter of the best definition in the space provided. *(4 points each)*

______ 1. to sift
______ 2. prickling
______ 3. to wheedle
______ 4. hue
______ 5. to anoint
______ 6. girth
______ 7. stature
______ 8. skirmish
______ 9. to strew
______ 10. arbiter

a. a shade of any color
b. a brief fight
c. a figure made of stone
d. a tingling or stinging feeling
e. to persuade by flattery or coaxing
f. to scatter, to throw about in a disorderly way
g. to sew with fine stitches
h. to pass through a sieve or strainer so as to separate the fine and coarse parts
i. to apply oil or ointment to
j. the circumference of a person or thing
k. a person selected to settle a dispute
l. height

NAME ______________________ CLASS __________ DATE __________ SCORE __________

UNIT 6: THE ELEMENTS OF THE EPIC

WORD ANALOGIES / Extending Vocabulary Skills

Directions: In the space provided, write the letter of the pair of words that best describes a *relationship* that is closest to that of the capitalized pair of words. (*5 points each*)

1. CANDOR : HONESTY ::
a. color : blue
b. sweet : sour
c. valor : bravery
d. tenor : baritone
1. ______

2. ARDOR : ALOOFNESS ::
a. passion : indifference
b. enthusiasm : spirit
c. odor : smell
d. disinterest : unconcern
2. ______

3. BEGUILE : MISLEAD ::
a. follow : lead
b. begin : finish
c. irk : satisfy
d. trick : cheat
3. ______

4. CLAMOR : TUMULT ::
a. claim : charge
b. snail : turret
c. tremor : steadiness
d. uproar : commotion
4. ______

5. APPEASE : ASSUAGE ::
a. irritate : alleviate
b. pacify : soothe
c. please : irk
d. pleasant : angry
5. ______

6. CONTEMPTIBLE : UNWORTHY ::
a. respectful : laudable
b. valued : worthless
c. shameful : admirable
d. expensive : valuable
6. ______

7. ENTREAT : BESEECH ::
a. command : plead
b. send : direct
c. demand : request
d. implore : beg
7. ______

8. HALE : HEARTY ::
a. quiet : noise
b. healthy : sound
c. robust : weak
d. sickly : sturdy
8. ______

9. INTERROGATE : QUESTION ::
a. quiz : answer
b. respond : examine
c. ask : query
d. venture : quest
9. ______

10. MAUDLIN : OVEREMOTIONAL ::
a. realistic : emotional
b. teary : unemotional
c. sentimental : tearful
d. gushing : serious
10. ______

11. PLUNDER : LOOT ::
a. raid : pillage
b. ransack : rebuild
c. blunder : error
d. guard : rob
11. ______

12. PREVAIL : TRIUMPH ::
a. yield : conquer
b. worst : best
c. surrender : overwhelm
d. succeed : overcome
12. ______

13. PRUDENT : CARELESS ::
a. extravagant : sensible
b. cautious : indiscreet
c. unwise : careful
d. caring : insensitive
13. ______

14. RENOWNED : UNKNOWN ::
a. prominent : noteworthy
b. outstanding : insignificant
c. unpopular : popular
d. famous : obscure
14. ______

15. SHUN : SEEK ::
a. reject : boycott
b. locate : find
c. avoid : pursue
d. hide : search

15. ______

16. DETAIN : HINDER ::
a. encourage : facilitate
b. contain : hold
c. retrain : educate
d. prevent : support

16. ______

17. VAUNT : CONCEAL ::
a. boast : cover up
b. shame : hide
c. brag : crow
d. flaunt : display

17. ______

18. DOMAIN : SOVEREIGN ::
a. empire : dominion
b. territory : monarch
c. subject : king
d. yardstick : ruler

18. ______

19. UNCOUTH : CRUDE ::
a. cultured : unmannerly
b. delicate : unrefined
c. cultivated : uncultured
d. gross : impolite

19. ______

20. BRACE : PISTOLS ::
a. volley : bullets
b. pair : guns
c. rifles : cannons
d. twins : triplets

20. ______

NAME ______________________ CLASS __________ DATE __________ SCORE __________

UNIT 6: THE ELEMENTS OF THE EPIC

UNIT REVIEW / Applying Skills I

A. READING AN EPIC

The following passage from Book 22 of the *Iliad* describes the encounter between Hector (Hektor) and Achilles (Akhilleus).

Directions: Read the passage carefully, and then answer the questions that follow.

Hektor stood firm, as huge Akhilleus neared. 97
The way a serpent, fed on poisoned herbs,
coiled at his lair upon a mountainside,
with all his length of hate awaits a man 100
and eyes him evilly: so Hektor, grim
and narrow-eyed, refused to yield. He leaned
his brilliant shield against a spur of wall
and in his brave heart bitterly reflected:
"Here I am badly caught. If I take cover, 105
slipping inside the gate and wall, the first
to accuse me for it will be Poulydamas,
he who told me I should lead the Trojans
back to the city on that cursed night
Akhilleus joined the battle. No, I would not, 110
would not, wiser though it would have been.
Now troops have perished for my foolish pride,
I am ashamed to face townsmen and women.
Someone inferior to me may say:
'He kept his pride and lost his men, this Hektor!' 115
So it will go. Better, when that time comes,
that I appear as he who killed Akhilleus
man to man, or else that I went down
before him honorably for the city's sake.
Suppose, though, that I lay my shield and helm 120
aside, and prop my spear against the wall,
and go to meet the noble Prince Akhilleus,
promising Helen, promising with her
all treasures that Aléxandros brought home
by ship to Troy—the first cause of our quarrel— 125
that he may give these things to the Atreidai?
Then, I might add, apart from these, a portion
of all the secret wealth the city owns.
Yes, later I might take our counselors' oath
to hide no stores, but share and share alike 130
to halve all wealth our lovely city holds,
all that is here within the walls. Ah, no,
why even put the question to myself?

I must not go before him and receive
no quarter, no respect! Aye, then and there 135
he'll kill me, unprotected as I am,
my gear laid by, defenseless as a woman.
No chance, now, for charms from oak or stone
in parley with him—charms a girl and boy
might use when they enchant each other talking! 140
Better we duel, now at once, and see
to whom the Olympian awards the glory."

These were his shifts of mood. Now close at hand
Akhilleus like the implacable god of war
came on with blowing crest, hefting the dreaded 145
beam of Pêlian ash on his right shoulder.
Bronze light played around him, like the glare
of a great fire or the great sun rising,
and Hektor, as he watched, began to tremble.
Then he could hold his ground no more. He ran, 150
leaving the gate behind him, with Akhilleus
hard on his heels, sure of his own speed.
When that most lightning-like of birds, a hawk
bred upon a mountain, swoops upon a dove,
the quarry dips in terror, but the hunter, 155
screaming, dips behind and gains upon it,
passionate for prey. Just so, Akhilleus
murderously cleft the air, as Hektor
ran with flashing knees along the wall.
They passed the lookout point, the wild figtree 160
with wind in all its leaves, then veered away
along the curving wagon road, and came
to where the double fountains well, the source
of eddying Skamánder. One hot spring
flows out, and from the water fumes arise 165
as though from fire burning; but the other
even in summer gushes chill as hail
or snow or crystal ice frozen on water.
Near these fountains are wide washing pools
of smooth-laid stone, where Trojan wives and daughters 170
laundered their smooth linen in the days
of peace before the Akhaians came. Past these
the two men ran, pursuer and pursued,
and he who fled was noble, he behind
a greater man by far. They ran full speed, 175
and not for bull's hide or a ritual beast
or any prize that men compete for: no,
but for the life of Hektor, tamer of horses.
Just as when chariot-teams around a course
go wheeling swiftly, for the prize is great,
a tripod or a woman, in the games 180
held for a dead man, so three times these two
at full speed make their course round Priam's town,
as all the gods looked on....

NAME ______________________ CLASS __________ DATE __________ SCORE __________

B. ANALYZING AN EPIC

Directions: For each question, place the letter of the best answer in the space provided. *(5 points each)*

1. In this selection, you learn about the character of Hektor through
a. the things he does
b. the things he says
c. the narrator's description
d. all of the above
1. ______

2. The information about Hektor in lines 97-102 is an example of
a. epithet
b. personification
c. heroic simile
d. foreshadowing
2. ______

3. The reference to Hektor as a "tamer of horses" in line 177 is an example of
a. epithet
b. personification
c. heroic simile
d. suspense
3. ______

4. When Akhilleus first appears in this excerpt, he is compared to
a. a beam of Pêlian ash
b. the sun
c. a lightning bolt
d. the god of war
4. ______

5. The simile beginning on line 164 compares
a. one spring to another spring
b. one spring to fire and another spring to ice
c. summer to winter
d. the springs to the washing pools
5. ______

6. The imagery in this same simile (lines 164-168) appeals to the sense of
a. sight
b. sound
c. touch
d. taste
6. ______

7. Hektor's statement in lines 141-142 reveals
a. his belief in the power of the gods
b. his inability to wait for an outcome
c. the gods' plan for him
d. the outcome of the fight
7. ______

8. The hawk mentioned in line 153 refers to
a. the flighty nature of men
b. the flight of Hektor
c. the meeting of Hektor and Akhilleus
d. Akhilleus's speed in running
8. ______

9. Irony is established by all of the following situations *except:*
a. Akhilleus attacking Hektor so fiercely that Hektor begins to tremble
b. Hektor, the bravest of the Trojan warriors, being chased by Akhilleus
c. Hektor appearing to stand bravely while he contemplates his fear
d. Hektor fearing what others will say of his cowardly behavior

9. ______

10. Two of the references to women in the excerpt, one in line 137 and the other in line 180, reveal the generally
a. high regard in which women were held
b. low esteem in which women were held
c. active role of women in the wars
d. gentle nature of Trojan men

10. ______

C. WRITING ABOUT THE EPIC

This excerpt makes clear that Homer had great respect for both Akhilleus and Hektor. Find details in the passage that show how Homer felt about both warriors.

Directions: Using the evidence you have found in the excerpt, write on a separate sheet of paper *one* paragraph, perhaps beginning with a statement such as: "Homer respects Hektor and Akhilleus because ____." *(25 points)*

D. ANALYZING LANGUAGE AND DEVELOPING VOCABULARY

Directions: In the spaces provided, mark each true statement **T** and each false statement **F**. *(5 points each)*

1. Later in the story, Achilles (Akhilleus) is fatally wounded in the heel by an arrow. The Achilles' tendon in the human heel probably was named after the Greek warrior. **1.** ______

2. Hektor's speaking to himself is an example of a monologue. **2.** ______

3. Hektor's reflection in lines 105-110 is an example of an heroic (Homeric) simile. **3.** ______

4. The description of Hektor as "Hektor, grim and narrow-eyed" in lines 101-102 is an example of an epithet. **4.** ______

5. Comparing Achilles' pursuit of Hektor to a chariot race (lines 178-183) is an example of an heroic (Homeric) simile. **5.** ______

NAME ______________________ CLASS __________ DATE __________ SCORE __________

UNIT 6: THE ELEMENTS OF THE EPIC

CRITICAL THINKING AND WRITING / Applying Skills II

A. RETELLING A STORY

Directions: In *two* paragraphs, retell Telemachus's attempt to "become his father's son" (lines 78 through 91). In the first paragraph, describe the actions he takes to convince the populace that he is a capable man. In the second paragraph, explain how Athena helps him. *(40 points)*

B. INTERPRETING CHARACTERS' ACTIONS

Directions: Write *one* paragraph to describe Odysseus's behavior when he first encounters Nausicaa (lines 440ff.). Why does he keep his identity secret until the last possible moment (line 646)? *(30 points)*

C. EVALUATING AN AUTHOR'S TECHNIQUE

Directions: In *one* paragraph, evaluate Homer's use of suspense. Describe how Homer holds the interest of his listeners after Odysseus arrives in Ithaca. Keep in mind Odysseus's disguise, the various people he meets, and the obstacles he faces. *(30 points)*

NAME ______________________ CLASS __________ DATE __________ SCORE ________

UNIT 7: THE ELEMENTS OF THE NOVEL

UNIT INTRODUCTION / Understanding the Elements of the Novel

Directions: For each question, place the letter of the best answer in the space provided. *(10 points each)*

1. The difference between a novel and a short story is that a novel
a. is longer
b. uses a number of conflicts, themes, and characters
c. usually goes into greater depth
d. all of the above
1. ______

2. A novel must
a. take place over a long period of time
b. follow the history of one family
c. contain all the elements of a story
d. involve important historical events
2. ______

3. Writing a novel
a. usually takes a long time
b. requires a group of authors
c. always involves research
d. is easy and fun
3. ______

4. Most great novels
a. are written by pairs of authors
b. have been written during the past half-century
c. exceed 600 pages
d. are informative and socially pertinent
4. ______

5. Brief and humorous stories in which animals speak and act like human beings are called
a. satires
b. allegories
c. fables
d. soap operas
5. ______

6. A writer's motivation for writing a novel is ultimately
a. making a lot of money
b. sharing a private vision
c. spreading propaganda
d. overthrowing the government
6. ______

7. A novella is
a. a medium-length narrative
b. a literary device involving ridicule
c. a novel of more than 500 pages
d. a novel that is made into an opera
7. ______

8. An example of dramatic irony might be
   a. an old man talking to a young boy
   b. describing a tree as "reaching up to God"
   c. an old woman washing clothes in a stream
   d. describing a pig wearing a dress as dainty and petite

8. ______

9. An example of situational irony might be
   a. a dog fetching a stick
   b. a doctor damaging his health
   c. an automobile accident
   d. a banker going home for dinner

9. ______

10. An author has a responsibility to
   a. try to change the world
   b. be as controversial as possible
   c. be true to his or her own vision
   d. write about himself or herself

10. ______

NAME ________________ CLASS ________ DATE ________ SCORE ________

UNIT 7: THE ELEMENTS OF THE NOVEL

ANIMAL FARM, Chapter I **George Orwell**

A. RECOGNIZING ELEMENTS OF THE NOVEL

Directions: For each question, place the letter of the best answer in the space provided. *(6 points each)*

1. You gather that *Animal Farm* will be a fable when you realize that
a. there is a stirring in the farm buildings after the farmer goes to bed
b. Mr. Jones forgets to close the popholes in the hen house
c. the farm animals gather to hear about Major's dream
d. this is a story in which animals speak and act like humans **1.** ______

2. Which of the following descriptive details is intended to be ironic?
a. Major has a wise and benevolent appearance.
b. Clover never quite got her figure back after her fourth foal.
c. The two cart-horses are careful where they sit.
d. Benjamin, the donkey, is the worst-tempered animal on the farm. **2.** ______

3. The main conflict in the story becomes evident when Major proclaims that
a. man is the only real enemy of animals
b. he will not live much longer
c. animals' lives are miserable, laborious, and short
d. the soil of England can support many more animals **3.** ______

4. As a solution to the conflict with humans, Major urges the animals to
a. refuse to serve men
b. keep the fruits of their labors
c. rebel against man's domination
d. purchase their own land **4.** ______

5. The climax of Chapter I occurs when
a. the animals join together to sing the song from Major's dream
b. the animals vote to accept the rats as comrades
c. Major tells the animals about his dream
d. Major says that all animals are equal **5.** ______

B. INTERPRETING MEANINGS

Part 1. *Directions:* For each question, place the letter of the best answer in the space provided. (5 points each)

1. The first part of Major's speech, before he is interrupted by the rats, is intended to be an allegory for a speech by
a. a labor union leader
b. a revolutionary leader
c. a political candidate
d. the leader of a nation **1.** ______

2. Major wants to settle the question of whether the wild animals are friends or enemies because
a. he wants the animals to be completely united
b. he is upset by the dogs' reaction to the rats
c. he fears that the wild animals will befriend men
d. he is unsure about the answer to this question **2.** ______

3. Major summarizes the differences between friends and enemies by emphasizing that
   a. man and the animals have a common interest
   b. there should be perfect comradeship among all animals
   c. whatever goes upon two legs is an enemy, and whatever goes upon four legs, or has wings, is a friend
   d. all animals are equal

3.______

4. Before Major relates his dream, he says:

> ...And remember also that in fighting against Man, we must not come to resemble him. Even when you have conquered him, do not adopt his vices. No animal must ever live in a house, or sleep in a bed, or wear clothes, or drink alcohol, or smoke tobacco, or touch money, or engage in trade. All the habits of Man are evil. And, above all, no animal must ever tyrannize over his own kind. Weak or strong, clever or simple, we are all brothers. No animal must ever kill any other animal. All animals are equal.

   This passage indicates that Major believes that
   a. the animals will want to imitate man
   b. man behaves as he does because he is powerful
   c. animals need rules of proper conduct
   d. these vices cause man to tyrannize others

4.______

Part 2. Orwell presents Major's speech as he would present that of a human speaker.

Directions: On a separate sheet of paper, assess Major's argument. Are his reasons for calling for an animal revolution convincing? Why, or why not? Cite the parts of his argument that are most compelling, and describe why they would be effective in persuading the animals to rebel. *(20 points)*

C. DEVELOPING VOCABULARY

Directions: Match each word in the left-hand column with the best meaning in the right-hand column. Place the letter of the best definition in the space provided. *(3 points each)*

______**1.** benevolent
______**2.** to ensconce
______**3.** cynical
______**4.** to abolish
______**5.** to tyrannize
______**6.** preliminary
______**7.** resolution
______**8.** plaited
______**9.** scullery
______**10.** paddock

a. braided
b. a fixed, firm purpose
c. the part of the kitchen where pots are scrubbed
d. kindly
e. coming before the main action
f. to recall or remember
g. to rule cruelly with unlimited power
h. a place where tools are kept
i. to place or settle comfortably or snugly
j. a small, enclosed field for animals
k. believing that people's actions are motivated by selfishness
l. to do away with completely

NAME ____________________ CLASS __________ DATE __________ SCORE __________

UNIT 7: THE ELEMENTS OF THE NOVEL

ANIMAL FARM, Chapter II **George Orwell**

A. UNDERSTANDING WHAT HAPPENED

Directions: In the spaces provided, mark each true statement **T** and each false statement **F**. *(3 points each)*

1. The pigs are the cleverest of the animals. **1.** ______

2. Boxer, Clover, and Mollie are the most faithful followers of Animalism. **2.** ______

3. The main cause of the rebellion is that the animals have not been fed. **3.** ______

4. Moses is the only animal to flee the farm. **4.** ______

5. The first thing the animals do after the rebellion is destroy Mr. Jones's tools and whips. **5.** ______

6. After the rebellion, all animals are allowed to behave as they like. **6.** ______

7. The animals do not destroy the farmhouse because they may want to live there in the future. **7.** ______

8. The animals are permitted to take whatever they need to eat. **8.** ______

9. The influence of Major's ideas is evident in the Seven Commandments. **9.** ______

10. None of the animals know what to do with the cows' milk. **10.** ______

B. RECOGNIZING ELEMENTS OF THE NOVEL

Directions: For each question, place the letter of the best answer in the space provided. *(6 points each)*

1. The major plot development of this chapter is that the
a. pigs become the leaders of the animals
b. animals stage a successful rebellion
c. animals break into the farmhouse
d. animals develop seven rules of conduct **1.** ______

2. The pigs most resemble human revolutionary leaders in that they
a. lead the animals in singing
b. establish rules of conduct
c. adopt the ways of their former rulers
d. develop a system of thought **2.** ______

3. Moses, the tame raven, who tells tales of Sugarcandy Mountain, is an allegory for what kind of human leader?
   a. a revolutionary
   b. a politician
   c. a business leader
   d. a religious leader 3.______

4. The rebellion is successful because
   a. the animals are guided by the rules of Animalism
   b. the pigs devise a clever plan
   c. the humans are unprepared for the sudden uprising
   d. Mr. Jones is out of town 4.______

5. The Seven Commandments may be important in the further development of the plot because
   a. some animals will want to disobey them
   b. they will provide a basis for the success of the farm
   c. they will prove to be unworkable
   d. they will be abolished 5.______

C. DEVELOPING VOCABULARY

Directions: Match each word in the left-hand column with the best meaning in the right-hand column. Place the letter of the best definition in the space provided. *(4 points each)*

______1. vivacious	a. located
______2. to expound	b. foaming
______3. preeminent	c. lack of emotion or interest
______4. apathy	d. to jump and skip about in play
______5. disheartened	e. to state or explain in detail
______6. situated	f. quick and light in movement
______7. to gambol	g. someone who causes another to suffer
______8. frothing	h. excelling others, surpassing
______9. nimble	i. cold
______10. tormentor	j. discouraged
	k. full of life and animation
	l. odd

NAME ______________________ CLASS __________ DATE __________ SCORE __________

UNIT 7: THE ELEMENTS OF THE NOVEL

ANIMAL FARM, Chapter III **George Orwell**

A. RECOGNIZING ELEMENTS OF THE NOVEL

Directions: For each question, place the letter of the best answer in the space provided. *(6 points each)*

1. At first, the animals are
a. unable to run the farm as well as Mr. Jones
b. enthusiastic about the results of the rebellion
c. reluctant to obey the Seven Commandments
d. divided over how much work everyone should do **1.** ______

2. The character who seems to be entirely trustworthy is
a. Napoleon **b.** the cat **c.** Boxer **d.** Squealer **2.** ______

3. Which of the following statements from the novel is meant to be ironic?
a. "Old Benjamin, the donkey, seemed quite unchanged since the rebellion."
b. "It was always the pigs who put forward the resolutions."
c. "Mollie refused to learn any but the six letters which spelled her own name."
d. "It is for *your* sake that we drink that milk and eat those apples." **3.** ______

4. The event most likely to foreshadow later plot developments occurs when
a. the animals finish the harvest in two days, less time than it had usually taken Jones and his men
b. Benjamin works at the same pace as he did before the rebellion
c. Napoleon takes control of the education of the newborn puppies
d. the sheep chant the new slogan for hours on end **4.** ______

5. The best summary of the conflict in this chapter is that
a. some animals are able to do more work than others
b. the pigs want certain privileges for themselves
c. the Seven Commandments are reduced to a single slogan
d. Snowball's committees are failures **5.** ______

B. INTERPRETING MEANINGS

Part 1. *Directions:* For each question, place the letter of the best answer in the space provided. *(6 points each)*

1. The animals accept the pigs' leadership because the pigs
a. possess superior knowledge **c.** produce the Seven Commandments
b. are united in their beliefs **d.** led the rebellion against Mr. Jones **1.** ______

2. The cat is active in the Re-education Committee in order to
a. avoid work **c.** catch sparrows
b. be helpful **d.** remain friendly with Snowball **2.** ______

3. The slogan, "Four legs good, two legs bad," is more popular than the Seven Commandments because it
a. correctly summarizes all of the principles of Animalism
b. keeps the animals safe from human influence
c. emphasizes that all animals are equal
d. is easier to remember 3.______

4. The most effective argument Squealer uses to justify the pigs' taking the milk and apples for themselves is that
a. many of the pigs actually dislike milk and apples
b. if the pigs fail to stay in good health, Jones will come back
c. the pigs manage and organize the farm
d. milk and apples are absolutely necessary for pigs 4.______

5. The author gives the following description of Old Benjamin, the donkey:

> ... He did his work in the same slow, obstinate way as he had done it in Jones's time, never shirking and never volunteering for extra work either. About the Rebellion and its results he would express no opinion. When asked whether he was not happier now that Jones was gone, he would say only "Donkeys live a long time. None of you has ever see a dead donkey," and the others had to be content with this cryptic answer.

The best explanation of Benjamin's meaning is that
a. hard work shortens your life
b. age brings wisdom
c. only time will tell the truth about a new system
d. it is safer to keep controversial opinions to yourself 5.______

Part 2. George Orwell describes the events of the novel in a straightforward way. He does not comment on the motives of the characters. How does he use irony to make you understand what really is going on?

Directions: On a separate sheet of paper, write a paragraph in which you give examples of the author's techniques for explaining the underlying meaning of events. *(10 points)*

C. DEVELOPING VOCABULARY

Directions: Match each word in the left-hand column with the best meaning in the right-hand column. Place the letter of the best definition in the space provided. *(3 points each)*

______1. parasitical
______2. to shirk
______3. cryptic
______4. to resolve
______5. propulsion
______6. manipulation
______7. maxim
______8. grudging
______9. seclusion
______10. acute

a. to release
b. sharp, severe, intense
c. a concisely expressed principle or rule of conduct
d. to find a solution to
e. reluctant, unwilling
f. having a hidden or unclear meaning
g. a way of entering
h. a forward motion
i. to neglect or evade because of laziness or negligence
j. living at the expense of others
k. the condition of being kept apart or separated from others
l. skillful handling or operation, artful control

NAME ______________________ CLASS __________ DATE __________ SCORE __________

UNIT 7: THE ELEMENTS OF THE NOVEL

ANIMAL FARM, Chapter IV **George Orwell**

A. UNDERSTANDING WHAT HAPPENED

Directions: In the spaces provided, mark each true statement **T** and each false statement **F**. *(3 points each)*

1. The other farmers help Mr. Jones because they feel sorry for him. **1.** ______

2. The farmers' predictions about Animal Farm come true. **2.** ______

3. The farmers fear there will be further animal rebellions. **3.** ______

4. The animals expect the humans to attack. **4.** ______

5. Benjamin supports the rebellion. **5.** ______

6. The Battle of the Cowshed lasts nearly an hour. **6.** ______

7. Boxer kills one of the stableboys from Foxwood. **7.** ______

8. The retreating humans try to capture Snowball. **8.** ______

9. The only animal killed is a sheep. **9.** ______

10. The animals decide to use the captured shotgun to defend the farm. **10.** ______

B. RECOGNIZING ELEMENTS OF THE NOVEL

Directions: For each question, place the letter of the answer in the space provided. *(6 points each)*

1. The major plot development in this chapter is that
a. Snowball leads the animals in defending the farm
b. animals on other farms take up Animalism
c. a group of humans tries to retake the Jones farm
d. Boxer performs heroically **1.** ______

2. Which of the following actions indicates that the novel is a fable?
a. Mr. Jones asks his neighbors for help.
b. Neighboring farmers spread stories of the animal rebellion at Animal Farm.
c. The neighboring farmers disagree among themselves.
d. The humans attempt to retake the farm. **2.** ______

3. If Animal Farm is intended to represent the Soviet Union in an allegory, what do Foxwood and Pinchfield represent?
a. armies that attacked the Soviet Union after the Russian Revolution
b. democracy and capitalism
c. leaders of non-Communist nations
d. neighboring European countries that feared a Communist revolution **3.** ______

4. The bravest pig proves to be
   a. Snowball
   b. Boxer
   c. Squealer
   d. Napoleon

4. ______

5. Boxer's character is developed in this chapter when he is shown to be
   a. a loyal supporter of the revolution
   b. a skilled military leader
   c. a hard worker
   d. a brave yet compassionate fighter

5. ______

C. DEVELOPING VOCABULARY

Directions: Match each word in the left-hand column with the best meaning in the right-hand column. Place the letter of the best definition in the space provided. *(4 points each)*

______ **1.** adjoined

______ **2.** to scorn

______ **3.** tractable

______ **4.** irrepressible

______ **5.** maneuver

______ **6.** vengeance

______ **7.** ignominious

______ **8.** impromptu

______ **9.** monstrous

______ **10.** posthumously

a. any movement or procedure intended as a skillful step toward a goal

b. situated next to

c. action taken in return for a wrong committed

d. to make fun of or look down upon

e. huge, enormous

f. without preparation or advance thought

g. shameful, dishonorable

h. taking place after death

i. hungry

j. easily managed or controlled

k. tired

l. uncontrollable

NAME ______ CLASS ______ DATE ______ SCORE ______

UNIT 7: THE ELEMENTS OF THE NOVEL

ANIMAL FARM, Chapter V **George Orwell**

A. RECOGNIZING ELEMENTS OF THE NOVEL

Directions: For each question, place the letter of the best answer in the space provided. *(6 points each)*

1. The major event in this chapter is
a. Mollie's deserting the farm
b. Snowball's planning the windmill
c. Snowball's leaving the farm
d. Napoleon's establishing his unchallenged leadership **1.** ______

2. George Orwell uses irony to indicate that
a. the animals refuse to mention the departed Mollie
b. the animals find Snowball's plans completely unintelligible but very impressive
c. Benjamin refrains from siding with either faction in the windmill dispute
d. Napoleon says that the windmill idea is nonsense **2.** ______

3. Which of thc following is meant to express irony?
a. Mollie says, "It isn't true!"
b. The pro-Snowball faction urges: "Vote for Snowball and the three-day wcck."
c. Squealer says that Napoleon had never really been opposed to the windmill.
d. The sheep chant, "Four legs good, two legs bad." **3.** ______

4. The main conflict in this chapter takes place between
a. Mollie and Clover **c.** Snowball and Squealer
b. Snowball and Napoleon **d.** Napoleon and Boxer **4.** ______

5. The character most loyal to the principles of Animalism is
a. Boxer **b.** Mollie **c.** Napoleon **d.** Squealer **5.** ______

B. INTERPRETING MEANINGS

Part 1. *Directions:* For each question, place the letter of the best answer in the space provided. *(5 points each)*

1. Mollie leaves the farm because she
a. likes to wear ribbons and eat sugar
b. is afraid that the humans will attack again
c. is unwilling to help the other animals
d. is afraid of the pigs **1.** ______

2. Napoleon brings out his ferocious dogs to
a. oppose a windmill for the farm
b. intimidate Snowball
c. acknowledge that Snowball is right
d. establish his unchallenged power **2.** ______

3. When Boxer first hears that Napoleon has cancelled Sunday debates, he
   a. immediately points out that debates are unnecessary
   b. convinces the other animals that Napoleon is right
   c. cannot think of anything to say
   d. decides to follow Mollie

3.______

4. In the end, Boxer settles his feelings about Napoleon's action by claiming that
   a. he will work harder
   b. if Napoleon says something it must be right
   c. he will not take sides in the dispute
   d. Napoleon is a great leader

4.______

5. Squealer answers the argument that Snowball fought bravely at the Battle of the Cowshed with this statement:

   > "Bravery is not enough....Loyalty and obedience are more important. And as to the Battle of the Cowshed, I believe the time will come when we shall find that Snowball's part in it was much exaggerated. Discipline, comrades, iron discipline! That is the watchword for today. One false step, and our enemies would be upon us. Surely, comrades, you do not want Jones back?"

   In this passage, Orwell calls attention to
   a. the role of discipline in changing society
   b. the human threat to Animal Farm
   c. the practice in totalitarian states of rewriting history to fit current policy
   d. Snowball's use of self-promotion in gaining power

5.______

Part 2. Mollie leaves the farm for what seems like a frivolous reason. Boxer resolves to remain loyal to Napoleon. Which horse do you think took the better course of action? Which do you admire more?

Directions: On a separate sheet of paper, write a paragraph stating your opinions and giving reasons for your point of view. Discuss the dilemma the author is posing between the duty of a citizen and the appeal of personal freedom. *(15 points)*

C. DEVELOPING VOCABULARY

Directions: Match each word in the left-hand column with the best meaning in the right-hand column. Place the letter of the best definition in the space provided. *(3 points each)*

______ 1. pretext
______ 2. blithely
______ 3. to ratify
______ 4. innovation
______ 5. aloof
______ 6. faction
______ 7. restive
______ 8. sordid
______ 9. articulate
______ 10. to disinter

a. able to express oneself easily and clearly
b. reserved and cool, distant
c. to argue against
d. a false reason or excuse given to conceal a real one
e. filthy, dirty, mean
f. in a carefree and unconcerned manner
g. to dig up, unearth
h. restless, uneasy
i. terrified, fearful
j. to confirm formally, to approve
k. a change made in the established way of doing things
l. a group of persons with common purpose

NAME ______________________ CLASS __________ DATE __________ SCORE __________

UNIT 7: THE ELEMENTS OF THE NOVEL

ANIMAL FARM, Chapter VI **George Orwell**

A. RECOGNIZING ELEMENTS OF THE NOVEL

Directions: For each question, place the letter of the best answer in the space provided. *(6 points each)*

1. The basic situation in this chapter is that the animals
a. prepare to defend the farm against humans
c. build the windmill
b. set up a system of trade
d. capture Snowball
1. ______

2. When Napoleon first violates the original Seven Commandments, the author introduces a complication by
a. trading with humans
c. using human tools
b. permitting the pigs to sleep in beds
d. pronouncing Snowball's death sentence
2. ______

3. Squealer's most effective argument is always that
a. the pigs' efforts require certain luxuries
b. none of the animals would want Mr. Jones to come back
c. brain work is harder than physical work
d. Napoleon is always right
3. ______

4. When Orwell describes how the humans begin to develop respect for Animal Farm, he utilizes which of the following literary devices?
a. allegory **b.** satire **c.** propaganda **d.** simile
4. ______

5. The climax of this chapter occurs when
a. Snowball's footprints are discovered near the windmill
b. the pigs move into the farmhouse
c. the harvest is taken in
d. the windmill falls down
5. ______

B. INTERPRETING MEANINGS

Part 1. *Directions:* For each question, place the letter of the best answer in the space provided. *(5 points each)*

1. The windmill is difficult to build because
a. Snowball is no longer there to direct the animals
b. the animals lack proper tools
c. the pigs refuse to do their share of the work
d. the animals are unable to use the available tools
1. ______

2. Napoleon changes his policy and decides to trade with neighboring farms because
a. certain necessities cannot be produced on the farm
b. he wants to better understand humans
c. he fears bankruptcy
d. he intends to spread Animalism
2. ______

3. Orwell indicates that Squealer's repeated warning about Mr. Jones's return is an empty threat by
   a. showing that the farm can defend itself
   b. revealing that Jones has given up hope of regaining his farm and has moved away
   c. suggesting that Napoleon has made a protective alliance with the other farmers
   d. describing how the animals are always united by the threat of Jones's return 3.______

4. The real reason for the collapse of the windmill is that
   a. Snowball destroys it
   b. Napoleon has changed Snowball's plans
   c. the windstorm blows it down
   d. the animals are unskilled builders 4.______

Part 2. Squealer challenges the animals who recall that resolutions were passed against some of Napoleon's new activities. He asks, "Have you any record of such a resolution? Is it written down anywhere?" Why do the other animals have no good answer to this argument? What message about education and the importance of written laws is the author trying to convey?

Directions: On a separate sheet of paper, write a paragraph explaining your answers to these questions. Explain how Orwell's message might be applied to a real situation in a nation. *(20 points)*

C. DEVELOPING VOCABULARY

Directions: Match each word in the left-hand column with the best meaning in the right-hand column. Place the letter of the best definition in the space provided. *(3 points each)*

______1. matted
______2. to procure
______3. broker
______4. commission
______5. bankrupt
______6. simultaneously
______7. repose
______8. to compensate
______9. perpendicularity
______10. arable

a. a percentage of the money earned on the sale of an item
b. occurring or done at the same time
c. suitable for growing crops
d. to get or bring about by some effort, to obtain
e. to allow something to happen
f. entangled in a thick mass
g. unable to pay one's debts
h. a person who buys and sells for other people
i. rest or sleep
j. to make up for
k. sudden activity
l. the quality of being vertical, or at right angles to a given line or plane

NAME ____________________ CLASS ________ DATE ________ SCORE ________

UNIT 7: THE ELEMENTS OF THE NOVEL

ANIMAL FARM, Chapter VII **George Orwell**

A. UNDERSTANDING WHAT HAPPENED

Directions: In the spaces provided, mark each true statement **T** and each false statement **F**. *(3 points each)*

1. Boxer's attitude is more influential than Squealer's speeches in persuading the animals to work harder. **1.** ______

2. Mr. Whymper suspects that there is a food shortage on Animal Farm. **2.** ______

3. Snowball is never actually seen on the farm. **3.** ______

4. The animals believe that Snowball is responsible for the mischief that takes place. **4.** ______

5. Squealer respects Boxer's honesty and willingness to work. **5.** ______

6. The animals who confess to crimes do so as a result of torture. **6.** ______

7. Boxer's faith in Napoleon begins to falter. **7.** ______

8. Clover plans to overthrow Napoleon. **8.** ______

9. Napoleon forbids the singing of "Beasts of England." **9.** ______

10. The animals prefer to sing the new song that Minimus has written. **10.** ______

B. RECOGNIZING ELEMENTS OF THE NOVEL

Directions: For each question, place the letter of the best answer in the space provided. *(6 points each)*

1. The main point in Chapter VII is that the animals must
a. decide on trading partners
b. rebuild the windmill
c. obtain sufficient food supplies
d. stop Snowball's treachery **1.** ______

2. Which of the characters instigates a rebellion against Napoleon?
a. Snowball
b. the hens
c. Boxer
d. the four younger pigs **2.** ______

3. Squealer's insistence that Snowball betrayed them at the battle of the Cowshed
a. describes an inner conflict
b. constitutes a climax
c. foreshadows danger
d. offers a resolution **3.** ______

4. The mood of the novel shifts from acceptance to horror after
   a. Napoleon stops the hens' rations
   b. Snowball's return is rumored
   c. the dogs attack Boxer
   d. Napoleon kills the animals who have confessed to treachery

4. ______

5. The animal who shows the clearest understanding of how things have gone wrong is
   a. Boxer
   b. the cat
   c. Clover
   d. Muriel

5. ______

C. DEVELOPING VOCABULARY

Directions: Match each word in the left-hand column with the best meaning in the right-hand column. Place the letter of the best definition in the space provided. *(4 points each)*

______ **1.** to embolden
______ **2.** infanticide
______ **3.** to capitulate
______ **4.** stupefied
______ **5.** to formulate
______ **6.** graphically
______ **7.** to cower
______ **8.** to secrete
______ **9.** pervading
______ **10.** retribution

a. spreading through all parts of
b. amazed, astounded
c. to crouch in fear or shame
d. to put into words
e. the killing of infants
f. in a regular way
g. to give courage to
h. the raising of infants
i. to give up, surrender
j. producing with words the effect of a picture
k. deserved punishment for evil done
l. to hide or keep secret

NAME ________________________ CLASS __________ DATE __________ SCORE __________

UNIT 7: THE ELEMENTS OF THE NOVEL

ANIMAL FARM, Chapter VIII **George Orwell**

A. RECOGNIZING ELEMENTS OF THE NOVEL

Directions: For each question, place the letter of the best answer in the space provided. *(6 points each)*

1. In a surprising action, Napoleon sells the timber pile to Frederick. In this episode, Orwell is utilizing a technique called
a. onomatopoeia **b.** reversal **c.** external conflict **d.** exposition **1.** ______

2. The line from the poem by Minimus that is intended to convey irony is
a. "Lord of the swill bucket!"
b. "Thou watchest over all,..."
c. "Faithful and true to thee,..."
d. "Calm and commanding eye,..." **2.** ______

3. Squealer proclaims victory, even though he was "unaccountably" absent during the fighting. This is an example of
a. alliteration **b.** situational irony **c.** dramatic irony **d.** allegory **3.** ______

4. The scene in which Frederick and his followers attack Animal Farm can best be described as an example of
a. internal conflict **b.** external conflict **c.** hostile setting **d.** mood **4.** ______

5. Following Orwell's description of the Battle of the Windmill, the tone of the scene becomes
a. mournful **b.** humorous **c.** whimsical **d.** joyful **5.** ______

B. INTERPRETING MEANINGS

Part 1. *Directions:* For each question, place the letter of the best answer in the space provided. *(6 points each)*

1. By indicating at first that he would sell the wood to Mr. Pilkington, Napoleon
a. hoped to win Pilkington's support
b. wished to spread the rebellion to Frederick's farm
c. hoped that Frederick would offer to increase his price for the wood
d. wished to spread Animalism to Pilkington's farm **1.** ______

2. Napoleon's plan backfires when
a. the windmill is destroyed
b. Frederick cheats him and Pilkington fails to come to his aid
c. Pilkington proves to be stronger than Frederick and a better potential ally
d. Napoleon loses the support of the animals **2.** ______

3. At the end of the chapter, the animals indicate that they still support Napoleon by
a. beginning to rebuild the windmill
b. singing "Beasts of England"
c. awarding him the Order of the Green Banner
d. expressing sorrow when he appears to be dying **3.** ______

4. When Squealer falls off the ladder in the middle of the night, Benjamin realizes that
   a. the pigs have been drinking whiskey
   b. Squealer has been secretly changing the commandments
   c. Squealer has been responsible for the things Snowball was accused of doing
   d. Squealer is the real leader of the pigs

4. ______

5. The following paragraph appears near the end of the chapter:

   By the evening, however, Napoleon appeared to be somewhat better and the following morning Squealer was able to tell them that he was well on the way to recovery. By the evening of that day Napoleon was back at work, and on the next day it was learned that he had instructed Whymper to purchase in Willingdon some booklets on brewing and distilling. A week later Napoleon gave orders that the small paddock beyond the orchard, which it had previously been intended to set aside as a grazing ground for animals who were past work, was to be plowed up. It was given out that the pasture was exhausted and needed reseeding; but it soon became known that Napoleon intended to sow it with barley.

   In this passage you learn that
   a. Napoleon was not so ill after all
   b. Napoleon intends to keep the animals working past retirement age
   c. Napoleon never gives away his plans
   d. Napoleon likes whiskey and intends to make his own

5. ______

Part 2. Throughout this chapter, Napoleon tries to promote the idea that the farm faces danger from enemies and traitors. Find examples of this in the text.

Directions: On a separate sheet of paper, write a paragraph explaining how Napoleon, and by extension, any dictator, uses real and imaginary enemies to control people. Cite examples of mistakes that Napoleon successfully conceals by using this method. *(10 points)*

C. DEVELOPING VOCABULARY

Directions: Match each word in the left-hand column with the best meaning in the right-hand column. Place the letter of the best definition in the space provided. *(3 points each)*

______ **1.** to decree
______ **2.** to skulk
______ **3.** impending
______ **4.** pensioner
______ **5.** hullabaloo
______ **6.** conciliatory
______ **7.** wistful
______ **8.** unscathed
______ **9.** unaccountably
______ **10.** lamentation

a. unhurt, unharmed
b. trying to gain good will by friendly acts
c. an outward expression of grief, a weeping or wailing
d. someone who writes
e. to hide out of fear or with evil intent, to lurk or sneak
f. a person who receives money in payment for previous services
g. in a manner that can't be explained
h. unwillingly
i. to announce a formal decision
j. a loud noise or disturbance
k. about to happen
l. longing, yearning

NAME ______________________ CLASS __________ DATE __________ SCORE __________

UNIT 7: THE ELEMENTS OF THE NOVEL

ANIMAL FARM, Chapter IX **George Orwell**

A. UNDERSTANDING WHAT HAPPENED

Directions: In the spaces provided, mark each true statement **T** and each false statement **F**. *(3 points each)*

1. Boxer was due to retire the following year. **1.** ______

2. The pigs set themselves above the other animals. **2.** ______

3. The animals constantly complain about insufficient food. **3.** ______

4. Moses the raven advises the animals to overthrow the pigs. **4.** ______

5. After Boxer collapses, he is taken to the animal hospital. **5.** ______

6. The van arrives for Boxer while the other animals are at work. **6.** ______

7. Boxer makes an attempt to break out of the van. **7.** ______

8. Squealer claims that he was present at Boxer's death. **8.** ______

9. At first, the animals fail to believe Squealer's explanation. **9.** ______

10. The pigs use the money from selling Boxer to buy whiskey. **10.** ______

B. RECOGNIZING ELEMENTS OF THE NOVEL

Dramatic irony occurs when readers have knowledge that the characters in a story do not have. For example, although Squealer frequently offers explanations of events to the other animals, Orwell is careful to let you know that something quite different is taking place.

Directions: Match Squealer's "official" story in the left-hand column with the truth in the right-hand column. Place the letter of the best answer in the space provided. *(6 points each)*

______ **1.** There is a "readjustment" in the animals' rations.

______ **2.** The animals now "worked shorter hours" than they had under Mr. Jones.

______ **3.** "The wounds on Snowball's back" in the Battle of the Cowshed "had been inflicted by Napoleon's teeth."

______ **4.** Napoleon was "making arrangements to send Boxer to be treated in the hospital at Willingdon."

______ **5.** Squealer "had...been present during Boxer's last hours."

a. Napoleon plans to send Boxer to the knacker's.

b. There is less to eat.

c. Boxer collapses when he is working alone.

d. Boxer dies alone at the knacker's.

e. Snowball secretly fought on the humans' side in the battle.

f. The animals now work like slaves.

g. Mr. Jones shot Snowball.

C. DEVELOPING VOCABULARY

Directions: Match each word in the left-hand column with the best meaning in the right-hand column. Place the letter of the best definition in the space provided. *(4 points each)*

_____ **1.** to formulate
_____ **2.** devotee
_____ **3.** complicity
_____ **4.** stratagem
_____ **5.** to profess
_____ **6.** knacker
_____ **7.** demeanor
_____ **8.** knoll
_____ **9.** to temper
_____ **10.** lamented

a. to declare openly, to affirm
b. grieved for, expressed sorrow for
c. outward behavior, conduct
d. to pretend
e. participation in wrongdoing
f. a trick or scheme for achieving some purpose
g. a small, round hill
h. a person who is a strong supporter of something
i. a person who buys and slaughters useless horses
j. to decorate
k. to soften, to restrain
l. to express in a systematic way

NAME ________________ CLASS ________ DATE ________ SCORE ________

UNIT 7: THE ELEMENTS OF THE NOVEL

ANIMAL FARM, Chapter X **George Orwell**

A. RECOGNIZING ELEMENTS OF THE NOVEL

Directions: For each question, place the letter of the best answer in the space provided. *(6 points each)*

1. Orwell's resolution of the novel as a whole can best be described as
a. cheerful **b.** pessimistic **c.** hopeful **d.** disinterested — **1.** ______

2. The new commandment stating that "some animals are more equal than others" is an example of
a. comic relief **b.** denouement **c.** satire **d.** conflict — **2.** ______

3. Changing the name of Animal Farm back to Manor Farm is meant to symbolize
a. the farm's prosperity
b. the failure of the revolution
c. a shift of power to the farm's human neighbors
d. the farm's return to its pre-rebellion situation — **3.** ______

4. The only farm animals who have prospered over the years are the pigs and dogs. What makes this fact ironic?
a. Only they have done no productive work.
b. They are the weakest physically.
c. They originally opposed the rebellion.
d. They are the least popular animals. — **4.** ______

5. Which event signals the climax of the chapter?
a. the change of the farm's name
b. Mr. Pilkington's toast
c. the final change in the commandments
d. the pigs' faces becoming human — **5.** ______

B. INTERPRETING MEANINGS

Part 1. *Directions:* For each question, place the letter of the best answer in the space provided. *(6 points each)*

1. What does Mr. Pilkington most admire about Animal Farm?
a. its use of up-to-date methods
b. its friendly relations with neighboring farms
c. its low rations, long working hours, and absence of pampering
d. the fine food and drink served by Napoleon — **1.** ______

2. For the pigs, the chief advantage of walking on two feet is that they can
a. use whips
b. wear human clothes
c. read newspapers
d. use a telephone — **2.** ______

3. The significance of Mr. Pilkington's *bon mot,* or clever remark, is that it
a. reveals him to be a close friend of Napoleon
b. proves that he sympathizes with the pigs
c. indicates that the pigs run the farm as harshly as the humans run theirs
d. reveals that Mr. Pilkington and Napoleon share the same problems — **3.** ______

4. Orwell's point in noting that the sheep could be retrained to chant a new slogan is that
   a. they never think for themselves, like many people who respond to slogans
   b. Napoleon always has dedicated followers
   c. Animalism is the guiding force in their lives
   d. they are the real leaders of the farm

4. ______

5. The following paragraph appears early in the chapter:

   > And yet the animals never gave up hope. More, they never lost, even for an instant, their sense of honor and privilege in being members of Animal Farm. They were still the only farm in the whole county—in all England—owned and operated by animals. Not one of them, not even the youngest, not even the newcomers who had been brought from farms ten or twenty miles away, ever ceased to marvel at that. And when they heard the gun booming and saw the green flag fluttering at the masthead, their hearts swelled with imperishable pride, and the talk turned always toward the old heroic days, the expulsion of Jones, the writing of the Seven Commandments, the great battles in which the human invaders had been defeated. None of the old dreams had been abandoned....If they went hungry, it was not from feeding tyrannical human beings; if they worked hard, at least they worked for themselves. No creature among them went upon two legs. No creature called any other creature "Master." All animals were equal.

   George Orwell's purpose in summarizing here the high ideals of the rebellion is to
   a. show that the fight has not been in vain
   b. review the benefits of the rebellion
   c. prepare you for Napoleon's final betrayal of these principles
   d. create a happy mood for the end of the novel

5. ______

Part 2. Orwell never states openly that the rebellion is a failure. Do you think it was?

Directions: On a separate sheet of paper, write a paragraph describing the effects of the rebellion. Cite details from the speeches of Mr. Pilkington and Napoleon to support your opinion. *(10 points)*

C. DEVELOPING VOCABULARY

Directions: Match each word in the left-hand column with the best meaning in the right-hand column. Place the letter of the best definition in the space provided. *(3 points each)*

______ 1. upstanding
______ 2. frugally
______ 3. imperishable
______ 4. deputation
______ 5. misgiving
______ 6. to dispel
______ 7. witticism
______ 8. gratified
______ 9. to intimate
______ 10. subversive

a. indestructible
b. to hint, to suggest indirectly
c. to scatter and drive away, to cause to vanish
d. gladly, willingly
e. attempting to undermine, overthrow, or destroy
f. to give up without a struggle
g. a humorous remark
h. a group of persons sent to represent others
i. honorable, upright
j. a feeling of fear, doubt, or suspicion
k. pleased, satisfied
l. sparingly, avoiding unnecessary spending

NAME ______________________ CLASS ________ DATE ________ SCORE ________

UNIT 7: THE ELEMENTS OF THE NOVEL

WORD ANALOGIES / Extending Vocabulary Skills

Directions: In the space provided, write the letter of the pair of words that best describes a *relationship* that is closest to that of the capitalized words. (*5 points each*)

1. GAMBOL : CAPER ::
a. dice : cards
b. frolic : sit
c. recline : cavort
d. jump : skip
1. ______

2. ADVOCATE : SUPPORT ::
a. champion : promote
b. encourage : discourage
c. oppose : propose
d. attack : hinder
2. ______

3. BENEVOLENT : MALEVOLENT ::
a. kindly : cruel
b. evil : good
c. violent : vicious
d. vindictive : malicious
3. ______

4. ACCORD : DISCORD ::
a. satisfaction : dissatisfaction
b. belief : disbelief
c. count : discount
d. agreement : disagreement
4. ______

5. COMPLICITY : CONSPIRACY ::
a. completion : conspiracy
b. complication : solution
c. scheming : plotting
d. complexity : simplicity
5. ______

6. CYNICAL : OPTIMISTIC ::
a. confident : contemptuous
b. skeptical : hopeful
c. believing : doubting
d. blind : perceptive
6. ______

7. EMBOLDEN : INSPIRE ::
a. inspirit : discourage
b. unnerve : invigorate
c. encourage : hearten
d. energize : dampen
7. ______

8. EMINENT : PREEMINENT ::
a. infamous : famous
b. ordinary : notorious
c. distinguished : illustrious
d. imminent : impending
8. ______

9. EXPOUND : DETAIL ::
a. expose : display
b. explain : describe
c. exaggerate : disparage
d. excise : delete
9. ______

10. INSOLUBLE : CRYPTIC ::
a. solution : problem
b. written : coded
c. ancient : grave
d. unsolvable : hidden
10. ______

11. PUNCTUAL : TIMELY ::
a. late : tardy
b. delayed : early
c. wounded : repaired
d. prompt : overdue
11. ______

12. PERPETUAL : ETERNAL ::
a. purple : royal
b. perpendicular : horizontal
c. transitory : fleeting
d. endless : brief
12. ______

13. PROFESS : DECLARE ::
a. deny : confirm
b. announce : contend
c. disclaim : assert
d. admit : proclaim
13. ______

14. RECONCILE : CONCILIATE ::
a. council : counsel
b. pacify : appease
c. antagonize : soothe
d. befriend : alienate
14. ______

15. SUBVERSIVE : TREACHEROUS ::
a. loyal : treasonous
b. covert : concealed
c. obvious : obscure
d. hidden : overt

15. ______

16. TRACTABLE : OBSTINATE ::
a. docile : stubborn
b. dogged : resolute
c. agreeable : compliant
d. controllable : obedient

16. ______

17. UNSCATHED : UNHARMED ::
a. intact : unimpaired
b. harmony : disharmony
c. perfect : damaged
d. injured : uninjured

17. ______

18. UNANIMOUS : ACCORDANT ::
a. majority : minority
b. win : lose
c. harmonious : united
d. unified : discordant

18. ______

19. VILE : WICKED ::
a. evil : surly
b. low : sinful
c. noble : coarse
d. admirable : contemptible

19. ______

20. VOLUNTARY : COMPULSORY ::
a. optional : deliberate
b. compelled : involuntary
c. free will : forced
d. volunteered : unforced

20. ______

NAME ______________________ CLASS __________ DATE __________ SCORE __________

UNIT 7: THE ELEMENTS OF THE NOVEL

UNIT REVIEW / Applying Skills I

A. READING A STORY

Directions: Read the passage below carefully. Then answer the questions that follow.

It was a bright cold day in April, and the clocks were striking thirteen. Winston Smith, his chin nuzzled into his breast in an effort to escape the vile wind, slipped quickly through the doors of Victory Mansions, though not quickly enough to prevent a swirl of gritty dust from entering along with him.

The hallway smelt of boiled cabbage and old rag mats. At one end of it a colored poster, too large for indoor display, had been tacked to the wall. It depicted simply an enormous face, more than a meter wide: the face of a man of about forty-five, with a heavy black mustache and ruggedly handsome features. Winston made for the stairs. It was no use trying the lift. Even at the best of times it was seldom working, and at present the electric current was cut off during daylight hours. It was part of the economy drive in preparation for Hate Week. The flat was seven flights up, and Winston, who was thirty- nine, and had a varicose ulcer above his right ankle, went slowly, resting several times on the way. On each landing, opposite the lift shaft, the poster with the enormous face gazed from the wall. It was one of those pictures which are so contrived that the eyes follow you about when you move. BIG BROTHER IS WATCHING YOU, the caption beneath it ran.

Inside the flat a fruity voice was reading out a list of figures which had something to do with the production of pig iron. The voice came from an oblong metal plaque like a dulled mirror which formed part of the surface of the right-hand wall. Winston turned a switch and the voice sank somewhat, though the words were still distinguishable. The instrument (the telescreen, it was called) could be dimmed, but there was no way of shutting it off completely. He moved over to the window; a smallish, frail figure, the meagerness of his body merely emphasized by the blue overalls which were the uniform of the Party. His hair was very fair, his face naturally sanguine, his skin roughened by coarse soap and blunt razor blades and the cold of the winter that had just ended.

Outside, even through the window pane, the world looked cold. Down in the street little eddies of wind were whirling dust and torn paper into spirals, and though the sun was shining and the sky a harsh blue, there seemed to be no color in anything except the posters that were plastered everywhere. The black-mustachio'd face gazed down from every commanding corner. There was one on the house front immediately opposite. BIG BROTHER IS WATCHING YOU, the caption said, while the dark eyes looked deep into Winston's own. Down at street level another poster, torn at one corner, flapped fitfully in the wind, alternately covering and uncovering the single word INGSOC. In the far distance a helicopter skimmed down between the roofs, hovered for an instant like a blue-bottle, and darted away again with a curving flight. It was the Police Patrol, snooping into people's windows. The patrols did not matter, however. Only the Thought Police mattered.

Behind Winston's back the voice from the telescreen was still babbling away about pig iron and the over-fulfillment of the Ninth Three-Year Plan. The telescreen received and transmitted simultaneously. Any sound that Winston made, above the level of a very low whisper, would be picked up by it; moreover, so long as he remained within the field of vision which the metal plaque commanded, he could be seen as well as heard. There was of course no way of knowing whether you were being watched at any given moment. How often, or on what system, the Thought Police plugged in on any individual wire was guesswork. It was even conceivable that they watched everybody all the time. But at any rate they could plug in your wire whenever they wanted to. You had to live—did live, from habit that became instinct—in the assumption that every sound you made was overheard, and, except in darkness, every movement scrutinized.

FROM *1984* by George Orwell

B. ANALYZING THE NOVEL

Directions: For each question, place the letter of the best answer in the space provided. *(5 points each)*

1. By stating in the first sentence that "the clocks were striking thirteen," George Orwell indicates that
   a. the clocks are broken
   b. it is late at night
   c. this is not the world you know
   d. this civilization is highly advanced

   1. ______

2. Irony is used in the first paragraph in
   a. the phrase "a bright cold day"
   b. the name of the apartment building
   c. the name "Winston Smith"
   d. the phrase "the vile wind"

   2. ______

3. The primary conflict that Orwell establishes is
   a. external conflict between several characters
   b. external conflict between a character and his environment
   c. internal conflict
   d. external conflict between a character and his brother

   3. ______

4. The mood of the opening might be described as
   a. despairing
   b. angry
   c. comfortable
   d. nostalgic

   4. ______

5. Characterization of Winston Smith is established in the opening passage chiefly by
a. physical description
b. his thoughts
c. his actions
d. the words of others
5. ______

6. The "enormous face" probably belongs to
a. the patrols
b. the Thought Police
c. Winston Smith
d. Big Brother
6. ______

7. Winston's reaction to the fact that his "every movement" is "scrutinized" is
a. fear
b. paranoia
c. rage
d. unknown to the reader
7. ______

8. In paragraph 4, the word that expresses disapproval of the Police Patrols is
a. "skimmed"
b. "snooping"
c. "hovered"
d. "like a blue-bottle"
8. ______

9. Parody and irony are used in the title of
a. Hate Week
b. Thought Police
c. Big Brother
d. all of the above
9. ______

10. The theme of the novel, as indicated by this excerpt, is
a. friendship
b. poverty
c. totalitarianism
d. destiny
10. ______

C. WRITING ABOUT THE NOVEL

Would you enjoy being a citizen in the world described in this excerpt from *1984?* Why or why not?

Directions: On a separate sheet of paper, using examples from the excerpt to support your opinion, write *one* paragraph. You might begin with a statement such as this: "I would not like to trade places with Winston Smith because ____." *(25 points)*

D. ANALYZING LANGUAGE AND DEVELOPING VOCABULARY

Directions: In the spaces provided, mark each true statement **T** and each false statement **F**. *(5 points each)*

1. Describing the wind as *vile* helps set the mood in paragraph 1. **1.**______

2. In paragraph 3, *sanguine* is an example of personification. **2.**______

3. Judging from the context, the meaning of *fitfully,* as used in paragraph 4, is "unable to sleep." **3.**______

4. In paragraph 5, Orwell suggests his feelings when he describes the telescreen's voice as *babbling away*. **4.**______

5. The connotation of *scrutinized* in paragraph 5 further expresses the theme established at the beginning of the excerpt. **5.**______

NAME ____________ CLASS ________ DATE ________ SCORE ________

UNIT 7: THE ELEMENTS OF THE NOVEL

CRITICAL THINKING AND WRITING / Applying Skills II

A. IDENTIFYING CHARACTERIZATION

Directions: Choose one of the minor characters in Animal Farm and, in *one* paragraph, show how Orwell uses this character to express human characteristics. Be sure to use specific examples from the text. *(30 points)*

B. CONTRASTING TWO CHARACTERS

Directions: Write *two* paragraphs to describe the characters of the two leaders Napoleon, and Snowball. How do their goals differ? What do they have in common? *(40 points)*

C. JUDGING THE AUTHOR'S USE OF SATIRE

Directions: Write *one* paragraph showing how Orwell uses exaggeration and ridicule to make a point about politics and human interaction.

How do the "commandments" change between Chapter II and Chapter X? Select other examples from the text to illustrate how the animal revolution becomes corrupt and distorted. When has the same thing happened in human history? *(30 points)*

USING THE ANSWER KEY

In keeping with the overall spirit of the ELEMENTS OF LITERATURE Testing Program, this Answer Key has been designed to be easy to use while remaining comprehensive enough to genuinely meet your classroom needs. In addition to answers, a special feature has been provided to offer assistance in working with any of your students who may find the analogy tests too difficult. This unique feature, "INTRODUCTION TO WORD ANALOGY TESTS / Teaching Students the Art of Inferring Word Correspondencies," follows on pages 245-246. The answers appear on pages 247-268.

INTRODUCTION TO WORD ANALOGY TESTS

Teaching Students the Art of Inferring Word Correspondencies

TEACHING ANALOGIES

The purpose of the analogy lessons is twofold: to provide practice in solving analogies and to teach vocabulary. Each lesson may be approached in a variety of ways—as a vocabulary exercise, as an open-book dictionary/thesaurus lesson, or as a paired-learning or small-group exercise. Based on the teacher's assessment of the class's vocabulary strengths and weaknesses and/or the difficulty of the vocabulary in any given lesson, the teacher should feel free to choose whichever approach will best meet the needs of a particular class. Any one of the approaches mentioned above will provide an opportunity for an interesting and challenging vocabulary experience.

READING ANALOGIES

One of the most common problems on standardized tests is the analogy. The analogy is popular because it requires careful, thoughtful reasoning rather than simple recall of memorized facts. Consider the following examples:

horse : colt :: cow : calf

This analogy is read: "horse 'is to' colt 'as' cow 'is to' calf." This is the most common form of the analogy and is coded A : B :: C : D. In this type of analogy, the fundamental relationship between A and B is analogous, or similar to, the relationship between C and D. In the example above, you can readily see that the *relationship* between horse and colt (adult to young) is analogous to the relationship of cow and calf.

Sometimes, to make the analogy more difficult to solve, the *sequence* of the terms will be changed:

horse : cow :: colt : calf

This form of analogy is coded A : C :: B : D. The two adult animals are contrasted with their respective young, but the essence of the analogy is the same as the earlier example.

When analogies are written on tests, they are in a multiple-choice format. Compare the two examples below. The first is written A : B :: C : D; the second is written A : C :: B : D.

Example 1. Lincoln : sixteenth ::

a. George : Abraham
b. assassinated : retired
c. fifteenth : Johnson
d. Washington : first

Example 2. Lincoln : Washington ::

a. George : Abraham
b. retired : assassinated
c. Virginia : Illinois
d. sixteenth : first

SOLVING ANALOGIES

To solve analogies, it is helpful to follow these steps. (Use Example 1 for Plan A; use Example 2 for Plan B.)

Plan A.

1. Read the stem. (Lincoln : sixteenth)
2. Try to identify the relationship. (Lincoln was the sixteenth president of the United States.)
3. Draw an arrow between the terms to establish a direction to the relationship. (Lincoln : sixteenth)
4. Read the choices for a pair of terms having a relationship that matches the relationship you identified in the stem. Be sure that the relationship is in the same direction as the relationship in the stem.

Plan B.

1. Read the stem. (Lincoln : Washington)
2. Try to identify the relationship. The apparent one, that of two presidents, will not yield a match. When this occurs, try matching the first term in the stem to the first term in each of the choices; try

matching the second term in the stem to the second term in the choices, and so on.

3. If you are not able to identify a relationship, skip it and go on to the next problem. If you have time, come back to any analogies that you skipped and spend more time on them.

CREATING ANALOGIES

There are three ways that writers make analogies more difficult to solve.

1. They alter the format from A : B :: C : D to A : C :: B : D (from "tea : leaf :: coffee : bean" to "tea : coffee :: leaf : bean"), thereby making the relationship more difficult to identify. Awareness and practice are the keys to coping with this problem area.
2. They use difficult or seldom-used words to express the relationship (herd : horses :: gaggle : geese). Wide reading, vocabulary study, and practice with analogies are the keys to coping with this problem area.
3. They use relationships which are unfamiliar or uncommon (Lincoln : sixteenth :: Washington : first). Again, practice with analogies, developing a relationship-oriented eye, and familiarity with the common analogy relationships are the keys to coping with this problem area.

TYPES OF RELATIONSHIPS

To help students become aware of the more common types of relationships that are used in analogies, the following list of relationships and examples is provided.

1. **Synonym Relationship**
   strong : powerful :: mighty : muscular
2. **Synonym-Antonym Relationship**
   strong : powerful :: weak : powerless
   strong : weak :: powerful : powerless
3. **Differ-by-Degree Relationship**
   yell : whisper :: wallop : tap
   breeze : hurricane :: mist : downpour
4. **Worker-to-Tool Relationship**
   butcher : cleaver :: surgeon : scalpel
5. **Person-to-Characteristic Relationship**
   miser : tight :: philanthropist : generous
6. **Object-to-Characteristic Relationship**
   pillow : soft :: concrete : hard
7. **Part-Whole-Part Relationship**
   brick : wall :: tile : mosaic
   finger : palm :: toe : arch
8. **Cause-Effect Relationship**
   drought : dehydration :: monsoon : flooding
9. **Group-to-Member Relationship**
   troop : scout :: pride : lion
10. **Person-to-Task Relationship**
    chef : cook :: ballerina : dance
11. **Worker-to-Object-Created Relationship**
    cooper : barrel :: novelist : novel
12. **Class-to-Species Relationship**
    snake : reptile :: bicycle : vehicle
13. **Hierarchical Relationships**
    lieutenant : sergeant :: corporal : private
14. **Object-to-Purpose Relationship**
    needle : sew :: scissors : cut
15. **Grammatical Relationship**
    go : gone :: be : been
    I : he :: my : his
16. **Symbolic Relationship**
    dove : peace :: hawk : war
17. **Association Relationship**
    toast : jam :: cup : saucer
    macaroni : cheese :: pie : ice cream
18. **Mathematical Relationship**
    6 : 2 :: 9 : 3

ANSWER KEY

UNIT 1: THE ELEMENTS OF A SHORT STORY

Page **1**
INTRODUCTION / Understanding Plot
1. a **2.** b **3.** a **4.** d **5.** d **6.** a **7.** d
8. b **9.** b **10.** c

Page **3**
Poison Roald Dahl
A. **1.** T **2.** F **3.** T **4.** T **5.** F **6.** F **7.** F
8. F **9.** T **10.** F
B. **1.** c **2.** a **3.** b **4.** a **5.** d
C. **1.** e **2.** g **3.** i **4.** b **5.** l **6.** a **7.** c
8. k **9.** f **10.** h

Page **5**
The Adventure of the Speckled Band Arthur Conan Doyle
A. **1.** b **2.** d **3.** a **4.** d **5.** a
B. Part 1. **1.** c **2.** d **3.** a **4.** b **5.** d
Part 2. Answers will vary, but students should include the following facts:
- Helen Stoner's description of the gypsies and her dying sister's use of the word ''band'' are misleading clues. The gypsies are on the plantation at the time of Julia's gruesome death and are looked upon with fear and suspicion.
- The cheetah and baboon which wander freely over the grounds and are feared by the villagers are not involved in the murder but also are described in such a manner that an inferior detective could have been misled by their presence.
- Theoretically, a lesser detective than Sherlock Holmes could easily have assumed that the gypsies were responsible for Julia's death, or that the cheetah or baboon frightened Julia to death.

C. **1.** T **2.** T **3.** F **4.** F **5.** T **6.** T **7.** F
8. T **9.** F **10.** F

Page **7**
The Birds Daphne du Maurier
A. **1.** F **2.** F **3.** T **4.** T **5.** T **6.** F **7.** T
8. F **9.** T **10.** T
B. **1.** b **2.** a **3.** c **4.** d **5.** a
C. **1.** b **2.** a **3.** d **4.** a **5.** c **6.** c **7.** a
8. b **9.** d **10.** b

Page **9**
INTRODUCTION / Understanding Character
1. d **2.** c **3.** b **4.** d **5.** a **6.** c **7.** b
8. b **9.** c **10.** d

Page **11**
A Christmas Memory Truman Capote
A. **1.** d **2.** a **3.** c **4.** a **5.** b
B. Part 1. **1.** c **2.** c **3.** d **4.** a **5.** b
Part 2. Students may include some of the following points:
- Buddy's friend often speaks like a child.
- She likes to play with Buddy.
- She is very superstitious.
- She cannot sleep the night before Christmas.
- The other adults in the story treat her like a child.

C. **1.** d **2.** c **3.** f **4.** i **5.** g **6.** a **7.** h
8. j **9.** b **10.** e

Page **13**
Mariá Tepache Amado Muro
A. **1.** T **2.** T **3.** F **4.** T **5.** T **6.** F **7.** T
8. T **9.** F **10.** F
B. **1.** b **2.** a **3.** c **4.** a **5.** c
C. **1.** a **2.** a **3.** d **4.** b **5.** c **6.** c **7.** a
8. d **9.** a **10.** c

Page **15**
Thank You, M'am Langston Hughes
A. **1.** b **2.** a **3.** b **4.** d **5.** b
B. Part 1. **1.** F **2.** F **3.** F **4.** F **5.** F
6. F **7.** T **8.** T **9.** F **10.** T
Part 2. Students who think Roger is glad not to see Mrs. Jones again may cite the following points:
- Roger may not want to see her again because he is ashamed of his robbery attempt.
- Roger probably does not like to be told what to do and might find Mrs. Jones too strict and demanding in the long run.

On the other hand, students who think Roger is unhappy about not seeing Mrs. Jones again may refer to the following:
- That Roger comes to like and respect Mrs.

Jones is indicated by the fact that he does not run out of her room even though he has the opportunity to do so.

- Roger is sorry he never sees Mrs. Jones again because she is kind and treats him like her own son.
- Mrs. Jones speaks very openly to Roger and tells him about her own life.
- Mrs. Jones gives Roger money for the shoes he wants and tells him kindly to behave himself.
- Roger probably realizes he needs a strong adult in his life who trusts him and treats him with respect.

C. **1.** g **2.** i **3.** e **4.** h **5.** b **6.** j **7.** a **8.** c **9.** d **10.** f

Page **17**

Blues Ain't No Mockin Bird Toni Cade Bambara

A. **1.** T **2.** T **3.** F **4.** T **5.** F **6.** F **7.** F **8.** T **9.** F **10.** F

B. **1.** a **2.** c **3.** a **4.** c **5.** d

C. **1.** b **2.** d **3.** a **4.** a **5.** c **6.** d **7.** b **8.** c **9.** a **10.** b

Page **19**

INTRODUCTION / Understanding Setting

1. d **2.** a **3.** b **4.** c **5.** a **6.** b **7.** c **8.** c **9.** a **10.** b

Page **21**

Top Man James Ramsey Ullman

A. **1.** a **2.** d **3.** d **4.** c **5.** c

B. Part 1. **1.** d **2.** c **3.** a **4.** d **5.** a

Part 2. Students favoring Nace may cite the following points:

- Nace's character is admirable.
- His long career and reputation as a great mountain climber make him the most deserving member of the group.
- Nace's victory would help to compensate for his friend's death.

Students favoring Osborn's success may include some of the following points:

- It is Osborn who shows endless courage and strength throughout the story.
- Osborn is young and bold, "a compact, buoyant mass of energy and high spirits."
- Osborn is always enthusiastic and positive. When a difference of opinion arises he usually capitulated with good grace.
- Later, when others are sick or injured, Osborn displays "inexhaustible" energy and gives "heart to all the rest."
- At the end, Osborn's humility leads him to claim that he failed to reach the summit, when in fact he has done so, in honor of Nace.

C. **1.** F **2.** F **3.** T **4.** T **5.** F **6.** T **7.** F **8.** T **9.** F **10.** T

Page **23**

Antaeus Borden Deal

A. **1.** F **2.** T **3.** F **4.** F **5.** T **6.** T **7.** F **8.** T **9.** F **10.** F

B. **1.** b **2.** c **3.** b **4.** b **5.** a

C. **1.** b **2.** a **3.** d **4.** b **5.** d **6.** b **7.** a **8.** c **9.** d **10.** b

Page **25**

A Man Called Horse Dorothy M. Johnson

A. **1.** a **2.** c **3.** c **4.** d **5.** b

B. Part 1. **1.** T **2.** F **3.** F **4.** F **5.** F **6.** F **7.** T **8.** T **9.** T **10.** F

Part 2. Answers will vary. Students may cite the following points:

- Horse learned how to behave like a man while he lived with the Crows. He rose from the lowest to the highest positions with the tribe. He progressed through the many different phases of Crow life—from killing a man, to marrying, to becoming a widower and then a son.
- When his wife and child died, according to custom, Horse is in a position to let Old Greasy Hand fend for herself, but he feels secure enough to allow himself the luxury of compassion for the old woman.

C. **1.** f **2.** g **3.** j **4.** h **5.** a **6.** c **7.** k **8.** i **9.** e **10.** d

Page **27**

INTRODUCTION / Understanding Point of View

1. d **2.** b **3.** c **4.** c **5.** c

Page **29**

Correspondence Carson McCullers

A. **1.** T **2.** F **3.** T **4.** T **5.** F **6.** T **7.** F **8.** T **9.** T **10.** F

B. **1.** d **2.** c **3.** d **4.** b **5.** b

C. **1.** T **2.** F **3.** F **4.** T **5.** F **6.** T **7.** F **8.** T **9.** F **10.** T

Page **31**

The Hat Jessamyn West

A. **1.** d **2.** b **3.** b **4.** c **5.** d

B. Part 1. **1.** c **2.** d **3.** c **4.** d **5.** a

Part 2. Students may include the following points:

- Cress's mother correctly understands that Cress wants the hat in order to be attractive to Edwin. From the beginning, Mrs. Delahanty thinks that the hat is meant to be worn by a "woman." She tells her husband, "I think Cress thinks this hat would make Edwin see her in a new light. Frail and feminine."
- At the end of the story, Mrs. Delahanty assumes that Cress must be upset because her ladylike image was ruined in front of Edwin. She thinks that Cress's image is based on how she looks. Cress, on the other hand, has based her image of herself not so much on beauty, but on appearing frail and helpless. This, she thinks, will cause Edwin, "who was always a victim himself," to be brave.

However, other students may bring up:

- The two women belong to different generations.
- Cress's temperament is more romantic than her mother's.

C. **1.** d **2.** b **3.** e **4.** a **5.** c **6.** f

Page **33**

The Old Demon Pearl S. Buck

A. **1.** T **2.** F **3.** F **4.** T **5.** F **6.** T **7.** F **8.** F **9.** F **10.** F

B. **1.** c **2.** a **3.** c **4.** a **5.** b

C. **1.** e **2.** j **3.** g **4.** h **5.** f **6.** i **7.** c **8.** a **9.** b **10.** d

Page **35**

INTRODUCTION / Understanding Theme

1. a **2.** b **3.** c **4.** a **5.** b

Page **37**

The Scarlet Ibis James Hurst

A. **1.** c **2.** a **3.** b **4.** a **5.** c

B. Part 1. **1.** T **2.** T **3.** F **4.** T **5.** T **6.** T **7.** F **8.** T **9.** T **10.** T

Part 2. Responses may vary, but should include the following points:

- Doodle is different in appearance and abilities from other people his brother knows.
- Doodle views the world differently and thinks differently. For example, he cries when he sees the beauty of the swamp. The narrator is not affected that strongly.
- When the boys tell "lies," Doodle is the most creative. His stories about the future are so "beautiful and serene" that all the narrator can do is whisper "Yes, yes."

C. **1.** b **2.** d **3.** a **4.** b **5.** d **6.** a **7.** b **8.** d **9.** c **10.** b

Page **39**

The Bridge Nicolai Chukovski

A. **1.** F **2.** T **3.** F **4.** T **5.** F **6.** T **7.** F **8.** F **9.** F **10.** T

B. **1.** d **2.** c **3.** c **4.** c **5.** a

C. **1.** c **2.** b **3.** a **4.** d **5.** d **6.** a **7.** c **8.** d **9.** b **10.** a

Page **41**

Red Dress Alice Munro

A. **1.** b **2.** a **3.** a **4.** b **5.** d

B. Part 1. **1.** c **2.** b **3.** d **4.** c **5.** a

Part 2. Since this essay question calls for the student's point of view, answers will vary. However, the following points will apply:

- Because her mother makes dresses for her, uses her special language ("au reservoir"), waits up for her at night, and does many other things to make her happy, the narrator feels obliged ("a mysterious and oppressive obligation") to show her mother that she is enjoying life, even though she may not be enjoying it at all.
- The narrator notes that, on the occasion of the Christmas dance, she had almost failed her obligation to her mother to be happy—and that there would be other occasions when, because things would not work out as well as they had at the dance, she would be very unhappy. But her mother would never know about these unhappy occasions because of the narrator's feeling of obligation to her mother to act always as though she were happy.

C. **1.** T **2.** T **3.** T **4.** F **5.** F **6.** T **7.** F **8.** F **9.** T **10.** T

Page **43**

INTRODUCTION / Understanding Irony

1. b **2.** b **3.** a **4.** c **5.** c

Page **45**

The Little Girl and the Wolf/The Princess and the Tin Box James Thurber

A. **1.** T **2.** F **3.** F **4.** F **5.** T **6.** T **7.** T **8.** F **9.** T **10.** T

B. **1.** b **2.** b **3.** a **4.** d **5.** b

C. **1.** c **2.** e **3.** l **4.** g **5.** h **6.** k **7.** j **8.** b **9.** a **10.** d

Page **47**

The Sniper Liam O'Flaherty

A. **1.** d **2.** b **3.** b **4.** c **5.** d

B. Part 1. **1.** d **2.** a **3.** c **4.** a **5.** d

Part 2. Students may include in their answers the following points:

- Liam O'Flaherty believes that war dehumanizes people. Implying that the sniper used to be a student, he shows how war has made "a man who is used to looking at death." Without thinking about it, he kills an old woman because she is an informer. And he utters "a cry of joy" when he kills his counterpart across the street. He then risks his life just to identify his victim.
- In addition, the author uses his setting as well as his characters to depict the dehumanization, tragedy, and senselessness of war.

C. **1.** b **2.** c **3.** a **4.** b **5.** d **6.** c **7.** b **8.** a **9.** d **10.** d

Page **49**

The Cask of Amontillado Edgar Allan Poe

A. **1.** T **2.** T **3.** T **4.** F **5.** T

B. **1.** b **2.** d **3.** b **4.** a **5.** d

C. **1.** T **2.** T **3.** T **4.** F **5.** F **6.** T **7.** F **8.** F **9.** F **10.** T

Page **51**

The Necklace Guy de Maupassant

A. **1.** d **2.** a **3.** d **4.** d **5.** c

B. Part 1. **1.** F **2.** T **3.** T **4.** F **5.** T **6.** T **7.** T **8.** T **9.** F **10.** F

Part 2. Students may note the following points:

- Mme. Loisel may be imagining that Mme. Forestier responds "frostily" because her perception is colored by her own emotions.
- Mme. Forestier is presented as a kind, generous, and sympathetic person. At the end of the story, she is "overcome" by Mme. Loisel's news.

C. **1.** b **2.** d **3.** a **4.** b **5.** c **6.** a **7.** d **8.** b **9.** b **10.** d

Page **53**

WORD ANALOGIES

1. **d** (haggard : gaunt :: stout : burly) Explanation: *Haggard* (looking weary and ill) and *gaunt* (thin and worn) are contrasted with *stout* (strong, bulky in figure) and *burly* (heavy and strong).

2. **b** (metropolis : countryside :: urban : rural) Explanation: *Metropolis* (a city, an *urban* area) is contrasted with *countryside,* (a *rural* area).

3. **c** (tributary : river :: root : tree) Explanation: A *tributary,* a contributing branch of a *river,* flows into a river in much the same way that a *root* contributes to, or channels moisture to, a *tree*.

4. **a** (bluster : words :: brandish : weapons) Explanation: When one *blusters* (is loud, noisy, and threatening, roaring like the wind), one uses *words*. When one *brandishes* (waves threateningly), one holds a *weapon*.

5. **c** (resolute : indomitable :: dogged : stubborn) Explanation: All four words are synonyms for preserving, determined, persistent, refusing to yield.

6. **c** (beleaguer : surround :: hamper : interfere) Explanation: When troops are *beleaguered,* they are *surrounded*. When an army's activities are *hampered,* they are *interfered* with and prevented from moving or acting freely.

7. **d** (uniform : similar :: unique : distinctive) Explanation: Things that are *uniform* are consistent and *similar*. Things that are *unique* are *distinctive,* and different from all others.

8. **b** (potency : languor :: strength : weakness) Explanation: *Potency* (*strength,* power) is contrasted with *languor* (lack of vigor or vitality, *weakness*).

9. **b** (pittance : abundance :: scanty : plenty) Explanation: *Pittance* (a small amount) and *scanty* (barely enough) are contrasted with *abundance* (a large quantity) and *plenty* (an ample supply).

10. **a** (summit : depression :: mountain : hollow) Explanation: *Summit* (the highest point) and its opposite, *depression* (a low place), are compared with their geographical equivalents, a *mountain* and a *hollow* (valley).

11. **b** (amble : careen :: stroll : lurch) Explanation: To *amble* is to *stroll,* to walk at a leisurely pace. To *careen* is to *lurch,* to move wildly at full speed, to sway suddenly.

12. **d** (oppressive : severe :: ruthless : pitiless) Explanation: All four words are synonyms for describing extreme actions done without concern or sympathy for others.

13. a (inanimate : languid :: lifeless : listless) Explanation: To be *inanimate* is to be *lifeless*. To be *languid* is to be *listless,* without energy, weak.

14. c (imprudent : dissolute :: barbaric : savage) Explanation: To be *imprudent* or *dissolute* is to be rash, incautious, and wasteful. To be *barbaric* and *savage* is to be crude, uncivilized, and brutal.

15. c (stolid : taciturn :: exuberant : verbose) Explanation: A *stolid* person (showing little or no emotion) would be *taciturn* (not liking to talk, uncommunicative). An *exuberant* person (high spirited) would be *verbose* (talkative, sometimes long winded).

16. a (disconsolate : woeful :: desolate : lonely) Explanation: a *disconsolate, woeful* person is beyond consoling and would likely feel *desolate* or *lonely,* forsaken, and abandoned.

17. c (morose : sullen :: gloomy : sulky) Explanation: These four synonyms describe a person who is ill-humored and withdrawn.

18. d (premonition : future :: reminiscence : past) Explanation: A *premonition* is a feeling that something (often bad) will happen in the *future*. A *reminiscence* is a recalling to mind of an event from the *past*.

19. b (imminent : impending :: simultaneous : concurrent) Explanation: An event that is *imminent* or *impending* is about to happen. Events that are *simultaneous* or *concurrent* will occur in the same time.

20. a (vulnerable : precarious :: insecure : uncertain) Explanation: All four words are synonyms for "open to harm, dependent upon change, or risk."

Page **55**

UNIT REVIEW

B. **1.** a **2.** a **3.** b **4.** c **5.** c **6.** c **7.** a **8.** d **9.** a **10.** b

C. Answers will vary. Students may include the following points:

- The author sympathizes with the child.
- Mama and Papa treat the boy with extreme lack of sensitivity, as if he were deaf and dumb.
- Mama expresses some degree of affection. Papa is hostile and cruel.
- Pity for the boy is balanced by dislike for the parents.

D. **1.** F **2.** F **3.** T **4.** F **5.** F

Page **59**

CRITICAL THINKING AND WRITING

A. Answers will vary, but students may include the following:

- Roger attempts to steal Mrs. Washington's purse, but loses his balance and falls. She brings him to her home.
- Forced to wash his face, he sees an opportunity to run, but decides to stay.
- Mrs. Washington feeds him and hands him ten dollars.

B. Answers will vary, but students may include the following:

- The setting of a peaceful town on a hot August day contrasts with the humiliating incident of the hat.
- Cress's love enhances the setting. She feels "the freshness of the sea breeze," and smells "the strange salt freshness of the sea."

C. Answers will vary, but students may include the following:

- "The Sniper" may be appreciated for its suspense and for its shock ending.
- "Poison" is riveting because it is hard to measure how much danger the characters are facing.

UNIT 2: THE ELEMENTS OF POETRY

Page **61**

UNIT INTRODUCTION / Understanding the Elements of Poetry

1. a **2.** b **3.** c **4.** d **5.** a **6.** b **7.** c **8.** d **9.** a **10.** b

Page **63**

INTRODUCTION / Understanding Imagery

1. a **2.** b **3.** d **4.** a **5.** d **6.** d **7.** c **8.** b **9.** d **10.** a

Page **65**

Imagery: Seeing Things Freshly

A. **1.** c **2.** a **3.** c **4.** b **5.** b

B. Part 1. **1.** T **2.** T **3.** F **4.** F **5.** T

Part 2. **6.** T **7.** F **8.** F **9.** T **10.** F

Part 3. Answers will vary. Students may include some of the following points, for example, from the Swenson poem:

- The typical image of a freeway changes after the reader becomes aware of the alien's unique perspective.
- The irony of the alien's belief that the cars are alive is not evident in the title.
- The title does not give a clue to the unusual content of the poem.

C. **1.** f **2.** i **3.** h **4.** g **5.** l **6.** a **7.** c **8.** b **9.** k **10.** d

Page **67**

INTRODUCTION / Understanding Similes and Metaphors

1. a **2.** c **3.** b **4.** d **5.** b **6.** c **7.** d **8.** c **9.** b **10.** a

Page **69**

Similes and Metaphors: Seeing Connections

A. **1.** c **2.** b **3.** a **4.** b **5.** d

B. Part 1. **1.** F **2.** T **3.** T **4.** F **5.** F

Part 2. **6.** T **7.** T **8.** F **9.** T **10.** F

Part 3. Answers will vary. Students must understand that the simile or metaphor they select is a condensation of an idea that would require greater explanation if written in prose. For example, in "Harlem" the phrase *fester like a sore* might replace

- a definition of *fester*
- the images that the word *sore* calls forth
- any situation untended or unheeded

C. **1.** g **2.** l **3.** a **4.** i **5.** d **6.** k **7.** b **8.** j **9.** e **10.** f

Page **71**

INTRODUCTION / Understanding Personification

1. c **2.** b **3.** a **4.** d **5.** d

Page **73**

Personification: Making the World Human

A. **1.** d **2.** c **3.** a **4.** a **5.** b

B. Part 1. **1.** F **2.** F **3.** F **4.** F **5.** T

Part 2. **6.** F **7.** T **8.** T **9.** F **10.** F

Part 3. Answers will vary. Students may include some of the following examples:

- the personification of living things used in the poems by Hillyer and Haines
- the personification of inanimate things in the poems by Spivack, Ratti, Stafford, and Inez

C. **1.** c **2.** g **3.** l **4.** h **5.** j **6.** i **7.** b **8.** k **9.** d **10.** f

Page **75**

INTRODUCTION / Understanding Rhythm

1. d **2.** a **3.** c **4.** c **5.** a **6.** d **7.** c **8.** a **9.** b **10.** d

Page **77**

The Sounds of Poetry: Rhythm

A. **1.** b **2.** a **3.** d **4.** b **5.** c

B. Part 1. **1.** F **2.** T **3.** T **4.** F **5.** T

Part 2. **6.** F **7.** T **8.** T **9.** F **10.** F

Part 3. Answers will vary, but students should include the following points:

- The first part of the poem has a brisk rhythm which suits the listing of hard jobs that must be done in rapid succession.
- The second part of the poem has a gentle, rolling rhythm which suits the dream-like relation of the woman's needs for peace and serenity.

C. **1.** f **2.** a **3.** j **4.** d **5.** l **6.** b **7.** c **8.** k **9.** e **10.** h

Page **79**

INTRODUCTION / Understanding Rhyme and Other Sound Effects

1. c **2.** a **3.** c **4.** b **5.** b

Page **81**

The Sounds of Poetry: Rhyme and Other Sound Effects

A. **1.** a **2.** d **3.** c **4.** b **5.** a

B. Part 1. **1.** T **2.** F **3.** T **4.** F **5.** T

Part 2. **6.** F **7.** F **8.** T **9.** T **10.** F

Part 3. Answers will vary, but students should include the following points:

- Frost's poem is pessimistic in mood; he foresees a painful end to life.
- Dickinson's poem is optimistic. She sees "heaven" and an opportunity to talk "with God" as events that await her at the end of life.

C. **1.** j **2.** e **3.** g **4.** h **5.** l **6.** f **7.** c **8.** a **9.** d **10.** k

Page **83**

INTRODUCTION / Understanding Tone

1. b **2.** c **3.** b **4.** a **5.** d

Page **85**

Tone: Revealing an Attitude

A. **1.** a **2.** d **3.** b **4.** b **5.** a

B. Part 1. **1.** T **2.** T **3.** F **4.** F **5.** F

Part 2. **6.** T **7.** T **8.** T **9.** F **10.** T

Part 3. Answers will vary, but students should include the following points:

- The dominant tone in "Lucinda Matlock" is joy and fulfillment. In "Mabel Osborne," the tone is one of bitterness and lack of fulfillment.
- It is clear that Lucinda Matlock would feel impatient with Mabel Osborne.

C. **1.** d **2.** l **3.** h **4.** a **5.** j **6.** c **7.** f **8.** k **9.** e **10.** i

Page **87**

INTRODUCTION / Understanding Ballads and Lyrics

1. c **2.** d **3.** b **4.** a **5.** d

Page **89**

Two Kinds of Poetry: Ballads and Lyrics

A. **1.** c **2.** d **3.** d **4.** a **5.** b

B. Part 1. **1.** F **2.** T **3.** T **4.** F **5.** T

Part 2. **6.** F **7.** T **8.** T **9.** F **10.** T

Part 3. Answers will vary. In their comparisons students might cite:

- The grief in "The Unquiet Grave."
- The repose of the dead in "The Unquiet Grave."
- The revenge of the mariner in "The Demon Lover."
- The unexpected death of the woman in "The Demon Lover."
- The bloody murder of the father in "Edward."
- The mother's counseling of murder and betrayal in "Edward."
- The murders and revenge in "Old Christmas."

C. **1.** h **2.** e **3.** a **4.** j **5.** b **6.** f **7.** k **8.** c **9.** d **10.** i

Page **91**

WORD ANALOGIES

1. **b** (stanza : poem :: paragraph : prose) Explanation: *Poems* are divided into sections called *stanzas*. *Prose,* written discourse, is divided into *paragraphs*.
2. **d** (poet : feelings :: statistician : numbers) Explanation: A *poet* works with *feelings*. A *statistician* works with *numbers*.
3. **a** (pivot : rotate :: revolve : swivel) Explanation: The four terms are synonyms for a twirling or turning motion.
4. **c** (revelation : disclosure :: unveiling : confession) Explanation: The four terms are synonyms for bringing something out into the open.
5. **a** (transparent : clear :: apparent : plain) Explanation: The four terms are synonyms for that which is readily observed or understood.
6. **c** (emissary : representative :: ambassador : messenger) Explanation: The four terms are synonyms for a person who represents either another person or a country.
7. **d** (cordiality : friendliness :: amiability : agreeableness) Explanation: The four terms are synonyms for warm, positive acceptance and goodwill.
8. **b** (defer : postpone :: expedite : facilitate) Explanation: To *defer* or *postpone* is to put off a task for later time. To *expedite* or *facilitate* is to hasten or accelerate the completion of a task.
9. **b** (degenerate : immoral :: virtuous : ethical) Explanation: *Degenerate* and *immoral* (perverted, dishonorable) are contrasted with *virtuous* and *ethical* (moral, honorable).
10. **c** (incessant : intermittent :: ceaseless : occasional) Explanation: *Incessant* and *ceaseless* (constant, uninterrupted) are contrasted with *intermittent* and *occasional* (irregular).
11. **d** (awed : astonished :: surprised : amazed) Explanation: The four terms are synonyms for "filled with wonder."
12. **a** (envious : jealous :: indifferent : uncaring) *Envious* and *jealous* (filled with envy) are contrasted with *indifferent* and *uncaring* (unconcerned, uninterested).
13. **a** (sarcastic : contemptuous :: complimentary: appreciative) Explanation: *Sarcastic* and *contemptuous* (stinging, bitter [as in speech]; disdainful) are contrasted with *complimentary* and *appreciative,* full of praise, approving.
14. **c** (ironic : inconsistent :: unexpected : curious) Explanation: The four terms are synonyms for describing unusual, strange, or unexpected events.
15. **d** (nostalgia : anticipation :: past : future) Explanation: *Nostalgia* (thinking about the *past*) is contrasted with *anticipation* (thinking about the *future*).

16. b (allusion : suggestion :: mention : hint) Explanation: These four terms are synonyms for reference (referring to) or intimation (not directly stating).

17. c (rent : torn :: ripped : tattered) Explanation: The four terms are synonyms for describing garments that are extremely worn and damaged.

18. d (patriarch : matriarch :: male : female) Explanation: A *patriarch* (*male* leader of a clan or family) is contrasted with a *matriarch* (*female* leader of a clan or family).

19. b (etymology : word :: genealogy : person) Explanation: *Etymology* is the history of a *word*. *Genealogy* is the history of a *person*.

20. a (track : path :: run : trail) Explanation: These four terms are synonyms, although track and run are less well known than path and trail.

Page **93**

UNIT REVIEW

B. **1.** c **2.** b **3.** b **4.** b **5.** d

C. Answers will vary. Students may include some of the following points for questions 1–5.

(1) Dickinson is describing *sunset*. The phrase ''Evening West,'' the many colors showing in the sky and water, and the final fading of the colors as stars appear, all contribute to form this vivid picture.

(2) The ''housewife'' is *not* orderly: she forgets to ''dust the pond,'' leaves threads in it, and litters the East with bits of green ''Duds of Emerald.''

(3) The metaphors ''Purple Ravelling'' and ''Amber thread'' stand for the reflected colors of the sky at sunset.

(4) Dickinson switches to apostrophe in line 3. She is personifying the sunset.

(5) The tone is *playful* (or joyful), in contrast to the reverential, serious tone of Wordsworth's poems.

D. **1.** F **2.** T **3.** T **4.** F **5.** F

Page **97**

CRITICAL THINKING AND WRITING

A. Answers will vary. Students may include some of the following examples:

- "Flannan Isle" and "Conquerors" are similar in that both take place in desolate settings.
- They are also similar in that the narrators delve deeply into the emotions elicited by the ''dark'' settings.
- Both settings are cheerless, although "Conquerors" suggests sadness and decay, while "Flannan Isle" expresses foreboding and possibly unearthly evil.
- In both poems the writers use run-on lines to avoid a sing-song effect.
- Both poems are slowly paced, invoking a dark, serious mood.

B. Answers will vary. Students may include some of the following examples:

- Personification is a metaphor which gives human qualities to something that is not human.
- Personification makes images more vivid because it gives greater significance to non-humans.

Examples include:

- The paper plates in John Haines's ''The Legend of the Paper Plates'':
  ''They trace their ancestry back to the forest.''
- Kathleen Spivack's ''March 1st'':
  ''I saw February still meandering around''
- John Ratti's ''My Mother Remembers Spanish Influenza'':
  ''It stopped at the foot of our hill for a second, and then rode on down the valley of the carbarn; where it waited out the night.''
- Colette Inez's ''Slumnight'':
  ''TV gunning down
  the hours
  Serves as sheriff
  in a room...''

C. Answers will vary. Some students might include an example like the following:

- I see no reason why the narrator in David Kherdian's ''Dear Mrs. McKinney of the Sixth Grade'' should feel regret about passing his teacher without speaking to her. If he had stopped, his childlike image of her might have been shattered.
- If I were writing a poem on this subject, I would emphasize that the student was right to keep his pleasant memories intact by leaving Mrs. McKinney in the past where she belongs. I also would say that Mrs. McKinney was aware of her students' love without being reminded.

UNIT 3: THE ELEMENTS OF NONFICTION

Page **99**

UNIT INTRODUCTION/Understanding the Elements of Nonfiction

1. c **2.** b **3.** b **4.** b **5.** d **6.** c **7.** a
8. b **9.** d **10.** c

Page **101**

INTRODUCTION / Understanding Personal Essays

1. b **2.** a **3.** d **4.** c **5.** d

Page **103**

The Giant Water Bug Annie Dillard

A. **1.** a **2.** b **3.** c **4.** c **5.** b

B. Part 1. **1.** b **2.** c **3.** d **4.** b **5.** d

Part 2. Answers will vary. Students may include some of the following points:

- They too would feel disgusted by witnessing the frog's death.
- Nature can be violent and cruel.
- The water bug's bite is its natural means of defense.

C. **1.** i **2.** e **3.** b **4.** a **5.** l **6.** k **7.** d
8. c **9.** h **10.** g

Page **105**

The Night the Bed Fell James Thurber

A. **1.** F **2.** T **3.** T **4.** F **5.** T **6.** T **7.** F
8. T **9.** F **10.** T

B. **1.** b **2.** d **3.** a **4.** c **5.** a

C. **1.** d **2.** k **3.** i **4.** e **5.** h **6.** c **7.** j
8. f **9.** b **10.** l

Page **107**

The Washwoman Isaac Bashevis Singer

A. **1.** T **2.** T **3.** T **4.** F **5.** F **6.** T **7.** T
8. F **9.** F **10.** T

B. **1.** d **2.** b **3.** c **4.** b **5.** a

C. **1.** d **2.** h **3.** j **4.** g **5.** b **6.** k **7.** a
8. e **9.** l **10.** c

Page **109**

Charley in Yellowstone John Steinbeck

A. **1.** d **2.** b **3.** d **4.** a **5.** c

B. **1.** b **2.** c **3.** c **4.** b **5.** d

C. **1.** b **2.** c **3.** a **4.** b **5.** d **6.** a **7.** b
8. c **9.** a **10.** b

Page **111**

INTRODUCTION / Understanding Reports on People and Events

1. b **2.** a **3.** b **4.** b **5.** c

Page **113**

FROM Coming into the Country John McPhee

A. **1.** T **2.** F **3.** F **4.** T **5.** T **6.** F **7.** T
8. T **9.** F **10.** T

B. **1.** c **2.** b **3.** b **4.** a **5.** d

C. **1.** d **2.** l **3.** e **4.** f **5.** k **6.** h **7.** g
8. a **9.** i **10.** b

Page **115**

Everything in Its Path Kai Erickson

A. **1.** T **2.** F **3.** T **4.** F **5.** F **6.** T **7.** T
8. T **9.** F **10.** T

B. **1.** a **2.** c **3.** c **4.** a **5.** b

C. **1.** c **2.** e **3.** j **4.** k **5.** l **6.** i **7.** a
8. d **9.** g **10.** f

Page **117**

Annapurna Maurice Herzog

A. **1.** b **2.** d **3.** a **4.** b **5.** c

B. Part 1. **1.** c **2.** b **3.** c **4.** d **5.** a

Part 2. Answers will vary, but should include evidence that Herzog shows equal concern for the safety and health of both the Frenchmen and the Sherpas.

C. **1.** b **2.** a **3.** d **4.** b **5.** c **6.** b **7.** d
8. a **9.** b **10.** c

Page **119**

INTRODUCTION / Understanding Biography and Autobiography

1. b **2.** b **3.** c **4.** b **5.** a

Page **121**

"Annie" Joseph P. Lash

A. **1.** d **2.** b **3.** b **4.** b **5.** b

B. Part 1. **1.** c **2.** c **3.** b **4.** b **5.** d

Part 2. Answers will vary. Students may include some of the following points to illustrate Annie's strength:

- Annie refuses to let herself be separated from Jimmie at the poorhouse.
- She keeps her curiosity alive throughout her ghastly experiences.

- She maintains her ambition despite ridicule by others.
- She finds the courage to appeal to Mr. Sanborn.

C. **1.** g **2.** d **3.** i **4.** j **5.** l **6.** a **7.** f **8.** k **9.** b **10.** h

Page **123**

Barrio Boy Ernesto Galarza

A. **1.** F **2.** F **3.** T **4.** T **5.** T **6.** F **7.** F **8.** T **9.** T **10.** F

B. **1.** b **2.** c **3.** c **4.** d **5.** b

C. **1.** e **2.** h **3.** k **4.** l **5.** i **6.** g **7.** b **8.** c **9.** j **10.** d

Page **125**

The Phantom of Yazoo Willie Morris

A. **1.** a **2.** c **3.** b **4.** a **5.** d

B. Part 1. **1.** b **2.** b **3.** c **4.** c **5.** d

Part 2. Answers will vary. Students may include some of the following points:

- The Old Scotchman's account is "considerably more poetic."
- The Old Scotchman uses "wondrous expressions."
- The Old Scotchman "made pristine facts more actual than actuality."
- The Old Scotchman "touched our need for a great and unmitigated eloquence."

Other students may cite:

- The Old Scotchman's account does not always match the real events.
- The Old Scotchman is always several innings behind.
- The Old Scotchman is "makin' all that stuff up."

C. **1.** a **2.** d **3.** c **4.** b **5.** b **6.** a

Page **127**

I Know Why the Caged Bird Sings
Maya Angelou

A. **1.** F **2.** F **3.** T **4.** T **5.** F **6.** T **7.** F **8.** T **9.** T **10.** F

B. **1.** b **2.** d **3.** a **4.** b **5.** b

C. **1.** f **2.** i **3.** b **4.** j **5.** l **6.** g **7.** a **8.** h **9.** e **10.** c

Page **129**

Life on the Mississippi Mark Twain

A. **1.** b **2.** a **3.** a **4.** d **5.** a

B. Part 1. **1.** c **2.** d **3.** c **4.** b **5.** d

Part 2. Answers will vary. Students may include the following points:

- Brown verbally abuses Twain but never swears, "for he had been brought up with a wholesome respect for future fire and brimstone." Nevertheless, Twain sees him as cruel and mean-spirited.
- Twain entertains the thought of killing Brown, and the only thing that stops him is the threat of prison.

Other students may cite:

- Twain praises the charitable work of the people of Memphis "in the gracious office of the Good Samaritan."

C. **1.** d **2.** a **3.** b **4.** c **5.** a **6.** c **7.** b **8.** a **9.** d **10.** a

Page **131**

WORD ANALOGIES

1. **c** (vivacity : zest :: somnolence : torpor) Explanation: *Vivacity* and *zest* (liveliness, energy) are contrasted with *somnolence* and *torpor* (sluggishness, sleepiness, laziness).

2. **a** (destitute : affluent :: impoverished : enriched) Explanation: *Destitute* and *impoverished* (poor, needy) are contrasted with *affluent* and *enriched* (wealthy, prosperous).

3. **c** (vituperation : scolding :: solicitude : caring) Explanation: One subjected to *vituperation* receives a *scolding*. *Solicitude,* on the other hand, expresses *caring* and concern for another's well being.

4. **d** (benediction : malediction :: blessing : curse) Explanation: A *benediction,* a *blessing*—literally "good words"—is contrasted with *malediction,* a *curse*—literally "bad words."

5. **b** (irredeemable : irrevocable :: reversible : changeable) Explanation: Something *irredeemable* or *irrevocable* is hopeless, unable to be changed or fixed. Something *reversible* or *changeable* is not permanent or hopeless.

6. **b** (sarcophagus : body :: cache : food) Explanation: A *sarcophagus* (a stone coffin) holds a *body*. A *cache* is a place for storing *food* or other supplies.

7. **c** (consecrate : desecrate :: dedicate : violate) Explanation: To *consecrate* is to *dedicate,* to make sacred. To *desecrate* is to *violate,* to treat as not sacred.

8. **c** (cryptic : obvious :: mysterious : evident) Explanation: *Cryptic* and *mysterious* (hidden, unclear) are contrasted with *obvious* and *evident* (clear, understandable).

9. a (illiterate : skills :: ignorant : knowledge) Explanation: If one is *illiterate,* one lacks certain *skills*. If one is *ignorant,* one lacks certain *knowledge*.

10. d (contemptuous : respectful :: disdainful : gracious) Explanation: *Contemptuous* and *disdainful* (lacking respect, scornful) are contrasted with *respectful* and *gracious*.

11. a (palpable : noticeable :: apparent : obvious) Explanation: These four terms are synonyms for easily perceived or conspicuous.

12. b (precarious : insecure :: perilous : risky) Explanation: These four terms are synonyms for being dependent upon chance or circumstances, at risk, and open for attack or injury.

13. d (storm : abates :: person : relents) Explanation: A *storm abates,* weakens, decreases in force or intensity. A *person relents,* becomes less harsh, severe, or strict.

14. a (insidious : treacherous :: truthful : honest) Explanation: *Insidious* and *treacherous* (capable of entrapment, not to be trusted, dangerous) are contrasted with *truthful* and *honest*.

15. b (resplendent : dilapidated :: bright : shabby) Explanation: That which is *resplendent* is *bright* and shiny and, by implication, in excellent condition. That which is *dilapidated* is *shabby,* worn, dull, and in disrepair.

16. d (facilitate : simplify :: hinder : complicate) Explanation: to *facilitate* is to *simplify,* to make things easier. To *hinder* is to *complicate,* to make things difficult.

17. b (inordinate : excessive :: unreasonable : surplus) Explanation: These four synonyms refer to excess above what is necessary, exorbitance.

18. c (verisimilitude : plausibility :: genuineness : authenticity) Explanation: *verisimilitude* and *plausibility* are conditions appearing to be true or believable. *Genuineness* and *authenticity* are conditions of actual truth, reality, and legitimacy.

19. a (estrange : unite :: alienate : reconcile) Explanation: *Estrange* and *alienate* (to separate, drive apart) are contrasted with *unite* and *reconcile* (bring together, restore to friendship).

20. d (sinister : wicked :: honorable : upright) Explanation: *Sinister* and *wicked* (evil, devilish) are contrasted with *honorable* and *upright* (noble, moral).

Page **133**

UNIT REVIEW

B. **1.** b **2.** c **3.** a **4.** c **5.** a
6. b **7.** d **8.** b **9.** a **10.** c

C. Answers will vary. Students may include some of the following points:

- Twain believes good writing should be honest. It should not glorify decaying ideals of the past.
- Twain criticizes Scott's writing as being overly flowery, wordy, and sentimental. In good writing, these qualities are avoided.
- Twain admires writing that reflects real, down-to-earth experience.
- Twain praises George Washington Cable and Joel Chandler Harris, two writers who write "modern English"; thus, he would favor writing that does not use old-fashioned expressions or style.

D. 1. T **2.** T **3.** F **4.** F **5.** T

Page **137**

CRITICAL THINKING AND WRITING

A. Answers will vary. Students may include some of the following points:

- Refuse from the Buffalo Mining Company had been building up in Middle Fork of Buffalo Creek since 1957.
- On February 26, 1972, the waste enclosure burst and the waste and accumulating debris flooded the hollow.
- In the disaster, 125 people were killed and 4,000 of the area's 5,000 inhabitants were left homeless.
- The National Guard, Red Cross, and Salvation Army aided the survivors immediately after the disaster.
- Later, HUD provided assistance in rebuilding homes.

B. Answers will vary, but students may include some of the following points:

- Both essays include ironic humor, exaggeration for comic effect, and comic imagery in details.
- The humor of both authors is gentle rather than stinging.
- The essays contrast in that Thurber uses satire to describe his family in "The Night the Bed Fell," while Steinbeck uses puns and anthropomorphism (i.e. humanization; attributing human characteristics to a non human) in "Charley in Yellowstone."

C. Answers will vary. Students may include some of the following points:

- Reasons for preferring one selection over another may include identification with or interest in the characters or episodes of the account, learning something from the experience of a childhood in another time or place, or feeling a warmth and interest in a particular character.

- The author's point of view in "The Washwoman" is that of the child, except for the introduction and ending.
- "Barrio Boy" has a child's point of view.
- "I Know Why the Caged Bird Sings" also has a child's point of view, but the author does occasionally comment on her experience from the perspective of an adult.
- The attitude of "The Washwoman" and "Barrio Boy" is one of warm recollection of childhood.
- "I Know Why the Caged Bird Sings" expresses warmth for the relatives but is tinged with bitterness at the conditions in which blacks lived at the time.

UNIT 4: THE ELEMENTS OF DRAMA

Page **139**
UNIT INTRODUCTION/Understanding the Elements of Drama
1. b **2.** b **3.** c **4.** a **5.** c **6.** c **7.** a
8. b **9.** d **10.** a

Page **141**
The Miracle Worker, Act One William Gibson
A. **1.** F **2.** T **3.** F **4.** T **5.** T **6.** F **7.** F
8. T **9.** T **10.** F
B. **1.** d **2.** c **3.** d **4.** b **5.** b
C. **1.** c **2.** g **3.** i **4.** a **5.** e **6.** d **7.** j
8. b **9.** h **10.** f

Page **143**
The Miracle Worker, Act Two William Gibson
A. **1.** a **2.** b **3.** d **4.** b **5.** b
B. Part 1. **1.** b **2.** d **3.** d **4.** a **5.** d
Part 2. Answers will vary. Students may bring up the following points:
- Captain Keller now trusts Annie to do her job. Previously, he considered her incompetent and impertinent.
- Kate Keller understands that spoiling Helen does not help. She realizes that discipline will pave the way for learning.
- James, scornful of Annie at first, has begun to respect her. He notices that Annie stands up to the Captain and makes him listen to her opinions.

C. **1.** j **2.** c **3.** e **4.** h **5.** i **6.** d **7.** b
8. f **9.** a **10.** g

Page **145**
The Miracle Worker, Act Three William Gibson
A. **1.** T **2.** F **3.** T **4.** T **5.** F **6.** F **7.** F
8. T **9.** T **10.** F
B. **1.** b **2.** c **3.** d **4.** b **5.** d
C. **1.** e **2.** h **3.** d **4.** b **5.** i **6.** a **7.** g
8. j **9.** f **10.** c

Page **147**
Visitor from Forest Hills Neil Simon
A. **1.** F **2.** T **3.** T **4.** F **5.** T **6.** T **7.** F
8. T **9.** F **10.** F
B. **1.** c **2.** b **3.** d **4.** a **5.** b
C. **1.** d **2.** f **3.** e **4.** b **5.** j **6.** g **7.** i
8. a **9.** h **10.** c

Page **149**
The Mother Paddy Chayefsky
A. **1.** d **2.** c **3.** a **4.** d **5.** b
B. Part 1. **1.** c **2.** d **3.** b **4.** c **5.** a
Part 2. Answers will vary. Students may bring up the following points:
- The mother fears the boredom and emptiness of an idle life.
- She is afraid of becoming dependent on her children.
- Independence will allow her to retain her pride and self-respect.

C. **1.** b **2.** g **3.** j **4.** k **5.** e **6.** h **7.** c
8. f **9.** d **10.** a

Page **151**
WORD ANALOGIES
1. **b** (covert : imperceptible :: surreptitious : unnoticeable) Explanation: All four terms are synonyms for describing undercover or secret activity.
2. **d** (allay : aggravate :: reduce : intensify) Explanation: *Allay* (to *reduce* or lessen) is contrasted with *aggravate* (to *intensify,* to make worse).

3. **a** (humiliate : embarrass :: belittle : humble) Explanation: All four words are synonyms for making someone feel ashamed.
4. **d** (indulgence : leniency :: denial : repression) Explanation: *Indulgence* and *leniency* (merciful, mild, kindness) are contrasted with *denial* and *repression* (negative, controlling, harsh).
5. **b** (bemoan : affliction :: lament : hardship) Explanation: One would *bemoan* (moan about) an *affliction* (a distressing condition) just as one would *lament* (weep, wail, or moan about) a *hardship*.
6. **c** (asperity : ferocity :: crossness : cruelty) Explanation: *Asperity* (harshness of temper) or *crossness* is contrasted with *ferocity* (wild force) or *cruelty*.
7. **a** (contention : intimation :: declaration : hint) Explanation: A *contention* or *declaration* (a direct statement) is contrasted with an *intimation* or *hint* (a suggestion or implication).
8. **d** (despondent : depressed :: discouraged : dejected) Explanation: All four terms are synonyms for feelings of extreme sadness, downheartedness, and hopelessness.
9. **b** (trepidation : resolute :: nervousness : confident) Explanation: *Trepidation* (*nervousness*) is the result of not feeling *resolute* (*confident*).
10. **a** (facetious : stolid :: humorous : unexcitable) Explanation: *Facetious* and *humorous* (funny, amusing) are contrasted with *stolid* and *unexcitable* (unemotional, solemn, and serious).
11. **b** (deferential : yielding :: emphatic : forceful) Explanation: *Deferential* and *yielding* (giving way, being unassertive) are contrasted with *emphatic* and *forceful* (strong, unyielding, assertive).
12. **d** (indolent : vigorous :: idle : energetic) Explanation: *Indolent* and *idle* (inactive, lazy) are contrasted with *vigorous* and *energetic* (active, dynamic).
13. **d** (profound : shallow :: deep : superficial) Explanation: *Profound* and *deep* (thoughtful, wise) are contrasted with *shallow* and *superficial* (lacking depth, uncritical, concerned only with the obvious).
14. **a** (apportion : allocate :: divide : distribute) Explanation: All four terms are synonyms for dividing into portions, setting apart for, designating.
15. **c** (compunction : regret :: scruple : uneasiness) Explanation: All four terms are synonyms for feelings one has when doing something one knows is wrong.
16. **b** (immune : vulnerable :: protected : unprotected) Explanation: *Immune* and *protected* (resistant, safe) are contrasted with *vulnerable* and *unprotected* (unsafe, defenseless).
17. **c** (laborious : rigorous :: difficult : challenging) Explanation: All four terms are synonyms for hard or demanding.
18. **a** (impertinent : brash :: disrespectful : impudent) Explanation: All four terms are synonyms for describing rude or unmannerly behavior.
19. **c** (requisite : necessary :: essential : required) Explanation: All four terms are synonyms for necessities.
20. **a** (confront : oppose :: face : challenge) Explanation: All four terms are synonyms for identifying aggressive, combative, belligerent actions.

Page **153**

UNIT REVIEW

B. **1.** a **2.** c **3.** a **4.** d **5.** b **6.** c **7.** d **8.** d **9.** a **10.** d

C. Answers will vary. Students may include all or some of the following points:
- Laurie may try to avoid heavy work.
- Laurie may try to avoid all work.
- Laurie may claim to be sick.
- Eugene may accuse her of faking.
- Laurie may get mad and exhibit anger and good health, thus proving Eugene's point.

D. **1.** F **2.** T **3.** F **4.** T **5.** F

Page **157**

CRITICAL THINKING AND WRITING

A. Answers will vary. Students may include all or some of the following points:
- The exposition is introduced similarly in each play; each play sets forth the basic situation in a speech by one character.
- In *The Miracle Worker,* Kate's speech to the baby Helen presents the exposition. In that speech, the audience learns about the baby's illness, the father's profession, the mother's concern, and Helen's deafness.
- In *The Visitor from Forest Hills,* Norma's telephone conversation reveals the exposition.
- In *The Mother,* the son-in-law's first long speech reveals that the mother wishes to be alone and the daughter wants the mother to live with her.

B. Answers will vary. Students may include all or some of the following points:
- The Boss speaks brusquely to the Mother. He appears to be a mean person.

- However, when the Boss tells the bookkeeper that he didn't have the heart to turn the Mother away, he seems like a nice person.
- The Boss faces the pressure of a deadline. When the Mother ruins half of the sleeves, the Boss cannot meet the deadline. He dismisses the Mother.
- It is conceivable that on a less stressful day, the Boss might have given the Mother another chance.

C. Answers will vary. Students may include all or some of the following points:

- The basic problem is Helen's gross table manners.
- The conflict arises when Annie tries to correct Helen's manners. Actually, there is a dual conflict: one clash occurs between Helen and Annie, and another between Annie and Captain Keller.
- The resolution occurs when the Kellers depart and Annie and Helen are left alone.

UNIT 5: WILLIAM SHAKESPEARE

Page **159**

UNIT INTRODUCTION / Understanding Shakespeare

1. c **2.** c **3.** d **4.** a **5.** d **6.** c **7.** a **8.** b **9.** d **10.** a

Page **161**

The Tragedy of Romeo and Juliet, Act I
William Shakespeare

A. **1.** F **2.** T **3.** T **4.** F **5.** F **6.** T **7.** T **8.** F **9.** F **10.** T

B. **1.** c **2.** d **3.** b **4.** c **5.** b

C. **1.** b **2.** e **3.** h **4.** c **5.** a **6.** g **7.** j **8.** f **9.** d **10.** i

Page **163**

The Tragedy of Romeo and Juliet, Act II
William Shakespeare

A. **1.** c **2.** a **3.** d **4.** a **5.** a

B. Part 1. **1.** c **2.** d **3.** d **4.** a **5.** b

Part 2. Answers will vary. Students may include some of the following quotations:

Friar: (lines 1–2)
''So smile the heavens upon this holy act
That afterhours with sorrow chide us not!''

Romeo: (lines 7–8)
''Then love-devouring death do what he dare—
It is enough I may but call her mine.''

Friar: (lines 9–11)
''These violent delights have violent ends
And in their triumph die, like fire and powder,
Which, as they kiss, consume.''

C. **1.** d **2.** c **3.** a **4.** f **5.** j **6.** h **7.** b **8.** e **9.** g **10.** i

Page **165**

The Tragedy of Romeo and Juliet, Act III
William Shakespeare

A. **1.** T **2.** F **3.** F **4.** F **5.** T **6.** T **7.** F **8.** F **9.** T **10.** T

B. **1.** c **2.** a **3.** c **4.** d **5.** b

C. **1.** l **2.** a **3.** i **4.** e **5.** b **6.** g **7.** c **8.** d **9.** f **10.** h

Page **167**

The Tragedy of Romeo and Juliet, Act IV
William Shakespeare

A. **1.** F **2.** T **3.** T **4.** T **5.** T **6.** F **7.** F **8.** F **9.** F **10.** T

B. **1.** a **2.** b **3.** c **4.** a **5.** d

C. **1.** f **2.** g **3.** a **4.** h **5.** c **6.** l **7.** d **8.** i **9.** k **10.** e

Page **169**

The Tragedy of Romeo and Juliet, Act V
William Shakespeare

A. **1.** c **2.** d **3.** a **4.** b **5.** c

B. Part 1. **1.** d **2.** a **3.** b **4.** b **5.** d

Part 2. Answers will vary. There are many feuding racial and national groups that students may pick. In a number of cases, the same kind of tragedy might occur today.

C. **1.** g **2.** i **3.** f **4.** l **5.** j **6.** d **7.** c **8.** k **9.** b **10.** h

Page **171**

WORD ANALOGIES

1. c (blessed : cursed :: favored : condemned) Explanation: Being *blessed* (*favored*) is contrasted with being *cursed* (*condemned*).

2. **a** (underling : subordinate :: vassal : serf) Explanation: An *underling* or *subordinate* is a low-ranking person, one who serves others.
3. **c** (crave : desire :: reject : spurn) Explanation: *Crave* and *desire* (to be in great need of, to want) are contrasted with *reject* and *spurn* (to leave alone or turn one's back on).
4. **d** (grudge : ill will :: malice : animosity) Explanation: These four terms are synonyms for hostility or bad feelings.
5. **b** (strife : conflict :: discord : turmoil) Explanation: These four terms are synonyms for contention, dissention, disagreement, and a very agitated or confused state.
6. **b** (attend : heed :: listen to : harken to) Explanation: These terms are synonyms: when one *attends* or *heeds*, one is *listening* or *harkening*.
7. **c** (misshapen : malformed :: contorted : twisted) Explanation: These four terms are synonyms for describing that which is irregular or ill-proportioned.
8. **a** (civil : amiable :: rude : ill-mannered) Explanation: *Civil* and *amiable* (polite and friendly) are contrasted with *rude* and *ill-mannered* (unfriendly and impolite).
9. **a** (grave : sober :: spirited : boisterous) Explanation: *Grave* and *sober* (subdued, quiet) are contrasted with *spirited* and *boisterous* (lively, noisy).
10. **d** (counsel : advice :: admonish : warning) Explanation: When one is *counseled* one receives *advice*. When one is *admonished* one receives a *warning*.
11. **a** (vex : annoy :: please : delight) Explanation: *Vex* and *annoy* (to agitate, trouble, bother) are contrasted with *please* and *delight* (to make happy).
12. **c** (discreet : prudent : impetuous : rash) Explanation: *Discreet* and *prudent* (careful, using good judgment) are contrasted with *impetuous* and *rash* (impulsive, careless).
13. **d** (despair : anguish :: solace : consolation) Explanation: *Despair* and *anguish* (discouragement, distress) are contrasted with *solace* and *consolation* (comfort, relief).
14. **b** (exquisite : mediocre :: superb : ordinary) Explanation: *Exquisite* and *superb* (magnificent) are contrasted with *mediocre* and *ordinary* (common).
15. **b** (devout : ardent :: passive : indifferent) Explanation: *Devout* and *ardent* (passionate, enthusiastic) are contrasted with *passive* and *indifferent* (not caring or reacting, unemotional).
16. **d** (prodigious : immense :: negligible : insignificant) Explanation: *Prodigious* and *immense* (huge, enormous) are contrasted with *negligible* and *insignificant* (trifling, unimportant).
17. **b** (conjure : ghost :: raise : spirit) Explanation: When you *conjure* up a *ghost*, you *raise* a *spirit*.
18. **c** (discourse : speak :: heed : listen) Explanation: To *discourse* is to *speak*; to *heed* is to *listen*.
19. **a** (baleful : sinister :: threatening : malicious) Explanation: The four terms are synonyms for something ominous, evil.
20. **d** (penury : poverty :: prosperity : affluence) Explanation: Poverty is contrasted with wealth.

Page **173**

UNIT REVIEW

B. **1.** a **2.** c **3.** d **4.** a **5.** b **6.** d **7.** a **8.** c **9.** a **10.** d

C. Answers will vary. Following is an example of a rewritten scene.

Emilia: He doesn't look so mad anymore.
Des: He's going to come right back. He told me to get ready for bed and to ask you to leave.
Emilia: Leave?
Des: That's what he said. So please go. Just give me my nightgown before you leave.
Emilia: I wish you'd never met him.
Des: I don't wish that. I love him so much that even when he's angry, I don't mind. Help me with these pins, will you?
Emilia: I put the new sheets on the bed.
Des: Fine. I'm losing my mind. If I should die, bury me in one of those sheets.
Emilia: You're losing your mind.
Des: I remember a woman who worked for my mother. Her boyfriend left her, and she went around singing a sad, old song. Tonight I can't get that song out of my head.
Emilia: Shall I get your nightgown?
Des: Never mind the nightgown. Just unhook my dress. Isn't Mr. Lodovico nice?
Emilia: He's very handsome.
Des: He's very polite.
Emilia: Polite! I know a woman who would walk barefoot across hot coals. . .
Des: Hang this up, will you? You'd better go. What's that?
Emilia: It's just the wind.
Des: Good night, Emilia. My eyes are itch-

ing. Does that mean I'm going to cry?

Emilia: Not necessarily.

Des: I've heard some people say that it does. Oh, these men! Emilia, do you think there are some women who cheat on their husbands?

Emilia: Of course.

Des: Would you?

Emilia: Why, wouldn't you?

Des: I certainly wouldn't!

Emilia: I wouldn't for a few little gifts here and there, but who wouldn't do it to help her husband get a fantastic job?

Des: I wouldn't do anything like that for the whole world.

Emilia: For the whole world? With the whole world you could do a lot for your husband. And he'd never have to know.

Des: I don't think any woman would do that!

Emilia: Some would, if the stakes were high enough. I really think it's the husband's fault if his wife strays. If he's bad-tempered or if he's jealous and restricts her freedom—why, women have feelings too and their husbands should know that they do. Let husbands be good to their wives—if not, let them know that if a woman behaves badly it is because she learns how to from her husband.

Des: Good night, Emilia! I hope that, instead of imitating someone's bad mistake, I'll be able to make things right again.

D. **1.** T **2.** T **3.** F **4.** T **5.** T

Page **177**

CRITICAL THINKING AND WRITING

A. Answers will vary. Students may include all or some of the following points:

- There is a feud between the Capulets (Juliet's family) and the Montagues (Romeo's family).
- Juliet is about to be engaged to Paris. A party is planned to celebrate the occasion.
- Romeo is in love with Rosalind, but is unhappy. To cheer himself, Romeo sneaks into the Capulet party.
- Romeo and Juliet meet at the party and fall in love.
- Tybalt, Juliet's cousin, sees Romeo at the party and vows to take revenge for the unwanted intrusion.

B. Answers will vary. Students may include all or some of the following points, depending on their point of view.

- The Nurse is hypocritical. She praises Paris in the same way she once praised Romeo.
- The Nurse is only looking after herself in siding with Juliet's parents on this question.
- The Nurse is a true friend. Her advising Juliet to marry Paris against her will simply represents her judgment as an adult who better understands the probable consequences of marrying Romeo. However, in giving Juliet this advice, she is simply accepting an easy answer to a complex problem.

C. Answers will vary. Students may include all or some of the following points.

Students who believe that Paris is an innocent victim may cite:

- Paris did not know Juliet loved Romeo.
- Paris loved Juliet.
- Paris thought Juliet's grief was caused by her cousin Tybalt's death.
- Paris dies in a duel with Romeo.

Students who believe that Paris is not an innocent victim may cite:

- Romeo offers Paris an opportunity to leave the tomb.
- Had Paris taken the time to speak quietly and reasonably to Romeo, as Romeo spoke to Paris, the duel might have been prevented.
- Paris, hot-headed and impulsive, provoked the duel and therefore was responsible for his own death.

UNIT 6: THE ELEMENTS OF THE EPIC

Page **179**
UNIT INTRODUCTION / Understanding the Elements of an Epic
1. c **2.** a **3.** b **4.** d **5.** b **6.** a **7.** a
8. d **9.** b **10.** c

Page **181**
The Odyssey, Books 1–4 Homer
A. **1.** d **2.** b **3.** a **4.** c **5.** b
B. Part 1. **1.** c **2.** c **3.** b **4.** d **5.** b
Part 2. Answers will vary. Students may include some of the following points:
- In lines 51–77, Athena presents the choices open to Telemachus and reminds him that he is "a child no longer."
- In lines 130–148, Athena further reminds Telemachus that he possesses many of his father's strengths, and shortly afterwards he prepares for his journey.
- In lines 157–174, Athena urges Telemachus not to be shy in approaching Nestor and asking him what he knows about Odysseus.

Other students may cite:
- In lines 89–90, Athena "lavished on him a sunlit grace/that held the eye of the multitude."
- Athena borrows a ship for Telemachus's journey and rounds up a crew.
- Athena openly contradicts Telemachus in lines 210–213 when he doubts the power of the gods.

C. **1.** g **2.** l **3.** d **4.** j **5.** h **6.** b **7.** c
8. a **9.** f **10.** k

Page **183**
The Odyssey, Book 5 Homer
A. **1.** T **2.** T **3.** T **4.** F **5.** F **6.** T **7.** F
8. T **9.** T **10.** T
B. **1.** b **2.** d **3.** a **4.** d **5.** c
C. **1.** d **2.** h **3.** k **4.** l **5.** f **6.** i **7.** b
8. g **9.** a **10.** c

Page **185**
The Odyssey, Books 6–8 Homer
A. **1.** b **2.** c **3.** c **4.** a **5.** a
B. Part 1. **1.** b **2.** c **3.** d **4.** a **5.** d
Part 2. Answers will vary. Students may include some of the following points:
- Odysseus modestly hides his nakedness when he first appears and when he bathes.
- Odysseus carefully weighs the best actions to take: he thinks before he acts.
- Odysseus speaks politely, skillfully, and diplomatically.
- Odysseus shows himself to be both charming and virtuous.

C. **1.** h **2.** j **3.** c **4.** e **5.** g **6.** l **7.** f
8. k **9.** a **10.** d

Page **187**
The Odyssey, Book 9 Homer
A. **1.** T **2.** T **3.** T **4.** F **5.** T **6.** F **7.** T
8. T **9.** F **10.** T
B. **1.** b **2.** d **3.** d **4.** d **5.** c
C. **1.** e **2.** h **3.** c **4.** b **5.** a **6.** l **7.** i
8. k **9.** g **10.** j

Page **189**
The Odyssey, Books 10–11 Homer
A. **1.** c **2.** d **3.** a **4.** b **5.** b
B. Part 1. **1.** d **2.** b **3.** b **4.** c **5.** b
Part 2. Answers will vary. Students may include some of the following points:
- The Lotus Eaters' drug makes those who take it forget about their duties and their homeland.
- Circe's drug is also destructive and has the further effect of turning men into pigs. The symbolism is a clear anti-drug message.

Other students may cite:
- Odysseus uses a drugged wine to overcome Polyphemus.

C. **1.** k **2.** b **3.** a **4.** l **5.** e **6.** g **7.** h
8. d **9.** c **10.** j

Page **191**
The Odyssey, Book 12 Homer
A. **1.** T **2.** F **3.** T **4.** F **5.** F **6.** F **7.** T
8. T **9.** F **10.** T
B. **1.** c **2.** d **3.** d **4.** d **5.** c
C. **1.** j **2.** l **3.** b **4.** h **5.** k **6.** g **7.** e
8. d **9.** a **10.** i

Page **193**
The Odyssey, Books 16–17 Homer
A. **1.** b **2.** a **3.** b **4.** c **5.** a
B. Part 1. **1.** d **2.** b **3.** b **4.** b **5.** c
Part 2. Answers will vary. Students may in-

clude some of the following points:

- Odysseus knows that the suitors are wasting his son's inheritance and are trying to marry his wife.
- He knows that Penelope grieves for him.
- He knows that his beloved Argos is terribly mistreated, and he is told that the dog's owner ''died abroad.''

Other students may cite:

- Penelope, Telemachus, Eumaeus, and Argos all respect his memory.

C. **1.** e **2.** g **3.** i **4.** j **5.** f **6.** k **7.** b **8.** a **9.** d **10.** l

Page **195**

The Odyssey, Book 19 Homer

A. **1.** T **2.** F **3.** T **4.** F **5.** T **6.** T **7.** F **8.** T **9.** T **10.** F

B. **1.** d **2.** b **3.** c **4.** a **5.** d

C. **1.** h **2.** d **3.** g **4.** l **5.** j **6.** b **7.** a **8.** k **9.** i **10.** e

Page **197**

The Odyssey, Book 21 Homer

A. **1.** d **2.** c **3.** d **4.** d **5.** b

B. Part 1. **1.** d **2.** b **3.** c **4.** b **5.** a

Part 2. Answers will vary. Students may include some of the following points:

- Odysseus enlists the help of the swineherd and cowherd to make sure he gets the bow and that it is given to him at the desired time.
- Odysseus makes sure his wife and the other woman will be free from harm.
- Odysseus asks Philoeteus to lock the outer gate so that no suitor will escape.
- Odysseus indicates to Telemachus that it is time to help, thus ensuring him another armed ally.

C. **1.** i **2.** e **3.** l **4.** b **5.** a **6.** h **7.** f **8.** k **9.** d **10.** j

Page **199**

The Odyssey, Book 22 Homer

A. **1.** F **2.** F **3.** F **4.** T **5.** T **6.** T **7.** T **8.** F **9.** F **10.** F

B. **1.** b **2.** c **3.** d **4.** c **5.** c

C. **1.** h **2.** f **3.** d **4.** k **5.** l **6.** b **7.** a **8.** e **9.** i **10.** j

Page **201**

The Odyssey, Book 23 Homer

A. **1.** c **2.** d **3.** c **4.** c **5.** a

B. Part 1. **1.** b **2.** a **3.** b **4.** c **5.** d

Part 2. Answers will vary. Students critical of Penelope may include the following points:

- Odysseus already has passed the test of stringing his bow, and he has dispatched the suitors who for so many years plagued Penelope and wasted her son's inheritance.
- Both Telemachus and Odysseus's old nurse, Eurycleia, already have accepted Odysseus.

Students writing in defense of Penelope may cite the following:

- For twenty years, Penelope has been wary of all who sought her hand. She did this in hopes of Odysseus's return, out of loyalty to him, and to protect herself and her family.
- Odysseus was cruel not to reveal his identity to Penelope earlier. The swineherd Eumaeus, Telemachus, and Odysseus's old nurse learned of Odysseus's return long before his wife did.

C. **1.** d **2.** f **3.** j **4.** l **5.** b **6.** i **7.** a **8.** e **9.** k **10.** g

Page **203**

The Odyssey, Book 24 Homer

A. **1.** T **2.** T **3.** T **4.** F **5.** T **6.** F **7.** T **8.** F **9.** F **10.** T

B. **1.** b **2.** c **3.** c **4.** b **5.** a

C. **1.** h **2.** d **3.** e **4.** a **5.** i **6.** j **7.** l **8.** b **9.** f **10.** k

Page **205**

WORD ANALOGIES

1. **c** (candor : honesty :: valor : bravery) Explanation: The synonyms candor and honesty, both positive attributes, are compared to the positive attributes of the synonyms valor and bravery.
2. **a** (ardor : aloofness :: passion : indifference) Explanation: *Ardor* and *passion* (enthusiasm, excitement) are being contrasted with *aloofness* and *indifference* (standoffishness, unconcern, disinterest).
3. **d** (beguile : mislead :: trick : cheat) Explanation: The four terms are synonyms for "to deceive or to fool."
4. **d** (clamor : tumult :: uproar : commotion) Explanation: The four terms are synonyms for ''a great deal of noise or confusion.''
5. **b** (appease : assuage :: pacify : soothe) Ex-

planation: The four terms are synonyms for "quieting, calming, making peaceful, comforting."

6. **a** (contemptible : unworthy :: respectful : laudable) Explanation: *Contemptible* and *unworthy* (despicable, undeserving) are contrasted with *respectful* and *laudable* (courteous, praiseworthy).
7. **d** (entreat : beseech :: implore : beg) Explanation: The four terms are synonyms for "to request," but imply great earnestness or need on the part of the asker.
8. **b** (hale : hearty :: healthy : sound) Explanation: The four terms are synonyms denoting good health.
9. **c** (interrogate : question :: ask : query) Explanation: The four terms are synonyms for requesting information, putting questions to someone.
10. **c** (maudlin : overemotional :: sentimental : tearful) Explanation: The four terms are synonyms—maudlin (overemotional), however, is more extreme than sentimental (tearful).
11. **a** (plunder : loot :: raid : pillage) Explanation: The four terms are synonyms for the thievery and vandalizing that goes on during riots or wars.
12. **d** (prevail : triumph :: succeed : overcome) Explanation: The four terms are synonyms for "to conquer."
13. **b** (prudent : careless :: cautious : indiscreet) Explanation: *Prudent* and *cautious* (wise, showing good judgment) are contrasted with *careless* and *indiscreet* (negligent, showing poor judgment).
14. **d** (renowned : unknown :: famous : obscure) Explanation: *Renowned* and *famous* (well known) are contrasted with *unknown* and *obscure* (unheard of).
15. **c** (shun : seek :: avoid : pursue) Explanation: *Shun* and *avoid* (keep away from) are contrasted with *seek* and *pursue* (search for, try to find).
16. **a** (detain : hinder :: encourage : facilitate) Explanation: *Detain* and *hinder* (delay, make difficult) are contrasted with *encourage* and *facilitate* (aid, make easy).
17. **a** (vaunt : conceal :: boast : cover up) Explanation: *Vaunt* and *boast* (brag) are contrasted with *conceal* and *cover up* (hide, secret).
18. **b** (domain : sovereign :: territory : monarch) Explanation: A *domain* or *territory* (land, country) could be ruled by a *sovereign* or *monarch* (king, queen).
19. **d** (uncouth : crude :: gross : impolite) Explanation: The four terms are synonyms for describing ill-mannered or rude behavior.
20. **b** (brace : pistols :: pair : guns) Explanation: A *brace* of *pistols* is a *pair* (two) of *guns*.

Page **207**

UNIT REVIEW

B. **1.** d **2.** c **3.** a **4.** d **5.** b **6.** c **7.** a **8.** d **9.** a **10.** b

C. Answers will vary. Students should include the following points:

- Both Akhilleus (Achilles) and Hektor (Hector) are depicted as heroic.
- Homer makes clear his admiration for both warriors when he writes that "he who fled was noble, he behind a greater man by far."
- Hektor's monologue offers a self-portrait of a man who is full of pride but is also repentant. One of his chief traits is courage.
- Homer characterizes Akhilleus as god-like—"the implacable god of war"—even though his actions are enraged and murderous.

D. **1.** T **2.** T **3.** F **4.** T **5.** T

Page **211**

CRITICAL THINKING AND WRITING

A. Answers will vary. Students should include the following:

- Athena advises Telemachus to go in search of Odysseus and try to find out if his father is dead or alive. She reminds Telemachus that he is no longer a child.
- Telemachus calls together the Acheans, seats himself in his father's chair, and proceeds to voice his complaints against the suitors.
- Athena uses her power by giving him "sunlit grace" and making him appear confident and well-spoken.

B. Answers will vary. Students should include the following points:

- Odysseus seems unaware of his terrifying appearance. He debates how to approach Nausicaa and decides he can best win her trust and cooperation by courting her, as a man to a woman, with sweet compliments that verge on outright flattery.
- Odysseus must proceed cautiously at first because he does not yet know if he has reached a friendly kingdom.
- Odysseus reveals his identity only after he is convinced that the Phaeacians are "gentle

folk'' who fear the gods and will not try to harm him.

C. Answers will vary. Students should include the following:
- A master of suspense, Homer builds tension after Odysseus arrives in Ithaca by posing the unspoken question: Will Odysseus be recognized?
- Odysseus's beggar disguise allows him to observe his kingdom and to determine who are his true friends and who are his enemies.
- Odysseus's clever strategy almost backfires near the end when Penelope turns the tables and decides to test her husband.

UNIT 7: THE ELEMENTS OF THE NOVEL

Page **213**
UNIT INTRODUCTION / Understanding the Elements of the Novel
1. d **2.** c **3.** a **4.** d **5.** c **6.** b **7.** a
8. d **9.** b **10.** c

Page **215**
Animal Farm, Chapter I George Orwell
A. **1.** d **2.** b **3.** a **4.** c **5.** a
B. Part 1. **1.** b **2.** b **3.** c **4.** d
Part 2. Answers will vary. Students may include some of the following points in their answer:
- It seems reasonable that animals would blame humans for all their suffering since men dominate animals and use them for their own benefit.
- Animals are subject to death at any time. Humans kill animals for their own well-being.
- People have no compassion for animals. They lack appreciation for their work and take their deaths for the benefit of humans for granted.

Other students may bring up the fact that some people refuse to kill and eat animals and object to the mistreatment of animals.

C. **1.** d **2.** i **3.** k **4.** l **5.** g **6.** e **7.** b
8. a **9.** c **10.** j

Page **217**
Animal Farm, Chapter II George Orwell
A. **1.** T **2.** F **3.** T **4.** T **5.** F **6.** F **7.** F
8. F **9.** T **10.** F
B. **1.** b **2.** d **3.** d **4.** c **5.** a
C. **1.** k **2.** e **3.** h **4.** c **5.** j **6.** a **7.** d
8. b **9.** f **10.** g

Page **219**
Animal Farm, Chapter III George Orwell
A. **1.** b **2.** c **3.** d **4.** c **5.** b
B. Part 1. **1.** a **2.** c **3.** d **4.** b **5.** c
Part 2. Answers will vary. Students may include the following points:
- Orwell uses irony to show that, although all the animals are supposedly equal, the pigs give themselves special privileges and become the leaders in a society of ''equals.''
- It is ironic that Boxer works even harder now that he is ''free.''

C. **1.** j **2.** i **3.** f **4.** d **5.** h **6.** l **7.** c
8. e **9.** k **10.** b

Page **221**
Animal Farm, Chapter IV George Orwell
A. **1.** F **2.** F **3.** T **4.** T **5.** T **6.** F **7.** F
8. F **9.** T **10.** F
B. **1.** c **2.** b **3.** d **4.** a **5.** d
C. **1.** b **2.** d **3.** j **4.** l **5.** a **6.** c **7.** g
8. f **9.** e **10.** h

Page **223**
Animal Farm, Chapter V George Orwell
A. **1.** d **2.** b **3.** c **4.** b **5.** a
B. Part 1. **1.** a **2.** d **3.** c **4.** b **5.** c
Part 2. Answers will vary. Students may include some of the following points:
- Boxer takes the better course of action because good citizens remain loyal to their leaders.
- Boxer should be admired because he is totally unselfish.

Other students may say that:
- Mollie is right in choosing to be loyal to herself rather than to a leader who uses force and terrorism to take control.

- Clover unjustly considers Mollie an "enemy of the people" and she is justified in escaping her dangerous environment.

C. **1.** d **2.** f **3.** j **4.** k **5.** b **6.** l **7.** h **8.** e **9.** a **10.** g

Page **225**

Animal Farm, Chapter VI George Orwell

A. **1.** c **2.** a **3.** b **4.** a **5.** d

B. Part 1. **1.** d **2.** a **3.** b **4.** c

Part 2. Answers will vary. Answers should center around the following:

- Most of the animals are unable to read.
- Many tyrants create a dependent citizenry by failing to provide education.
- The uneducated are always ripe for exploitation.
- It is unlikely that an uneducated individual could organize and lead a rebellion or stand up to an authoritarian leader.
- Laws are often used against the uneducated and underprivileged.

C. **1.** f **2.** d **3.** h **4.** a **5.** g **6.** b **7.** i **8.** j **9.** l **10.** c

Page **227**

Animal Farm, Chapter VII George Orwell

A. **1.** T **2.** F **3.** T **4.** T **5.** F **6.** F **7.** F **8.** F **9.** T **10.** F

B. **1.** c **2.** b **3.** c **4.** d **5.** c

C. **1.** g **2.** e **3.** i **4.** b **5.** d **6.** j **7.** c **8.** l **9.** a **10.** k

Page **229**

Animal Farm, Chapter VIII George Orwell

A. **1.** b **2.** a **3.** c **4.** b **5.** d

B. Part 1. **1.** c **2.** b **3.** d **4.** b **5.** d

Part 2. Answers will vary. Answers should center around the following:

- Napoleon makes the animals believe that the heroic Snowball is an enemy and traitor.
- Napoleon smooths over his mistakes and consolidates his position as dictator by having his portrait and the poem of praise by Minimus inscribed on the barn wall.
- Napoleon executes three hens who claim to have been inspired by Snowball to kill Napoleon.
- Napoleon, like all dictators, knows that concern about a common threat (real or imagined) from neighbors instills fear and binds citizens to the group in power.
- When the wheat crop is full of weeds, the rumor is spread that Snowball is responsible.
- By using slogans such as "Death to Frederick" and "Death to Pilkington," scapegoats are created and internal problems are blamed on outsiders.
- The animals are led to believe that Snowball is plotting the destruction of the windmill and farm.

C. **1.** i **2.** e **3.** k **4.** f **5.** j **6.** b **7.** l **8.** a **9.** g **10.** c

Page **231**

Animal Farm, Chapter IX George Orwell

A. **1.** T **2.** T **3.** F **4.** F **5.** F **6.** T **7.** T **8.** T **9.** T **10.** T

B. **1.** b **2.** f **3.** g **4.** a **5.** d

C. **1.** l **2.** h **3.** e **4.** f **5.** a **6.** i **7.** c **8.** g **9.** k **10.** b

Page **233**

Animal Farm, Chapter X George Orwell

A. **1.** b **2.** c **3.** d **4.** a **5.** d

B. Part 1. **1.** c **2.** a **3.** c **4.** a **5.** c

Part 2. Answers will vary, however answers probably will indicate that the rebellion failed. Students may include some of the following points:

- The lower animals on Animal Farm, do more work and receive less food than any animals in the county.
- The pigs treat the other animals the same way, or worse, than humans treat their animals.
- Napoleon seeks to wipe out the memory of Old Major and everything he stood for.

C. **1.** i **2.** l **3.** a **4.** h **5.** j **6.** c **7.** g **8.** k **9.** b **10.** e

Page **235**

WORD ANALOGIES

1. **d** (gambol : caper :: jump : skip) Explanation: The four terms are synonyms for playful jumping or skipping.
2. **a** (advocate : support :: champion : promote) Explanation: The four terms are synonyms for "to encourage or argue for."
3. **a** (benevolent : malevolent :: kindly : cruel) Explanation: A *benevolent* act is *kindly* (helpful). A *malevolent* act is *cruel* (hurtful).
4. **d** (accord : discord :: agreement : disagreement) Explanation: *Accord* and *agreement* are contrasted with *discord* and *disagreement*.

5. **c** (complicity : conspiracy :: scheming : plotting) Explanation: Someone guilty of *complicity* or *conspiracy* is involved with scheming or plotting.

6. **b** (cynical : optimistic :: skeptical : hopeful) Explanation: *Cynical* and *skeptical* (doubting, thinking negative) are contrasted with *optimistic* and *hopeful* (looking on the positive side).

7. **c** (embolden : inspire :: encourage : hearten) Explanation: The four terms are synonyms for "to motivate."

8. **c** (eminent : preeminent :: distinguished : illustrious) Explanation: the four terms are synonyms for describing someone who is above the norm, famous, highly positioned and highly regarded.

9. **b** (expound : detail :: explain : describe) Explanation: The four terms are synonyms for "adding additional information."

10. **d** (insoluble, cryptic :: unsolvable : hidden) A problem that is *insoluble* (*unsolvable*) may be so because of the *cryptic* (*hidden* or obscure) solution.

11. **a** (punctual : timely :: late : tardy) Explanation: *Punctual* and *timely* (being on time) are contrasted with *late* and *tardy*.

12. **c** (perpetual : eternal :: transitory : fleeting) Explanation: That which is *perpetual* is *eternal* (will last forever). That which is *transitory* is *fleeting* (temporary).

13. **d** (profess : declare :: admit : proclaim) Explanation: The four terms are synonyms for stating or expressing ideas/thoughts.

14. **b** (reconcile : conciliate :: pacify : appease) Explanation: The four terms are synonyms for "bringing together," "calming."

15. **b** (subversive : treacherous :: covert : concealed) Explanation: *Subversive* or *treacherous* (disloyal) acts are usually *covert* or *concealed* (hidden, secret).

16. **a** (tractable : obstinate :: docile : stubborn) Explanation: *Tractable* and *docile* (passive, easily managed) are contrasted with *obstinate* and *stubborn*.

17. **a** (unscathed : unharmed :: intact : unimpaired) Explanation: The four terms are synonyms for "not injured or damaged."

18. **c** (unanimous : accordant :: harmonious : united) Explanation: The four terms are synonyms for "in agreement."

19. **b** (vile : wicked :: low : sinful) Explanation: The four terms are synonyms describing evil or immoral actions.

20. **c** (voluntary : compulsory :: freewill : forced) *Voluntary* and *freewill* (of one's own accord or choice) are contrasted with *compulsory* and *forced* (required, mandatory, without choice).

Page **237**

UNIT REVIEW

B. **1.** c **2.** b **3.** b **4.** a **5.** a **6.** d **7.** d **8.** b **9.** d **10.** c

C. Answers will vary. Students may include the following points:

- The setting is grim and forbidding.
- Being watched at all times is unsettling and an invasion of privacy.
- There is an atmosphere of tension and danger, foreshadowing dreadful events to come.

D. **1.** T **2.** F **3.** F **4.** T **5.** T

Page **241**

CRITICAL THINKING AND WRITING

A. Answers will vary. Students may use some of the following examples:

- Benjamin, the donkey—cynicism and apathy.
- Mollie, the mare—vanity.
- Boxer—simple-mindedness and unquestioning loyalty.

B. Answers will vary. Students may include the following points:

- force *vs.* persuasion
- public organization *vs.* secret police
- words *vs.* actions

C. Answers will vary. Students may include the following points:

- In the Russian Revolution, the revolutionaries became totalitarian just as the pigs became oppressors of the other animals.
- American Indians began to adopt the attitudes and habits of the white man, just as the pigs developed human habits and vices, both to their detriment.